Considerable Appeal

By K. M.

ISBN 0-9755739-0-X
First Printing 2004
Cover art and design by Samantha E. Ruskin
Photo by S. J. Wilson

Published by:
Dare 2 Dream Publishing
A Division of Limitless Corporation
Lexington, South Carolina 29073

Find us on the World Wide Web
http://www.limitlessd2d.net

Printed in the United States and the UK by

Lightning Source, Inc.

This book is dedicated to my wonderful friend, Jude, who has been my inspiration, my courage, and my strength, and without whom I would not be the person I am today.

CONSIDERABLE APPEAL

Sequel to **Undeniable**

By K M

Considerable Appeal

Chapter 1

The courtroom was quiet as the presiding judge contemplated the arguments of both counsel. It was nearly noon, and all parties were increasingly anxious to break for a much-needed lunch recess. The early winter January day outside was bright and sunny, albeit a bit blustery for the normally mild Central Florida climate. Brilliant beams of sunlight filtered through the 22nd floor large windows, bathing the court chambers in a golden glow as a subdued hush settled over the occupants of the state-of-the-art courtroom.

Judge Calloway glanced over at the plaintiff's table, noting the anticipatory stance of the lead attorney. Addressing the tall form who was patiently awaiting his response, he rubbed his fingers briskly against his forehead and queried the matter further. "Counsel, what relief would you seek, provided, of course, that I grant your motion to freeze the funds deposited by the defendant into the registry of this Court?"

The lead counsel allowed the corners of her mouth curl ever so slightly, sensing imminent victory. "Your Honor, should you grant our motion, we would then immediately seek an order releasing those funds directly to the plaintiff."

"On what basis?" Judge Calloway tapped his finger solidly on the dark wooden bench top.

Blue eyes shifted as the junior partner looked over toward her second chair associate. The dark head nodded almost imperceptibly, and the young associate handed over several bound sets of case law, statutes, and pertinent rules of procedure. "Your Honor, since a final judgment was entered against the defendant, he was required to post a

3

bond, if he was so inclined, in order to continue operating his business pending appeal. Instead, the defendant chose to post cash rather than the required bond, which was clearly not contemplated by current law." The lead counsel approached the judge's bench and handed a set of bound materials to the trial clerk, then provided a copy to opposing counsel. "Your Honor, if I may direct your attention to tab four of the materials, the statute clearly requires and provides for the posting of a bond, not cash. Furthermore, in our original attempts to collect on the judgment, we determined that the defendant maintains very limited additional assets. Absent the cash posted with this Court, his remaining assets are clearly not enough to cover the amount of the judgment itself."

The judge slowly looked up from the proffered materials and focused on the plaintiff's lead attorney. "Am I to understand, counselor, that you are alleging that the defendant posted cash to the registry of this Court in order to shield his assets from garnishment or levy?"

Dark eyebrows shot up in disguised innocence. "We are certainly not alleging deliberate evasion on the part of the defendant, Your Honor. We are merely saying that the correct procedure as required by law was not followed, and that the deadline for doing so has long since passed."

The judge now turned his attention toward opposing counsel, clearly displeased by the defendant's apparent attempt at deception. Nevertheless, his words belied an implied warning. "Mr. Davis, the Court will assume that such a posting of cash, rather than a bond, was an inadvertent oversight of applicable law." He sat back in his over-sized leather chair for a moment, then proceeded. "All right. I'm granting Plaintiff's motion. The funds are frozen pending further hearing on disbursement. The parties may submit a proposed order, and the plaintiff has ten days to file a motion for release of the frozen funds. The defendant may oppose." Judge Calloway gave a frank look to defense counsel. "Mr. Davis, if the defendant opposes, there must be specific legal grounds for such opposition, otherwise, absent such legal showing, I will tell you now that there is no basis to maintain the funds in this Court's registry or to release them back to your client."

The defense counsel, sufficiently chastised, responded weakly. "We understand, Your Honor."

Finally, Judge Calloway gaveled the Court in recess and all occupants of the courtroom rose as he proceeded to exit through the small doorway behind his bench.

Back at counsel table, the young associate had been watching the proceedings with avid interest and considerable amazement. In her opinion, the junior partner had been absolutely brilliant, the lead counsel's tall, elegant frame emanating confidence throughout the entire proceeding. As the judge departed the courtroom, green eyes tracked over to fix on cool blue, a wide smile gracing the young associate's fair features. "That was great."

"Thanks." Jessica Harrison packed up her briefcase. "Do me a favor, will ya? Prepare a proposed order for today's hearing, then prepare draft motion to release those funds and let me see it."

"You got it." Robin Wilson gathered all remaining items from the counsel table and followed the junior partner the through the courtroom's dark wood double doors. "Hey, Jess. One thing I don't get. Why didn't you go after them on shielding their assets? You know they did it on purpose."

Jess stepped out into the long, now empty corridor. "Because I could get what I wanted without embarrassing the opposing counsel. I may very well be up against him in the future, and it's better not to have bad blood, if possible." She glanced over at Robin. "Always take the high road if you can help it. You'll get a reputation as an honorable lawyer. If you start out with a negative reputation, it's very hard to get rid of it."

The associate considered the sound advice and realized that Jess was teaching her things that strict book experience, and even practical experience could not. "I'll remember that. Thanks." As they approached the elevators, Robin's stomach, somehow sensing the noon hour, growled softly. "Um, Jess? Could we maybe get lunch before heading back?"

A wide, knowing smile was her response. "I suppose we could do that." The smile then turned a bit serious. "But, maybe we should eat separately. We're trying to be careful, remember?"

The young associate sighed in slight frustration. "I remember, but surely it can't hurt just this once. We're not even at the firm. No one will notice."

Jess, she is definitely your weakness. All things considered, the junior partner acquiesced much too easily on the matter. "I guess it'll be okay just this once. How about we go to that Italian restaurant across the street and get some pasta?"

Green eyes lit up. "Great." The elevator doors opened. "But, I'm buying."

Jess stepped into the elevator car. "You're buying? Any special reason?"

"It's part of our deal. I buy you lunch every day." Robin suddenly blushed as she entered the elevator.

Jess stared at Robin and pushed the first floor button. *Buy lunch every day?* Quizzical blue eyes regarded twinkling green. *I don't get it.*

Robin grinned, picking up on Jess's momentary confusion. "The other part of our deal is that you make sure my stomach is happy every day." The associate felt herself blush all over again.

Stomach happy every day? Jess was lost in contemplation as the doors to the elevator opened on the 12th floor and a deputy sheriff stepped aboard. The older woman momentarily broke from her thoughts and noted the now very amused green eyes staring back at her. *I still don't get it.* Perhaps it was the surroundings, but for the life of her, Jess just couldn't pick up on whatever it was that Robin was subtly trying to say. Either that, or Jess was particularly dense that day. It was hard to say.

Robin stifled a giggle in continued amusement. *I guess I have to spell it out for her.* "Jess, I know how your appetite can get."

The junior partner considered the proffered clues. *Lunch every day. Stomach happy. Appetite.* Dark eyebrows furrowed in thought. *Nope, still don't get it.* A blue eye peeked beneath her dark bangs. *I still don't get....* Suddenly, both blue eyes grew very wide. *Oh.* Jess glanced over and around the deputy sheriff for a clear view of Robin who was now biting her lip to hide an obvious grin. *Oh.* The older woman felt a faint blush creep up her face despite the presence of an oblivious deputy sheriff. *Oh boy.* Azure eyes glared in Robin's direction. *You are so dead.*

The elevator doors opened on the first floor and all occupants exited the elevator car. The deputy sheriff headed toward the jury assembly room, while the young associate led the way into the vaulted lobby. "So, Jess, it's settled, then? I'm buying?"

The junior partner walked up beside the associate. "Yes, Robin. You're buying." A smirk. "After all, it's part of our deal, right?" Now, crystal blue eyes were the ones twinkling in clear amusement. "And I can assure you that I'll definitely uphold my end of our bargain later on."

Jess's tone of voice caused Robin to swallow involuntarily. *Oh boy. I am definitely in trouble.* And that particular thought was not entirely unappealing.

****

"Are you all set to move this weekend?" Jess fiddled with the edge of her napkin. "Need any help with anything?"

6

Robin smiled, knowing how hard it was for Jess just to sit back and not be involved. "Everything's set. The apartment movers are scheduled for Saturday." Pale eyebrows lifted slightly. "We won't be in your way while we're moving, will we?"

"Nope." A thought occurred to the older woman. "Um...Robin, exactly how much stuff do you have?"

"Quite a lot." Robin replied seriously. "We may have to rearrange some things." The waiter brought their entrees and set them on the table in front of them.

"You don't need everything from your apartment, you know. I have everything we need."

"True." Robin continued. "But there's a certain fluffy sofa that I'm quite fond of." She grinned. "I guess I could put it in the spare room. Along with the TV. And my desk. And the dresser. And...."

Jess cut in. "Looks like that room's gonna be rather crowded." She expertly twirled her spaghetti on her fork, then took a bite.

The blonde head shook. "Actually, I've rented storage space at that mini-warehouse place down the street. I'm gonna put most of my stuff there."

"You know, Robin, you can have any room you want. If you want to move things around and have more space, we can do that."

The associate sipped her citrus tea. "Nope. The spare room's fine."

Jess set her fork down, then spoke in a very warm tone of voice. "Hey. I mean this. I want you to feel comfortable. You can have the extra bathroom, which I never use, all to yourself, and you can take whatever bedroom you want. I realize that there may be times when we each want our privacy, and I really want for you to have a place all to yourself." She resumed eating, but didn't look up. "I might get on your nerves or something."

Robin smiled at the endearing sentiment. "Thanks. I'm sure I'll be quite comfortable in the spare room, but yes, I will take the hall bathroom." She took a bite of her ziti and regarded the taller woman. "I'm sure you won't get on my nerves, Jess." A green eye peered up somewhat shyly. "I might get on yours, though."

"Never."

Robin wouldn't let the subject drop just yet. "You'll tell me, though, if I do, right?"

Jess squinted her eyes. The thought honestly never occurred to her. "Yes, I promise, if you promise to do the same."

"Yes." Robin was suddenly nervous. What if it turned out they couldn't get along together? Living with someone all the time, then working together all day could become overwhelming. *What if it messes things up between us?* Her expression was noticeably pensive.

"Hey, kiddo." Jess caught Robin's sudden change in demeanor. *Second thoughts? Damn.* "Everything okay?"

Robin nodded. "Yeah. Promise me something, Jess."

"Anything." Jess meant it.

"I know you're used to living by yourself. If you find that having me under foot is too much for you, and you'd rather I live somewhere else, say something to me right away, okay?" Green eyes focused squarely on blue. "I don't want to jeopardize things between us. I don't want to be in your way."

Jess listened intently, then strictly upon impulse, reached across the table and grasped Robin's hand. "I want you to hear me, and I want you to believe me." She took a breath, determined to explain what she had only recently realized, herself. "Living by myself was an empty existence. I know that now." The older woman smiled almost sadly. "I would absolutely love for you to be under foot. I'd cherish that." She fixed her gaze firmly on the younger woman's to convey the final insight. "You never, ever could be in my way, Robin. Never."

Robin felt the grip on her hand suddenly tighten, and she fought an unexpected tightness in her throat. "Thank you." She whispered, then steadied herself. "But you'll tell me just the same, right?"

Let me try it another way. "Let's make a deal." Jess rubbed her thumb back and forth over Robin's fingers. "If either of us has a problem with something the other one does or doesn't do, we'll tell each other right away. We won't sit on it or try to spare each other's feelings." She tilted her head to one side. "Will that work?"

"Yes." The younger woman smiled. "That'll work."

"Good." Jess released the smaller hand. "Now, let's finish eating and get back to the office. You have a lot of work to do this afternoon, kiddo."

Robin chuckled. "Right. Thanks to you." She grinned with undisguised affection. "I knew all along you just wanted me around to do your grunt work for you."

In a far corner of the Italian restaurant, Paul Franklin sat back in his seat and closely watched the interaction between the two women. *Hand holding?* He observed the warm smiles and affectionate glances with fascination, then arched a sandy brown eyebrow as an unspoken thought came to mind. *How interesting.*

****

8

Jess watched the apartment movers bring in a fifth cartload of boxes. "I thought you were putting most of your things in storage."

"I am." Robin directed the movers into the spare bedroom. "This is just the stuff I need."

The older woman followed Robin down the long hallway. "I have a spare closet in the office if you need more space." Jess was trying hard to be helpful.

"No, Jess." The two women entered the spare room. "There's enough space in here for my things. Thanks, though."

Just then, several movers brought in a full-sized frame, headboard, box spring and mattress and began setting up the bed against the room's opposite wall. Jess watched in riveted fashion, then narrowed her eyes. *A bed? She needs a bed?* Dark eyebrows raised almost comically. "Um...Robin? You're not...planning on using that, are you?"

The smaller woman turned to face Jess. "Using what?"

"That." Wary blue eyes stared at the now half assembled bed.

Robin followed Jess's gaze. "Oh. That." She held back a grin. "Only if I need to."

Only if she needs to? A slight pout. "Explain, please."

One of the movers assembling the bed gently cleared his throat, reminding Robin of his presence in the room. Green eyes promptly closed as an imminent blush made its way all the way to her ears. "Come with me." She led Jess out into the hallway, briefly debating whether to tease the older woman further, then had a bit of sympathy. *She's so adorable when she pouts.* "It's a daybed, Jess."

"A daybed?" There was still obviously a need for further clarification.

"Right. Just in case you might want to be alone to take a nap, or if I get sick or something."

Azure eyes peeked uncertainly beneath her dark bangs. "If you got sick, you wouldn't have to be by yourself. I'd take care of you."

A warm smile. "You did that once before."

"I remember."

Robin grasped Jess's hand and squeezed it. "Let's make a deal, okay?"

"I'm losing track of our deals, Robin." Jess quipped.

The smaller woman chuckled. "Well, if you forget, I'll remind you." She then became more serious. "Jess, I don't want to crowd you, so if you want to be alone, or if you need space, just let me know and I'll go in there." Robin motioned toward the spare room. "It would only be for those times." Jess had a blank look on her face, so Robin continued. "There might be some times when we each need our own space. Do you know what I mean?"

Jess nodded, but was otherwise silent.

She's really thrown by this. "But those times would be very rare."

That brought a small grin. "Very rare?"

"Right." Robin grinned back. "Hardly ever."

Hardly ever is good. "All right. Deal." Jess swung their still-joined hands playfully in front of her. "I really do want you to feel comfortable here, and have a place that's just for you to go to, if you need to do that sometimes." An eyebrow arched. "As long as it's not a permanent arrangement."

Green eyes twinkled. "No. It would be very temporary."

"Excuse me, ladies." A mover led the way through the narrow hallway carrying another piece of furniture.

"Um...Robin?" Jess eyed the continuous stream of items making their way into the spare bedroom. "How much stuff do you have?"

"Just my bedroom furniture, a TV, alarm clock, lamp, stereo, bookshelf, and of course my clothes and some bath items." The younger woman smiled innocently. "Why?"

"No reason." Jess turned to head back into the living room. "Though I do believe most of that stuff will get rather dusty from disuse, don't you?"

Robin could feel the smirk on the older woman's face as she walked away, then raised a pale eyebrow in thought. *She has a point.*

****

Jess sat quietly at her desk, leaning back comfortably in her burgundy leather chair as she reflected on the past weekend's events. *Moving events.* The early morning winter sun now barely peeked its first rays above the horizon, casting red and orange glows along the downtown city skyline and offering a certain serenity in its wake. The Roberts & McDaniel office suite was quiet, no one yet appearing inside to begin the workday among the usual hustle and bustle of a busy law office. Jess enjoyed this time of day the most. It allowed for quiet contemplation and placing things in the proper perspective. She swiveled slightly in her chair and gazed out the floor to ceiling window at the rising sun, idly noting the golden yellow hues now bathing the masses of steel and concrete building towers directly in her view, and casting long, almost eerie shadows in the process. *Moving day.*

Muted sunlight reflected off a mirrored faux window on the tower next door, nearly hypnotizing her mind as she shifted her blue eyes to the building's granite columns, then finally to the high archways serving as a type of gateway to the city proper. A faint, almost imperceptible niggling inside her mind delicately made its presence known amidst the quiet stillness of the dawn's early morning. *Moving day.* What, indeed, had come over her that day? Robin had gotten moved in and settled okay. Jess remembered feeling at first exuberant that they were finally living together, then once Robin had moved her things into the spare room, Jess suddenly felt...what? Distance? Insecurity? Uncertainty? *It was that damn bed.* Somehow, she hadn't counted on that. It was a bit symbolic, perhaps, that there was still an excuse not to be totally together, and it was rather silly at the same time because that wasn't at all what Robin had intended. *But still....*

All things considered, it was immensely better now that Robin was living with her. Not that Robin hadn't practically been living with her before, but now...now they both had the same address and the same telephone number and the same...*home.* Hadn't Jess wanted that all along? Still, Robin seemed to want some distance. Or maybe it was just that they each needed different things. *That's it.* Robin appeared to need her own space, while Jess needed to be close. She let her gaze linger on the now backed-up interstate below and considered that idea further. The irony of the situation almost caused her to laugh out loud. She never before was one to need anything or anyone. *Not since James, and that was such a long time ago.* Now, it seemed that she needed Robin, and she needed her to be close...very close. To be honest, it held such considerable appeal that any other alternative seemed almost unacceptable. She tapped a long finger absently against the side of the cherry wood desk. So, all right, she and Robin would have to work on the space thing. Fine. *I can live with that. Not an insurmountable problem. Right?* It crossed her mind that it was absolutely astounding that she was this attached to Robin...a woman even...a beautiful, loving, caring person. Jess arched an eyebrow. *The love of my life.*

She fiddled with the clasp of the bracelet Robin had given her for Christmas, finally unlatching it and slipping it off her wrist to inspect it further. She fingered the blue and white sapphires that glinted in the early morning sunlight, then flipped the band over to reveal the tiny inscription inside, reading it to herself all over again. *Forever.* Robin wanted that, after all, right? Didn't they both want that? Jess traced the word with the tip of her index finger. *Forever.* The niggling inside her mind now grew noticeably louder, and she finally acquiesced to the ever-increasing and unrelenting internal chatter.

Well?

'*Well, what?*' The alternate internal voice was not amused at the early morning intrusion.

What are you waiting for?

'*You're going to have to be more specific, here. I'm not a mind-reader.*' A small internal chuckle at the apparent joke.

Don't be coy. You got what you wanted. Now get on with it.

The alternate internal voice, as usual, attempted evasion. '*I'm sorry, I don't know what you mean.*'

This is growing rather tedious. Your continued attempts at ignorance are wearing thin. However, if you need it spelled out for you, then fine.

'*Get on with it then, will ya? I don't have all day.*'

Fine. Robin's moved in.

'*Brilliant.*' The alternate internal voice dripped with sarcasm. '*Now, tell me something I don't already know.*'

It's time.

'*You are obviously determined to drive me crazy today. I hate riddles. Time for what?*'

Listen very closely. Robin's moved in. It's time to make the final commitment. Again, what are you waiting for?

'*She just moved in, for Pete's sake. Give me a little time, here.*' The alternate internal voice nearly pleaded.

You bought the ring, didn't you?

A moment's reflection. '*I bought the ring, yes, but I haven't decided whether it's appropriate to give it to her.*'

Having second thoughts?

'*Never.*' The answer was firm.

Then, I repeat. What are you waiting for?

'*It's a big step. People will notice. We'd have to explain. The firm could go against us.*'

All insignificant.

The alternate internal voice grew testy. '*Easy for you to say, buddy. It's not your job on the line.*'

Does it really matter? In the grand scheme of things, isn't Robin worth losing everything?

A bit of uneasiness over the situation. '*She wouldn't want that. And what about her? All the questions. What about her family's reaction?*'

Precisely.

'*I'm sorry. You're talking in riddles again. Did I mention that I hate that?*' The alternate internal voice was growing increasingly belligerent. *Precisely what?'*

They are all convenient excuses, aren't they? You seem to want to have it both ways. You want Robin to move in, you want her in your bed....

'Hold it right there, buddy.' The alternate internal voice warned. *'I resent your implication.'*

The truth hurts, doesn't it?

'It's not the truth.' The alternate internal voice insisted.

Call it what you want, then. The fact is, you want Robin right where she is, but you're afraid to make the ultimate commitment.

'I'm not afraid of that.'

No?

'No.'

Then what is it?

'I told you.' The alternate internal voice reiterated the same tired excuses. *'People will notice. Her family. The firm.'*

You're stalling. All of that is irrelevant. Robin is worth everything and you know it. What are you really afraid of?

'I'm not answering that.' The alternate internal voice sought to dismiss the matter.

Don't avoid it. What are you really afraid of?

Silence.

Is it the idea of a commitment in general?

'No.'

Is it the idea of two women committed to each other for the rest of their lives?

The alternate internal voice hesitated just a bit. 'No.'

No?

'Okay, I admit it's a little unconventional, but no.'

Is it Robin?

'Absolutely not.' The alternate internal voice was certain.

Then what is it? Rejection?

No answer.

Answer, please.

A long internal sigh. 'It's just that Robin might not want the outward acknowledgment of our relationship. She might not want the questions, the possible alienation by her family and others, and all the complications.'

Because of you.

'Yes.' The alternate internal voice replied somberly. 'Because of me.'

You're both grown-ups. You can handle it. She said forever. Don't you think she knows what that means?

'She said forever, but I believe she meant that she'll love me forever, not that she commits to me forever. There's a big difference, you know.'

Cut it out.

'I beg your pardon.' The alternate internal voice was now indignant.

Cut it out. What are you really afraid of? Go ahead. Spit it out.

The alternate internal voice became hostile. 'You're really starting to get on my nerves.'

Then, quit playing games. You're afraid of something. What is it?
More silence.
Admit the truth.

'You want the truth? Fine. Here it is.' The alternate internal voice annunciated the next words very succinctly. 'She's not over him.'

So, we're back to David again, are we?

'Yes.' The alternate internal voice practically hissed the acknowledgment.

You're afraid she won't commit to you because deep down in her heart, she still loves him and she can't let go.

'Yes. Happy now?' The alternate internal voice was extremely agitated. 'She can't even forgive God for taking him away. How could she just forget all that and commit to me?'

You're not giving her any credit. She's seeing Dr. Richmond. She'll work through that.

'Maybe, maybe not.'

Fine. What else?

'What else, what?' The alternate internal voice was deliberately obtuse, now thoroughly annoyed at the direction the internal conversation was taking.

Don't feign innocence yet again. What else are you afraid of?

'Damn it! You're bugging the hell out of me.'

Answer the question, please.

'Fine.' The alternate internal voice nearly spat out the response. 'Here is your answer. She might not commit to me because she wants to be free to eventually leave.'

I see. So, let's boil this down in a nutshell, shall we? You're afraid that Robin will reject your ring not necessarily because of all the potential questions, or because of her family, or even because of the firm's possible concerns, but because she still loves David, and once she understands that through her visits with Dr. Richmond, she will want to be free to leave you without the ties of commitment hanging in the way. Have I summarized that up accurately?

'*Yes, oh all-knowing mighty and powerful one. You've got that right.*' The alternate internal voice snarled. '*Now, get the hell off my back!*'

Easy, there. Just think about one last thing, all right?

The alternate internal voice momentarily calmed. '*Fine. What?*'

What have you got to lose? And, what have you got to gain? It's worth the risk, isn't it?

No answer.

Just think about it.

'*Fine.*' Long fingers traced the sapphires on the bracelet one more time before replacing the bangle on the owner's wrist, the owner, herself, suddenly very weary. '*Now, please just go away. I'm rather tired of this conversation.*'

****

Later that same morning, Robin put the finishing touches on a Motion to Compel and stood up to give herself a quick stretch. Her fingers reflexively went to the diamond heart-shaped pendant around her neck, feeling the smooth solid gold channel band and beveled cut in-laid diamonds. *Jess's heart.* It was absolutely the most endearing gift Robin had ever received, and without a doubt, the most precious. *Does she know?* Robin took a moment to ponder the significance of the gift. *Does she know how I treasure it?* Another, deeper thought came to her. How exactly would Jess feel about a commitment? Not just a declaration of love, but a forever kind of commitment? Naturally, her mind took the next detour. *The ring.* It was true, Robin had bought the ring purely on impulse, not really considering the implications or complications of such a move. Her light brows creased as she contemplated the action further. If she gave Jess the ring, they'd be forced to go public with their relationship....*Well, only, of course, if Jess chose to wear it.*

What to do. She tapped two fingers in staccato fashion on the desk top. There was a white elephant in the room and she knew it. Robin had only had one session with Dr. Richmond so far; getting completely past the anguish of David's accident would take time. She only hoped she'd finally be able to let go of the overwhelming guilt. She shook her head. *As if that were possible.* Petite fingers ran briskly through her short blonde hair in slight frustration, the sparkling waters of the lake below capturing and then holding her now diverted attention. After many long moments of reflection, she finally concluded that she couldn't make a commitment to Jess, or expect one in return, while the issue was as yet unresolved. It wouldn't be fair. *I'd drag her down with me.* However, once that particular issue was off the table....

What to do. Robin sat back down in her chair and crossed her feet at her ankles in front of her. There were no easy answers. The litany of issues ranging from public acknowledgment, to career risks, to family reactions, to overcoming her feelings of unworthiness...if that was the appropriate word, abounded. *And a label?* Could she live with that? Wasn't Jess worth it? And for that matter, did it really matter what anyone else thought? Isn't a label just that? A label. Nothing more. *Perhaps.* The reality was, Robin loved Jess, the person, and the fact that Jess is also a woman did not in any way change that reality. Robin picked up her pen and bit the top lightly between her teeth, finally making her decision. Aside from the career risks, everything else was merely extraneous. Jess was worth everything, even a label.

So, what to do. What about that ring? If they could get past the firm's concerns, it would all boil down to timing. The ultimate question was, when would the right time be? That question, Robin discovered, had no easy answer.

A light knock at her partially open door caused her to snap her head up and turn away from her musings. "Come in."

Michelle Richards poked her head inside the doorway. "Hi. Got a minute?"

"Sure." Robin waved her inside. "What's up?"

Michelle sat down in the chair in front of the desk. "I was hoping you could cover an ex-parte hearing for me tomorrow. I've got a client conference that just came up, and I really need to get these out-of-state commissions appointed for a couple of depositions in Atlanta."

As Robin listened, her hand unconsciously tugged at the pendant necklace she wore. "Sure, just leave the papers with me. I'll take care of it tomorrow." She smiled.

"Great." The diamond pendant caught the senior associate's eye. "That's gorgeous." She pointed toward the necklace.

Robin swallowed. "Thanks."

"Is it new?"

I can do this. "Um...yeah." Robin picked up her pen and twirled it lightly between her fingers, then quickly added. "It was a gift."

Michelle spent another moment appraising the diamond piece. "From...someone special?" She glanced up at Robin expectantly.

"From a friend." *That's technically true.* The pen twirled faster.

Deciding not to pry, and since she had a lot more work to

accomplish before the day was through, Michelle stood up to leave. "Well, whoever it is certainly has nice taste. It looks good on you." She turned toward the door. "Oh yeah, I almost forgot. What's the name of the apartments where you live? I'm thinking of getting a new place, and I remember you said once that the rent was pretty reasonable."

Robin opened her mouth to answer, but nothing came out. The pen, however, tumbled helplessly to the floor. *Be honest.* "I...um....recently moved from there, but the name of the apartments is Heron's Cove." She casually retrieved her pen from underneath the desk.

Michelle smiled gratefully. "Thanks. So, where did you move?" The senior associate was merely making polite conversation.

I knew she was going to ask that. The pen, quite on its own, resumed its twirling. "I moved over to Jess's place. She offered, since she has such a big house, and I decided try it out. I get a lot more room for the money." Robin was quite proud of the plausible answer she'd concocted.

As expected, Michelle's eyes grew very wide. "Jessica Harrison? You moved there?"

A mental sigh. *I need to get used to this.* "Yeah. It works out well."

The senior associate grew pensive. "I don't know, Robin. I think you have to watch out. You know how difficult she can be sometimes. It seems she'd be hard to get along with."

The pen clattered lightly against the side of the desk. "I think it'll be fine, and I really do like the house." Robin forcibly grabbed her pen and set it down on her legal pad, then deftly brushed aside any further conversation on the matter. "So, when you have those papers ready for the hearing tomorrow, just drop them by." She offered a warm smile that belied her unease. "I'll take care of it."

"Okay. Thanks." And with that, Michelle exited the office, leaving Robin nervously sitting at her desk and wondering just how long she and Jess could keep up the charade.

Who are we kidding? People are going to find out.

****

In spite the fact that it was the first weeks of a typically dreary January, the work week was actually moving along quite nicely. It seemed that people needed to take their time and put the holidays solidly behind them before getting all geared up again and charging full-steam ahead into the busy business fray. It was now mid-week, and to her mild surprise, Jess had actually accomplished quite a bit, having made major progress on an appellate brief she'd been working on since before the holidays. In light of her good fortune, she decided to knock off work at a reasonably decent hour and head on home.

Giving in to an unusual and rare impulse, she stopped along the way and picked up some Chinese take-out, then pulled her silver Mercedes into the garage of The Ranch. She strolled inside the sprawling house and found Robin in the living room unpacking a small box left over from her recent move. "Hey, kiddo." The taller woman parked her briefcase in the foyer and set her Chinese take-out on the dining room table.

"Hi." Robin looked up. "You picked up something for dinner?" She stopped her unpacking and stepped over to the dining room table. "I'm starving."

A shocked expression. "Imagine that." Jess winked, then headed into the kitchen to retrieve the plates and utensils.

"Very funny." Robin called back, then curiously peeked inside one of the take-out bags. "So, what'd you get?"

Jess brought out the dinnerware and began unpacking the assorted food. "Chinese. A little moo goo gai pan and some mu shu pork."

Robin flipped open a container. "And?"

Blue eyes looked up. "And what?"

"What else did you get?"

"Um..." A blank look. "Egg rolls?"

Light eyebrows furrowed. "Okay. And?"

A considerably confused expression replaced the previous one. "Um...won ton soup?" The older woman pulled out the soup in question.

"Oh." Robin opened another bag and peered curiously inside. "Hmmm."

"You wanted the egg drop?"

"Oh. No. Won ton's fine." The younger woman searched the bag further, then mumbled to no one in particular. "I thought for sure it'd be here."

"What?" Jess emptied the contents of the remaining bag. "Fortune cookies? They're right here." She produced several small packages of the referenced cookies for inspection.

"No." Perplexed green eyes studied blue. "I guess it's really not here." The younger woman seemed rather surprised at the revelation, then focused her attention on the displayed food. "Okay. I'll get the drinks. Is iced tea all right?"

"Sure." Jess watched with a close eye as Robin padded her way

18

into the kitchen. Once the younger woman was safely out of sight, Jess quickly retrieved another bag from beneath a chair and pulled out a container, promptly dishing its contents onto her own plate.

After a moment, Robin returned with two glasses of iced tea and sat down at the table. "I think I'll try the mu shu pork, first." A delighted grin. "I really love making those little crepe thingies." She began unwrapping the pancakes, then spread ample amounts of mu shu sauce over them before adding the pork filling. In her subsequent attempt to reach for the fried rice, Robin caught sight of the older woman's plate. She abruptly stopped her motion in progress and fixed her gaze squarely on the plate's contents. "Um...Jess?" Green eyes narrowed considerably. "What is that?"

Jess stopped mid-chew and looked up rather innocently. "Um...what is what?"

A petite finger pointed at Jess's dinner. "That. On your plate."

Jess attempted to evade the question. "It's Chinese food, Robin." She resumed eating.

"I can see that." A blonde eyebrow arched in suspicion. *I knew it was here.* "Specifically, though, what is it?"

"It's just the food I bought." Jess gave the non-committal reply, then nonchalantly took another bite.

"Right." Robin paused to further assess the situation, her sea-green eyes narrowing once again. "You..." Robin wagged a finger in Jess's direction. "Are very sneaky."

Innocent blue eyes peered back. "Sneaky?"

"Yes. You tried to sneak it in so I wouldn't notice, didn't you?"

The dark head shook vehemently. "No, I didn't."

"Don't bother denying it, Jess." A frank look. "I'm on to you."

Rats. Jess now knew she'd indeed been caught. "Okay, Robin, so maybe I did, but I had a really, really good reason."

Robin stifled a grin. "You did?"

"Yes." Jess took another bite. "Wanna hear it."

"Well..." A long, exaggerated sigh. "If you must." Robin proceeded to neatly roll her mu shu pancake, then took a bite.

"Okay. It's like this. I was standing at the take-out counter, minding my own business, when the order for guy standing behind me came out of the kitchen. It was just sitting there, and I saw it."

The younger woman listened with rapt attention. "You saw it?"

"Yes."

Robin took another bite. "The shrimp?"

Jess blinked several times. "Yes."

"With the lobster sauce?"

Jess blinked once more. "Yes."

Robin took a sip of her tea. "And so you decided to get some, too."

"Yes."

"I see." Robin spooned some fried rice onto her plate, then dished out a small amount of moo goo gai pan. "I'm glad you admitted that." She patted Jess's arm sympathetically. "Do you feel that this is becoming a problem for you?" An unmistakable twinkle made its way to her eyes.

Jess gave Robin a bemused look, then debated whether to play along. *Why not?* "Well, I believe that there is a problem, yes."

A pale eyebrow rose, then quickly fell. "Admitting you have a problem is the first step toward recovery."

"Well, it's not really my problem." Jess jabbed a succulent shrimp with her fork and lifted it off her plate. "See, there is a certain person who, as preposterous as it sounds, thinks that my...shall we say...fondness for a particular seafood-related item is some sort of fetish." She waved the tasty piece of shrimp in Robin's direction. "Of course, I totally disagree."

Robin ignored the shrimp in front of her nose and cocked her head slightly. "Go on."

"Well, naturally, since this person fails to grasp the finer points of my cuisine of choice, I'm forced to sneak meals of this particular seafood-related item whenever I can." Jess added a second delectable shrimp to her fork, then continued further. "I'm trying very hard to deal with this person's difficulty in accepting my completely normal, socially acceptable and perfectly reasonable fondness for this particular seafood-related item." Now, an aggrieved sigh. "Alas, I've finally come to the conclusion that the only solution to this unfortunate problem is to declare each and every day 'shrimp day.' I'm even considering making it a house rule." Jess finished her monologue by plopping the forkful of prized shrimp into her mouth with a deliberate flourish, ostensibly emphasizing her point.

All Robin could do was stare at Jess in true and utter disbelief. Things had apparently progressed much further than she had originally thought. "I have just one thing to say to you."

A dark eyebrow arched. "And what's that?"

"You're hopeless."

"Well, I think we've already established that, Robin." Jess quipped. A long moment of silence followed, then blue eyes peeked hesitantly across the table. "Um...want some?" Jess pointed at her plate, the peace offering clear.

Robin couldn't help but grin. "Well..." She considered the offer for what it was. "Perhaps just a taste."

"Okay. Here." The older woman scooted over closer to Robin and lifted a fork full of the now infamous shrimp with lobster sauce to the younger woman's mouth, watching with delight as Robin ate the proffered food. Maybe it was their proximity, but Jess couldn't resist leaning in closer and giving the sweet lips in front of her a quick kiss in the process.

"Mmmm. That was very good." Robin commented.

Jess beamed. "The shrimp?"

"No." An affectionate smile. "The kiss."

"Oh." The older woman considered the response, then offered to sweeten the deal with a little incentive. "There's more."

"More shrimp?" Robin was secretly enjoying the playfulness.

Jess shook her head. "More kisses." She leaned in for another, now lingering, kiss.

After a moment, Robin pulled back and stared into crystal blue eyes, finally deciding to wrap up her carefully crafted negotiations. "You know." She whispered. "I'd be inclined to agree with a house rule declaring every day 'shrimp day' if it were to also include the kisses."

Sensing imminent victory, Jess quickly accepted the counter-offer. "Deal." Not surprisingly, for the next several moments, the once popular shrimp was all but forgotten.

****

The fire was softly blazing in the fireplace after dinner was finished, the yellow-orange flames flickering quietly and casting dim shadows around the darkened living room. Robin splayed her petite body out on top of the Oriental rug that lay just beyond the ceramic tile floor in front of the hearth, and gently rested her head on a large throw pillow for support. Green eyes silently watched the now glowing embers as the blaze steadily burned down. Jess approached the fireplace cautiously, carrying several large pieces of oak hardwood, and put a new log on the swiftly dying fire. The resulting crackling preceded a quick flare-up of new flames which danced robustly within the hearth, the reinvigorated blaze sending welcome waves of heat out into the spacious living area.

"Better?" Jess grabbed another throw pillow and stretched out on the floor beside Robin.

"Much. Thanks."

The long body curled snugly around the smaller frame. "Sometimes this house can be a little drafty when it's cold outside."

Robin turned her head toward Jess and grinned. "Did I just hear you admit that it was cold outside?"

The older woman realized her gaffe and rushed to correct. "I meant the house can be drafty when it is cool outside, Robin. That's what I meant."

The grin widened. "Right. Cool outside." The smaller body turned fully toward the fire. "Do you mind me hogging your living room like this?"

There was a small sigh as Jess realized that Robin still didn't consider the house her home. *I guess it's just gonna take some time.* She spoke her next words very softly. "For the record, kiddo, this is your living room, too, and you can do anything you want in it." A thought popped into her mind and she quickly amended her statement. "Well, anything within reason, of course." She grinned somewhat devilishly and snaked a long arm contentedly around the younger woman's waist.

Robin reveled in the resulting warmth. "I just don't want to be in your way."

Another small sigh. *Let's set this straight once and for all.* "Hey." A large hand reached over and gently turned Robin's face toward her own. "Look at me, sweetheart. In case I haven't communicated this very well, let me say it to you again. You are not in my way. You will never be in my way. And even if you were to be in my way, which you won't, I would not have a problem with it." She brushed Robin's cheek tenderly with her thumb and whispered. "You got that?"

The blonde head nodded in acknowledgment. "Got it."

"Good." With that, Jess changed the subject. "So, are you pretty much unpacked now?"

"Just about. I have one small box of knick-knacks, but I think I'll put that up in the spare closet. Otherwise, everything's unpacked."

Jess tightened her grip on the smaller woman's waist and cuddled up close. Robin seemed quieter than normal, and Jess had learned from previous experience that it usually meant that there was something on her mind. "Want to talk about it?"

Robin took a deep breath. "I always wonder how you know."

The taller woman propped herself up on one elbow and rested the side of her head in her hand. "I just know." Something registered in her mind as she stroked the blonde hair from Robin's eyes, and she finally understood. "You have another session with Dr. Richmond tomorrow."

"Yeah."

That was non-committal. Robin hadn't talked about her first and only session, and Jess hadn't wanted to pry. "If you'd rather not talk about it, honey, it's okay. You don't have to, you know." Jess brushed her knuckles lightly against Robin's cheek.

The younger woman shifted to lay flat on her back and gazed into understanding eyes now turned an incredible shade of blue in the flickering firelight. "It's just that I'm going to have to talk about us with Dr. Richmond, and I guess I'm not used to discussing that with anyone."

"Does it bother you, talking about us?"

This is hard to explain. "A small hand reached for the larger one still resting on her waist and interlocked their fingers. "I worry what people will think when they know, then I realize that it's really silly to worry about it. Dr. Richmond is a therapist. She doesn't care personally about that."

The unspoken thought hung in the air between them until Jess finally put voice to it. "But others will care."

A somber nod. "Yes. Others will care."

Jess leaned in and kissed a blonde eyebrow, then whispered, her azure eyes reflecting an almost imperceptible hint of sadness. "Would it really matter to you if people knew?"

A long sigh, then an honest answer. "I don't know." And Robin really didn't know. She thought she knew, but now, she wasn't so sure. On the one hand, she really didn't want to have to sneak around and hide her relationship with Jess, and on the other hand, she knew the practical consequences of disclosing it. "It would hurt your career. Maybe both of ours. The firm wouldn't understand."

Okay. "Let me ask you something, and you don't have to answer it if you don't want to. If you took the career part away so it was not an issue, how would you feel if people knew about us?"

Robin thought about that. "I wouldn't like being the subject of comments or being labeled, but ultimately, if we didn't have to worry about the career aspect and the firm's reaction, I think I could handle it."

Jess proceeded cautiously. "So, provided there wasn't the career issue or the firm's concerns, you're saying you wouldn't mind a public acknowledgment?" *The ring is a public acknowledgment.*

Robin squeezed Jess's hand. "I decided something. People can know or not know. It doesn't matter, as long as I'm with you."

Jess asked the final question, mentally checking off all real and imagined obstacles. "What about your family?"

A heavy sigh. "I've also decided that although I'll have to deal with them, they don't control me or my life." Green eyes studied blue, a similar question now on Robin's mind. "What about you, Jess? How would you feel?"

The older woman stared into the fire, taking a moment to order her thoughts. "My mother knows and it's okay. I don't know how my brother and his wife would react, but like you said, they don't control me or my life." She paused for a second and snuggled closer to Robin, then resumed her previous train of thought. "As far as everyone else is concerned, what I do is none of their business. It's true, I wouldn't like being the subject of comments either, or being labeled, but they can say whatever they want. If they don't understand, so be it." Her voice softened to a whisper. "They couldn't possibly understand how I feel about you."

Robin nodded, but nevertheless had to ask. "You're saying that you would still want to be with me, even if people knew and even if they didn't understand?"

"Let me put it this way." Jess smiled near a petite ear. "Yes."

Okay. Robin then brought up a related topic. "Michelle came by my office today. She was admiring my necklace."

An eyebrow arched. "What did she say?"

"She liked it." Robin thought back to their conversation. "She asked who it was from." Now, Robin felt a bit guilty. "I didn't lie, but I told her it was from a friend."

Jess reflected on that. "That was the wise thing to do. We still have the firm's concerns to think about."

"Michelle also asked which apartments I live at. It seems she wants to find a new place, and she heard me talking once about how my rent was reasonable." Robin turned in Jess's embrace, repositioning herself so that her head now rested in the crook of the older woman's neck. "I told her that I moved in here."

"Oh. What was her reaction to that?"

"She was a bit surprised, but otherwise she didn't make too much of it. She did, of course, try to warn me that you could be a little hard to get along with." The smaller woman grinned against Jess's skin.

"Did she, now?"

"Yes."

"And did you agree with that assessment?" A blue eye peeked

down at Robin.

"I didn't comment, but if I had to answer, I probably would have said that other than certain culinary matters, and of course, animal-related footwear, you are quite easy to get along with." Green eyes peeked back.

"I see." Jess nuzzled against the blonde hair and breathed in the sweet scent. "We'll have to work on those matters, then. I think in time, you'll come around to my point of view."

Robin smirked. *Not likely.* She took on somewhat serious expression. "So, do you think it's all right that people know I'm living here?"

Jess trailed her fingers up and down Robin's shirtsleeve. "It's not exactly a secret, you know. Besides, it doesn't matter. We're roommates, after all, remember?"

That brought a decided grin. "Right. Roommates." The younger woman shifted and braced herself up on one arm, sea-green eyes now dancing in the waning firelight. "You know, Jess." She drawled. "When I was moving in here last weekend, I'm pretty sure I scoped out the whole house and I still didn't see it."

Dark eyebrows knit together. "See what?"

"My present, of course."

Jess's mouth fell open. "Your...."

"Present." Robin supplied again. "You know, my birthday's next week."

Blue eyes focused steadily on green in a clear challenge. "And?"

"Nothing." Robin shrugged. "Have I told you about this sporty looking BMW that...." She was effectively cut off by a large hand covering her mouth.

"I think you might have mentioned it a time or two, Robin." Jess removed her hand. "Let me just say that if I got you a present, and I'm not saying I did, but if I did, I certainly wouldn't hide it around here for you to find."

Green eyes twinkled. "Well, I guess you do have a point. A car really is too big to hide around here anyway, isn't it?"

Jess was utterly and truly charmed. *A car indeed.* "Come here." She reached up and pulled the younger woman down closer to her, claiming her lips in the process.

The two bodies were otherwise engaged for the remainder of the evening, as the fire finally burned its way down to barely glowing embers only to extinguish itself fully in the stillness of the night.

****

The day started out like any other day, with the usual deadlines to meet and minor crises to avert. Jess had just finished winding up a two-hour conference call with a rather difficult client when a light knock on the door drew her attention. "Come in."

Harry Roberts opened the heavy wood door and entered the well-appointed partner-sized office. "You got a minute, Jess?" He didn't wait for a reply, closing the door behind him and making himself comfortable in the chair next to the large floor to ceiling window.

"Sure, Harry. What's up?" The junior partner folded her hands on top of her cherry wood desk and waited.

Harry suddenly seemed a little uncomfortable. "Gee, I wish I'd gotten some coffee on the way over here." He gruffly mumbled the statement, obviously stalling a bit before proceeding with what brought him over to Jess's office.

A wary eyebrow arched. *What's up, Harry?* Jess picked up her telephone and called her secretary. "Angie, Mr. Roberts is in my office. Could you bring him a cup of coffee, please? Black." The junior partner looked to Harry for confirmation, and upon seeing the nod, hung up the phone and asked the previous question once again. "So, Harry, what's up?"

The head of the litigation department shifted in his seat, then decided to broach the subject quickly. "I hear you've taken on a tenant."

Jess mentally cringed. *Shit. What's the damn problem?* "Yes." She responded evenly. "A while back, Robin and I had discussed the possibility of her moving into the house, and she finally decided to do that." The junior partner felt the need to explain further. "The fact is, Harry, Robin's family is up north, and she is here by herself. You also know that I've had that whole house to myself all these years. It seemed a waste not to make full use of it. Robin and I talked about her moving in, and we decided we'd give it a try."

Harry's features softened. As Jess's mentor, he was well aware of her previous situation with James and remembered all too well the emotional damage done to one of his brightest attorneys by that no-good leech. He assumed his familiar mentor role. "That's fine, Jess. I certainly do understand. It's probably a good thing for Robin, as well. I know it can be difficult starting out in a strange city by yourself, and I'm sure you wouldn't mind the company in that big house of yours."

Although Harry didn't come right out and say it, Jess knew that he was being sympathetic. She smiled inwardly at his concern. In times past, Harry had been more of a father figure to her than a mentor. In fact, he was more of a father to her than her own father had been. She continued with her explanation. "Robin and I seem to work well together, which in my case, as you know, is saying a lot." She gave him a self-deprecating smile. "Considering that, we thought we could probably get along all right sharing the same house."

"You two have gotten close, haven't you?"

That question came out of the blue. *Damn.* Harry seemed amazingly perceptive all of a sudden. *Stay calm.* "We're friends, yes." Jess's voice betrayed none of her increasing anxiety.

Just then, Angie knocked on the door and opened it, bringing in with her Harry's cup of black coffee. She handed it to him, then subtly surveyed the situation inside the office. Her boss seemed a bit tense, and the head of litigation was a little uneasy, as well. *Hmmm. Wonder what's going on.* In her brief stay, Angie managed to glean that something quite interesting was indeed being discussed. She left the office and proceeded directly to her desk, immediately phoning her best friend, Betty, who just happened to serve as the secretary to none other than Harry Roberts. What's a day without a little minor gossip?

Back inside the office, Jess sensed that there was more to Harry's visit than just idle chit chat about the state of her housemates. "There isn't a problem, is there?" *There better not be.*

Harry took a long sip of his coffee, then very deliberately set the cup down on the corner of the cherry wood desk in front of him. He looked Jess squarely in the eye. "I want you to be careful." The tone of his voice carried a well-intentioned warning. "You are a partner. Robin is an associate. You are, in essence, her employer. She is your employee. If you two are friends and want to share a residence, that's fine, so long as it doesn't lead to a conflict of interest."

Jess straightened up in her burgundy leather chair. "What type of conflict of interest are we talking, here?"

Harry paused, then leaned forward slightly. "It would not be a good thing for this firm if there were undercurrents of favoritism. Robin does mostly your work. You review her performance. The Management Committee makes the final determination on retention, but it is based on the partners' reviews of the associate's overall work product and achievements." He took a moment to allow his comments sink in. "It's a fine line. I know you will make every effort to be objective when it comes to an associate's review and work load, personal friendships aside."

"I understand." And Jess absolutely did understand, all too well.

Harry continued. "With experience and training, Robin will be a very good attorney. She already is, and I'm betting that's due in large part to the interest you've shown in taking her under your wing. She will benefit from your experience, but she must also be given constructive feedback so she knows how to improve. I know you've been doing that, and it would be best to continue with that same approach, both to benefit Robin and to avoid any misimpression of favorable treatment." He smiled gently. "You're an excellent attorney, Jess, one of the best here, and I have every confidence in you and in your judgment on this matter."

The junior partner sat very still listening to Harry. When it boiled right down to it, he was really looking out for her, and his words were spoken with a fatherly concern she'd come to depend on throughout the years. He also was looking out for the firm, of that there was no doubt, and there was no mistaking the underlying, albeit subtly implied, warning. "I see your point, Harry. When it pertains to job performance, I guarantee that I will be completely objective."

"Good." Harry finished his coffee and stood up. "Now, how about you joining Barbara and me for dinner next week. Our treat." He paused, then added. "When you see Robin, ask her if she'd liked to come along, too, if she's free. My wife has told me on more than one occasion how much she enjoyed talking with both of you at the holiday party last month."

Jess smiled. "Thanks. I'd love to join you and Barbara. Let me mention it to Robin and see if she'll be free next week, then I'll get back to you on that."

"Great." With the conversation now concluded, Harry turned and left the junior partner's office, closing the door solidly behind him.

The tall form sank back into her leather chair as if a heavy weight now rested on her shoulders. Things were starting to close in. She knew they would. All along, she knew it would just be a matter of time. The trick always had been to beat the eventual odds. The fact that Harry, although never admitting it, was concerned with the appearance of her friendship with Robin spoke volumes. Suddenly, almost as an afterthought, something else made its way into her rational thinking. Something which caused even Jess to flinch as Harry's words echoed in her mind. *You are Robin's employer. She is your employee. It's a fine line.* Large hands now rested over repentant blue eyes, a profound weariness abruptly setting in. It all had become abundantly clear. Harry wanted to make sure that Jess didn't cross the line.

The problem was, she already had.

Chapter 2

The lazy Saturday morning came with clouding skies and drizzling rain, the light pattering of raindrops on the bedroom window finally rousting the petite form from a heavy sleep. She slowly opened her eyes, momentarily squinting at the somewhat dreary gray light, then finally turned and noted the time on the clock radio. *That late?* Drowsily, she rolled over toward the center of the waterbed and promptly noticed that that she was alone. Her companion had apparently already gotten up, probably hours ago. As she pondered her solitary situation a moment longer, a subtle aroma made its presence known. *Coffee.* All thoughts of resuming her slumber suddenly vanished. She sniffed in the enticing scent, twitching her nose slightly, then quickly rose and donned her robe and slippers.

Groggily, Robin padded her way into the kitchen, finding the freshly brewed gourmet blend she so eagerly sought. She poured herself a large cup, added liberal amounts of cream and sugar, then set about locating her conspicuously elusive housemate. She stifled a yawn as she checked the dining room, and upon finding it vacant, next ventured out into the large living room. There, perched in a corner of the plush sofa, Jess sat quietly reading the morning paper, coffee cup in hand. The taller woman had one long leg casually swung over the other, gently rocking a foot back and forth as she studied the day's headlines. Robin entered the living room, and before she had proceeded too far, stopped dead in her tracks. She stared at the older woman, mouth slightly open, and then broke out into uncontrollable giggles, nearly spilling her coffee in the process.

Blue eyes peeked up above the Saturday comics section. "Morning." Jess studied the softly giggling woman. "Something you

29

find...funny?"

Robin sat down in a nearby chair and momentarily composed herself. "No." The giggling resumed.

Amused blue eyes watched with interest. "You obviously find something funny." Jess set down the newspaper and continued to swing her foot back and forth, casually taking a sip of a coffee. "Care to share?"

The younger woman suppressed a grin. "I was just admiring your...slippers." A chuckle escaped as she assumed a somewhat similar posture, crossing her legs and swinging one bunny slipper covered foot back and forth.

A satisfied smirk edged across the older woman's face. "Yes, I must say they are quite comfortable."

"I can see that." Robin set her half-empty cup down on the coffee table and appraised her housemate's footwear with a critical eye. "I....um...didn't think that Tweety Bird was quite your style." She tried, but failed, to suppress another giggle.

Both dark eyebrows rose in seeming dismay. "Don't you like them?"

Green eyes glanced from Jess back down to the slippers in question. "They're lovely. They're just so..." Robin searched for the appropriate word. "Yellow."

"Yellow." Jess mouthed the word, then set her empty coffee cup down on the oak table and inquired further. "Do you have a problem with...yellow?"

"Um...no." A bemused expression. "Absolutely not." It became apparent that Robin was simply unable to contain her amusement. Her giggles turned into full laughter, forcing her to wipe her eyes several times before she was finally able to get herself under control. She once again glanced at the bright yellow slippers and crinkled her nose slightly. "They are a little distracting, though, don't you think?"

"Really?" Innocent blue eyes regarded the referenced slippers. "I hadn't noticed." A yellow slipper clad foot swung briskly in front of the sofa.

Robin almost lost it all over again. "Um...Jess?" She absolutely had to ask. "You don't intend on wearing those from now on, do you?"

Jess put a hand to her chest in obvious offense at the question. "Why, of course, Robin." Blue eyes subtly twinkled. "I see no reason not to." One long leg shifted conspicuously and crossed the other, wildly swinging the opposite yellow slipper in front of Robin in the process. "Do you?"

She is so sneaky. Green eyes narrowed considerably. "If this is some sort of attempt to get me to give up my bunny slippers, it's not going to work."

An appalled expression. "I'm shocked that you would even think such a thing, Robin." Blue eyes fixed on green. "You have your slippers. I have mine."

Robin wagged a playful finger in Jess's direction. "You thought that if you wore the most outrageous slippers, I would reconsider my decision to keep wearing my bunny slippers, didn't you?"

The dark head shook vehemently. "No, I didn't."

"Yes, you did." A smirk. "I'm on to you, Jess."

"You're paranoid, Robin. I recall very specifically that you, yourself, said that my slippers were lovely." Jess was confident she had gained the upper hand on the matter. She regarded her yellow slippers with fondness. "I quite like them."

Robin simply stared at the older woman. "You think you're so smart, don't you?"

Jess grinned mischievously. "Yes, I think I'm smart, but it has absolutely nothing to do with my slippers."

Robin moved over and knelt in front of Jess. "You're impossible."

"Impossible? I beg to differ, Robin. I was sitting here minding my own business reading the paper, when all of a sudden, you finally wake up, almost at noon I might add, and come out here and start insulting my new slippers."

Robin bent down and inspected the yellow slippers more closely. "You're right. I apologize." She reached up and slowly uncrossed Jess's legs. "I shouldn't have made fun of your slippers like that." Petite hands skillfully removed one yellow slipper, then the other, tenderly caressing the bare feet as each slipper fell to the floor. "Actually, what I should have done was..." An impish grin appeared. "This." With lightning quickness, Robin shot up and took off running, yellow slippers in hand.

That's it! Jess bolted from the sofa and ran after Robin, down the long hallway and toward Robin's new room. When she reached the end of the hall, the door was closed tight. "Robin?" She called through the door. "Give them back."

No answer.

Jess knocked insistently. "Robin, I know you're in there. Give them back."

Robin cracked the door slightly and peered out. "Fair is fair. You stole mine, remember?"

"I gave them back."

31

"Only after I threatened to ban you to the guestroom."

Ahaa. A smug grin. *Gotcha.* Jess nudged her way inside the room. "Just remember, Robin, two can play at that game."

Uh oh. Robin swallowed as she became all too aware of her miscalculation. "You wouldn't."

Jess smirked, "This is a lovely room, Robin. I'm sure you'll very comfortable here tonight." Sensing imminent victory, she offered one last time to resolve the situation. "You could give them back and avoid this, you know."

A blonde eyebrow lifted in thought. "Perhaps we could call a truce just for today." Robin sat down on the daybed and tossed off her bunny slippers.

"A truce?" Jess was intrigued.

"Yes." Robin grinned. "Perhaps we could declare this 'no slippers day.' She raised both eyebrows expectantly. 'What do you say?"

Jess joined her on the bed. "And, just so I'm clear, what are the benefits of 'no slippers day'?"

The petite body reclined against the throw pillows. "I'm quite sure you could think of something."

Jess leaned forward and covered the small body with her own, pondering the matter for just a moment. "Nope." She grinned. "I can't think of anything."

Robin opened Jess's robe and pushed it off her shoulders. "Think harder, then." She leaned up and nibbled on a conveniently placed earlobe.

Jess closed her eyes at the contact. "Nope. I'm still at a loss here, Robin."

Small hands lifted Jess's shirt top and brushed against a bare stomach. "Then, I would say you definitely need to concentrate."

The dark head rested on Robin's shoulder as the gentle touches continued. "I'm afraid I'm fresh out of ideas." The older woman then gasped as she felt those same small hands slowly begin to remove her drawstring flannel boxers.

"You need to think really, really hard, Jess." Robin completed the task at hand and grazed her fingertips across a particularly sensitive area.

"Nope." Jess nearly croaked. "I'm drawing a complete blank."

Soft lips pressed against Jess's collarbone. "Are you absolutely sure?"

"Um...." Jess was, indeed, unable to think clearly. "Could you give me a little hint?"

Robin's response was to pull Jess closer to her, claiming her lips in an intense kiss. "Does that, perhaps, help you?" Robin asked in a now breathless whisper.

Fiery blue eyes seared into green as Jess grinned. "Yes, Robin. I believe that did it. I suddenly feel...inspired." She hastily assisted Robin out of her robe and flannel nightshirt and once again met the younger woman's enticing lips. "Who knew..." She murmured through her insistent kisses. "That 'no slippers day' had so many possibilities."

Robin closed her eyes, vaguely aware of the gentle pattering of rain outside, before warm hands and moist lips displaced any further thought and carried her away to other more interesting places. *Who knew?*

Indeed.

****

Although it was now early afternoon, neither Jess nor Robin had yet eaten breakfast. Robin was positively starving, and even Jess, despite her self-inflicted morning fast, had to admit that she could indeed use a little sustenance. They both showered and dressed, then met in the kitchen to prepare a light brunch.

"So, what are your plans for today?" Jess poured herself another cup of freshly made coffee and sat down at the kitchen table.

Robin beat several eggs and waited for the skillet to heat up. "Well, that depends on you. Are you here, or do you have to go in to the office?"

"Sorry, kiddo. No hooky time for me today. I need to get some work done this afternoon." Blue eyes held a hidden sparkle. "However, you do need to keep tomorrow open."

All too innocent green eyes glanced up. "Tomorrow?"

"Yes." A frank look. "And don't pretend you don't know what tomorrow is. You've only been reminding me about it for months, and not so subtly either." The older woman lifted an eyebrow to further her point.

Robin was playfully indignant. "I only mentioned it a couple of times."

"Whatever." Jess waved a dismissive hand. "Just make sure you take care of your Sunday chores today and anything else you have to do, and keep tomorrow wide open." A blue eye winked conspiratorially.

The smaller woman poured the beaten egg mixture into the skillet, then prepared the ham and cheese and added it to the eggs. "You're not going to tell me why?"

"Nope."

"Could you, maybe, give me a teensy weensy little hint?" Green eyes peered at Jess hopefully.

"Nope."

An exasperated sigh. "Okay. Fine." Robin set the now cooked omelette down in front of Jess. "If that's the way you're going to be...."

"Yes." The dark-haired woman grinned smugly. "That's the way I'm going to be." She watched as Robin prepared another omelette. It was a bit difficult, Jess had to admit, keeping the surprise she'd planned for the next day a secret. She took a bite of her omelette and studied the younger woman further. Robin would be twenty-six. *Seven years difference.* Jess thought about that. Was seven years really that much difference? Thirty-three wasn't exactly old, was it?

"Hey." Robin caught the faraway look in Jess's eyes as she sat down a the table with her own plate. "Is the omelette all right?"

"Oh." Jess snapped out of it. "Yeah. It's great." She gave Robin an affectionate smile, then resumed eating. *A little shrimp would be good.*

Green eyes observed the older woman surreptitiously. *I bet she's thinking shrimp would be good.* "Not for breakfast, Jess."

Blue eyes grew wide. *How did she know what I was thinking?* "What?"

The blonde head shook. "If you want to make every day 'shrimp day' that's fine, but I absolutely draw the line at having shrimp for breakfast."

"It's brunch, Robin. Besides, you don't know that's what I was thinking."

The younger woman simply cocked her head and gave Jess a candid look. *I know.*

Okay. Fine. "Dinner, then. No arguments."

Fine. "No arguments."

They both ate the remainder of their meals in contented silence, somewhat lost in their own thoughts but entirely comfortable, nonetheless. Once brunch was finished, Robin stood up and began clearing away the dishes.

Jess stopped her. "I'll get those. You fixed the omelettes." She padded over to the sink. "Now, remember, do all your chores today, okay?"

"Yes, Mom." Robin grinned, then turned to leave the kitchen.

"Oh, and Robin?" The taller woman flipped a look back at the retreating form. "I do believe you still have some things that belong to me."

Robin stopped mid-stride. *Rats.* "Well, I suppose I do." A blonde eyebrow arched thoughtfully. "How about a trade?"

"A trade?" Jess put the plates in the dishwasher. "What type of trade?"

"Let's say a double scoop of ice cream at the ice cream parlor in exchange for certain very yellow slippers."

"You're offering to trade me for something that is already mine?" Dark eyebrows shot up in disbelief. "Did I hear you correctly?"

"Yes." A self-satisfied grin. "Take it or leave it."

Jess, you are so hooked. "Fine. Deal."

Robin sauntered out of the kitchen. *She's so easy.*

****

"Where are we going?" Robin drove her blue Miata out onto the main highway.

"Can't tell ya. Keep driving." Jess directed Robin through the mid-day Sunday traffic.

"First you kidnap me, then you make me drive my own kidnapping."

"I did not kidnap you. As I recall, you came along quite willingly after I told you that we were going to stop at the ice cream parlor later on." The older woman watched the traffic. "Turn left, here." She then grinned happily. "Besides, since it's your birthday, I get to kidnap you if I want to."

Green eyes focused on the road. "So you admit you kidnapped me."

A quick roll of the passenger's blue eyes. "I am merely giving you directions to get to an ultimate destination which I only know." A smug grin. "That is all."

"Right." The younger woman smirked. "You seem to have gotten better at direction giving lately, I'll give you that."

The game of one-upmanship continued. "I'm steering you clear of one-way streets, Robin." Jess quipped. "I know how difficult they are for you to navigate."

A sideways glance. "You are such a brat."

"Yeah, yeah. Keep driving."

"Can't you just give me one little hint?" Robin whined.

"No."

The younger woman stopped at a red light and tapped her fingers lightly on the steering wheel. "You didn't plan a surprise party, did you?"

"No. No surprise party."

"Are we going to a movie?"

"No."

The light turned green and Robin proceeded through the intersection. "We're going to Disney World?"

A frank look. "Does this look like the way to Disney World?" The question really required no response. "Turn down this street." Jess indicated another congested highway.

Robin pursed her lips in continued thought. "This looks like the way to the mall. We're not going to the mall, are we? Because, Jess, I don't want to ride the train again."

"As much as I would love to ride the train, Robin, and I haven't had my train fill in a very long time, we are not going to the mall." A long finger pointed up ahead. "See that sign on the right? Turn in there."

Robin read the referenced sign and then looked at Jess with a questioning gaze. "This is the BMW dealership."

"Correct. Pull in."

The younger woman sobered. "Jess, I was just teasing you about this. I wasn't...."

Jess gently interrupted. "Just pull in and park the car, okay?"

The Miata pulled into the lot toward the main showroom. Robin put the car in park and started once again to object. "Jess...."

"Just listen to me, all right?" The older woman turned fully in the passenger seat, her tone soft but focused as she continued. "First, tell me a couple of things. Suppose that you were going to get a new car. Would you trade this one or sell it separately?"

Robin swallowed. "Um...trade it."

"Okay. What about car payments? Would you want to keep your current payment range or could you go a little higher?"

"I could go a little higher."

"All right." Jess proceeded cautiously. "What about a down payment? Would you be able to put anything down?"

The younger woman took a deep breath. "No. Not now. I was saving for that. It's only been four months, and Christmas kind of bit into my savings a little." *Okay, a lot, especially due to one particularly expensive item.* She shook her head, now very uneasy. "Jess, I...."

A large hand went up. "You're supposed to be listening,

remember?" A warm smile followed. "Just go on inside, okay? You said you've had your eye on one car in particular. Go find it and give it a test drive." The older woman's voice was genuinely sincere. "Here's the deal. After you test drive the car, if you decide you like it, then your down payment is taken care of. It would be up to you to negotiate your trade and your monthly payments. How does that sound?"

Robin was speechless. It was never her intent to push Jess into paying, even partially, for her new car. After a long moment, the younger woman finally found her voice. "Jess, this is...too much. Really, I was only teasing you. I never meant to pressure you into this."

The dark-haired woman gave Robin a tender smile before speaking again. "Honey, listen. You haven't pressured me into anything. Believe me, if I didn't want to help you with this, I wouldn't do it." Large fingers wrapped around smaller ones. "I want to do this. I want you to have a new car, if you find one you like." She ducked her head and looked into green eyes. "Will you let me do this?"

Robin sighed. "I feel like I'm taking advantage of you."

That drew an unexpected grin. "You are absolutely not taking advantage of me. I want to do this. Besides, I get the best part of the deal."

Golden eyebrows furrowed. "How do you figure?"

"Well...." Jess drawled. "First, I won't have to listen to you going on and on and on about this purported car every five minutes." Smiling blue eyes met green. "And second, if you get a new car, when I ride in it, I won't be squished anymore."

"Hey." Robin grinned for the first time. "I only mentioned it a couple of times." She paused as Jess's words registered. "Was that a crack about my height?"

Innocent blue eyes sparkled. "Not at all. Just stating the facts." Jess winked, then smiled affectionately. "Now go on, kiddo. Pick out a nice car for yourself."

Robin felt a gentle squeeze at her hand, sighing as she realized that the older woman was completely serious in her offer. Her gaze locked onto the crystal blue eyes in front of her, and she swallowed in an attempt to keep her emotions in check. "You are..." She glanced upward, searching her mind for an appropriate word, then whispered. "Amazing." She smiled, then let go of Jess's hand. "Will you come in with me?"

"Absolutely." The taller woman started to open the car door but was stopped as small arms encircled her and held onto her tightly.

"Thank you, Jess." Robin's voice was now shaky with emotion. "Very much."

Jess hugged back, reveling in the connection between them. "You're very welcome, sweetheart. Happy Birthday." She leaned back. "Ready?"

A nod, then a very excited grin. "Ready."

They walked into the rather large showroom, and Jess asked to see the manager while Robin admired several of the showroom vehicles. A few moments later, a tall gentleman appeared from one of the offices. "Ms. Harrison, good to see you again."

"Mr. Whitman." Jess extended her hand, then motioned toward Robin. "This is Robin Wilson. She'll be looking at some of your cars today. In accordance with our arrangement, the down payment I deposited with you yesterday will apply toward whichever car she chooses."

The manager smiled. "Very good. Ms. Wilson, let me have one of our sales personnel assist you with your selection and then accompany you on a test drive." He quickly waved an eager salesman over, then turned his attention toward Robin. "We'll discuss the specifics of an actual deal upon your return."

Robin nodded politely, but if truth be told, was quite overwhelmed. She turned to Jess and whispered. "You came here yesterday and set this up, didn't you?"

Jess stared sheepishly at the floor. "Yes."

"I thought you had to go into work."

"I did. I just took a detour first."

"Oh." The blonde head shook in amazement. "I knew you were very sneaky."

The corners of Jess's mouth curved into the most adorable crooked grin. "Anything for my birthday girl."

Robin was sure she blushed.

It was barely two hours later when all negotiations were completed and the two women left the car dealership in Robin's brand new sporty metallic blue BMW convertible.

****

Jess dimmed the lights and ducked into the kitchen, leaving Robin standing alone in the dining room. After a moment, the taller woman emerged carrying a cake adorned with several carefully lit candles. She set it down on the dining room table directly in front of Robin and grinned happily. "Happy Birthday."

"You made me a cake?" The birthday girl's eyes lit up excitedly.

Jess's expression held a trace of guilt. "Actually, no, but I got it at the Italian bakery. It has a special filling."

"Ooooh, special filling." Robin stared at the cake. "You even got the candles right. Two on the top and six on the bottom."

"I learned that from you, remember?" Jess grinned proudly, especially pleased that she had been able to display the rather complicated candle placement system correctly. "Let me sing." She proceeded to sing the entire birthday song to Robin, doing a very impressive job at it.

The birthday girl raised an appraising eyebrow. "You did that better than I did at your birthday."

Jess shrugged as if it were nothing special. "Now, go ahead and make a wish and blow out your candles."

Petite hands rested on the front of the table as Robin first took a deep breath, then made a wish and blew out the grand total of eight candles, watching slightly mesmerized as tiny wisps of smoke trailed haphazardly upward from the burnt candle tips. In an odd flashback, she remembered a time when she and Jess had only known each other a little over a week, and the older woman had appeared at her front door for their first home-cooked dinner together, bearing a housewarming gift. *The centerpiece.* Robin smiled internally as she recalled the wish she'd made that first night, after their evening together had concluded and she had gently blown out the centerpiece's candle. With sudden clarity, she realized that her wish of so many months ago had indeed come true. *I am happy.* She also realized that her wish of tonight was a mere extension of her original wish. *Happiness together forever.* It seemed like such a simple wish, and perhaps a bit idealistic, but to Robin, it was everything. The question was, would it really be possible?

"Hey." Jess waved her hand back and forth over the candles, dispersing the wisps of smoke in the air. "That must be some wish if you have to think about it so hard."

The blonde head nodded thoughtfully as Robin brought herself back to the present. "You could say that." She grabbed the cake knife and grinned. "So, what do you want? A big piece or a little piece?" A blonde eyebrow rose, waiting for the response.

"It's got amaretto crème filling and French vanilla icing so I'll definitely have a big piece." Azure eyes sparkled. "Besides, if I don't get mine now, you'll end up eating the rest of it yourself." The taller woman quipped. "You always do."

Robin pointed the cake knife in Jess's direction. "Just for that, you get an extra big piece." She cut the cake into neat, but large pieces and put each piece on a plate, handing one to Jess. "You have to finish the whole piece." Robin proceeded to take a bite of her cake, slowly tilting her head back and closing her eyes in pure bliss as she tasted the delicious amaretto filling. Finally, she opened her eyes once again and practically breathed her delight. "God. That is...heavenly. You sure do know how to choose a good cake." She took another bite and repeated the process.

Jess watched the display transfixed. *That is one of the most sensual things I have ever seen.* A long finger reached over and wiped a tiny bit of frosting from the corner of Robin's mouth. *French vanilla icing.* A dark eyebrow edged up. *That has definite possibilities.* She licked the frosting from her finger, then began eating her own piece of cake.
Hmmm. Maybe we'll both have seconds.

****

It turned out to be an early evening, as both women were quite exhausted from the day's events, their stomachs still rather full from the delicious dessert. They each had put away two pieces of cake. It was that good. Now, Robin lay in the waterbed curled snugly in Jess's embrace. She ran the palm of her hand up and down one of the long arms that held her, feeling the soft cotton fabric of the flannel sleep shirt and taking comfort in its warmth. "Thank you for today." She whispered.
Jess smiled in the dark. "You're welcome, sweetheart. I hope you had a good day."
The smaller body shifted slightly in Jess's arms. "I had a fabulous day. First, a car, then ice cream." She burrowed her head contentedly into the crook of Jess's neck. "And finally, amaretto crème filled cake."
"Don't forget the French vanilla icing."
Robin felt herself blush. "That was the best part." She grinned against the soft skin, then took on a slightly serious tone. "Jess, about the car, I...."
"I thought we settled that."
Robin sighed uneasily. "I saw how much you put down on it, and I think it's too much." She didn't want to hurt Jess's feelings, but the amount really was quite significant.
A long finger traced a petite shoulder blade. "If I put it down, it wasn't too much. Let me say this to you again, so you know really I mean it. I wanted to do it, I wanted for you to have that car, and I

wanted to find a way to make it possible for you to have it." She brought her hand underneath Robin's chin and tilted it upward. "See, I got everything I wanted and it wasn't even my birthday." Her wide smile was barely visible in the faint night's light.

It's still too much. Soft lips reached up and kissed Jess tenderly. "You are the sweetest person. Have I ever told you that?"

Equally soft lips responded in a similar fashion. "You might have mentioned it a time or two." The older woman grinned, then brushed her fingers through Robin's short blonde hair, playing with it idly between her fingertips. "So, how did your phone conversation go with your folks tonight?

Should I get into it? "It was fine. They called to wish me a happy birthday. I told them I got a new car. They were surprised, but they thought it was generally a good thing."

Perhaps it was the remote way the younger woman referred to the conversation, or maybe it was just Jess's sixth sense when it came to Robin, but something sounded off. "What else?"

There was a long sigh. "How can you tell?"

Jess shrugged. "I just can."

She's going to freak. "My father took it upon himself to set up an interview for me at his golfing buddy's law firm. They want me to come up next week for the meeting." As expected, she felt the body beneath her stiffen. "I told them I didn't want to go to the interview, and that I wanted to stay right where I am. I told them I like it here." Robin was silent for a long moment as she fiddled with the edge of Jess's sleep shirt, then mumbled under her breath. "I just knew they weren't going to give up."

"So then, they aren't going to cancel the appointment?" Jess's voice was even.

"No." The answer was very quiet.

"I see." And, in fact, Jess did see. *It's crystal clear what's going on here.* Indeed, it was quite apparent that Robin's parents were simply not going to let up until Robin fully explained to them her real reasons for wanting to stay in Florida. And that begged a further question. Was Robin reluctant to disclose their relationship to her parents because she wanted to be free to end it at some point?

The younger woman continued. "They don't understand, even though I've told them time after time that I don't want to go back there. I don't see why they just don't accept that."

I do. It was now or never. Jess either had to speak up or forever bite her tongue on the matter. It was a delicate situation. These were Robin's parents, and Robin should handle things with them without any

41

interference from her so-called roommate. But still, Jess saw in the situation what Robin apparently could not. *Or maybe, she just doesn't want to see it.* After a brief pause, the older woman decided to just spit it out. "You're lying to them."

A stunned blonde head lifted. "What?"

"You're lying to them." Jess repeated. "They know something's going on with you, and they're worried about you. They want you near them so they can be sure you're really okay." Her tone was almost sad. "They know you're keeping something from them, and they don't know what it is."

Gray-green eyes glared at Jess in the dark. "That is not fair."

"Isn't it? The only way they're going to fully understand your reluctance to go back there is if you tell them."

Robin began shaking. "I...I can't do that."

Jess looked away, interpreting Robin's admission as proof of her own earlier assessment as to the reasons why. *I know you can't.* "And that's why they'll never give up."

Robin rolled over and laid flat on her back, staring unseeing at the darkened ceiling. She knew, of course, that Jess was right. Her parents couldn't possibly understand something that they didn't know. She spoke in a soft voice. "If I tell them, it might not go well."

"That's possible."

Robin bit her bottom lip lightly. "It might solve one problem, but create others."

"That's true."

"If I tell them, they might...." Robin's voice quavered.

Jess had compassion. She closed her eyes, now regretting trying to push the younger woman into doing something when it was really Jess's own selfish insecurity that caused the pushing in the first place. "Shhh. Come here." She wrapped the small body in her arms. "I'm sorry. I didn't mean to pressure you into something you weren't ready for."

Petite hands clung tightly to Jess. "No. You had every right to think that. I did say that I'd deal with them and I wouldn't let them control my life. It's just that the reality of what that meant hit me. It hit me that I'd have to tell them sooner, rather than later, and that I'd have to be prepared to deal with their reaction."

"If you're not ready...."

"No. You're probably right." Robin's voice was more resolute, but still held a touch of uncertainty. "I suppose I should face this with them. Waiting won't make it any easier." She became introspective. "If I don't tell them, they'll just keep at it, and I'll end up fighting with them all the time. But, if I do tell them, it might go badly."

"It has to be up to you. I'll support you whatever you decide." The older woman was amazingly understanding, considering the implications either way.

Robin tightened her grip on Jess's waist. "I want to think about it, okay?"

"Okay."

Jess held Robin until sleep claimed them both, each soberly aware of the ramifications should Robin decide to take the contemplated course of action. At least the truth would be out. The problem was, neither Robin nor Jess could decide if that was really a good thing.

****

Jess stirred from a hazy sleep. She cracked one eye open, noting the time glowing in the dark on the digital clock, and became aware of a muffled sound that barely made its way into her consciousness, but nevertheless, failed to register. She shifted underneath the covers and attempted to resume her pleasant slumber, when she heard the sound again. This time, it fully woke her as she dwelled momentarily in the place between wakefulness and sleep. *What...?* Groggily, she turned over and faced the petite form lying on the other side of the waterbed, hearing the light sniffling one more time. "Robin?" The taller frame scooted over toward the younger woman. "Is everything all right?"

"Yeah." The small voice whispered. "Go back to sleep."

Jess heard the sniffling continue. "Robin, honey, you're crying. What's the matter?"

How can I tell her? "Nothing." The voice was barely audible.

"Shhh." Long arms gathered up the younger woman and held onto her very tightly. "Talk to me, sweetheart." Jess whispered and stroked the blonde head soothingly. "I'm here."

For some unexplained reason, what was meant as reassurance instead brought a flood of tears, dampening Jess's flannel sleep shirt considerably.

"Please, honey." Jess was now very agitated. "What's wrong?" She rocked the younger woman, trying to calm her.

A moment passed, then a shaky reply. "I'm afraid you won't understand."

Uh oh. "You know you can say anything to me." Jess whispered reassuringly.

"It's all right." The sniffling lessened. "Don't worry about it. It was just a bad dream, that's all."

That's all? Despite the obvious attempt to minimize the matter, the small body shuddered beneath the larger one, still quite shaken. Jess tried again. "Would you like to talk about it?"

Robin was silent. *Should I?* She could hear the strong beating of Jess's heart beneath ear, and somehow, it comforted her. *All right.* She cleared her throat, then cautiously began. "I had a dream about the night...the accident happened." She waited for any reaction from Jess, or the expected stiffening of the body beneath her own, but it didn't come. Instead, Robin felt the older woman hold on to her more tightly as she listened quietly. *I feel so safe here.* "It was really foggy outside that night. In my dream, I hung up the phone after David's father called, and I drove over to the hospital where I was supposed to meet his parents. Only, when I got there, they weren't there." She paused. "Instead, your mom and your brother were there, but I wasn't surprised by that."

Is this going where I think it's going? Jess kept a strong hold on Robin and continued to listen.

"The emergency room doctor came out and told us...." The small body started shaking and the tears came again. "You were the one in the car, Jess, not David. It was you, and the doctor told us the paramedics did everything they could, but you didn't make it." Robin was nearly distraught.

Damn. "Shhh. Honey. It was just a dream. I'm here. We're both here and everything's okay." Jess rocked the smaller woman again in her arms. "I'm all right."

Robin swallowed and tried to calm herself, not succeeding very well. "It just seemed so real, and it was like I expected it all along. I expected it to be you and not him. I don't know why that was."

Jess tried to think of something to say. "But it wasn't real. It was only a dream."

"You don't understand."

"What don't I understand, sweetheart?" The low voice was very soft and caring as Jess brushed the tears from Robin's face.

"I saw you."

"You saw me?"

Robin nodded, then took a deep, steadying breath. "Um...that night, when I met David's parents at the hospital and the doctor told us he didn't make it, they wouldn't let me or his mother see him. His father had to...." She swallowed hard. "He had to identify him. They said that we shouldn't see him like he was...that we wouldn't want to remember him like that." Robin began crying very hard. "But in my dream, I saw you. I went behind the curtain and you were lying there and you were...." Her voice trailed off, unable to put words to the scene.

"Oh, sweetheart." *God, this is morbid.* Jess blinked back a tear and shuddered, herself. "That must have been...very upsetting for you." She resumed rocking the younger woman in her arms, and clutched the blonde head to her chest to offer some measure of comfort. "You know that was a dream, right? I'm right here, and I'm okay."

Tear-filled eyes looked up. "But you don't know what will happen, Jess. David didn't know."

What Robin said was absolutely true. *Damn. I need a will.* Up until now, it hadn't mattered. The State would take care of everything and distribute it to the surviving next of kin. "You're right. We don't know."

"Promise me something." Gray-green eyes locked intently with silver-blue in the dark. "If we ever don't agree on something or get angry with each other, you won't leave upset, even if I say things to you that I shouldn't say."

"I won't get angry at you."

"Promise me." The request was more demanding.

"Robin, honey, you could never...."

"No." Small hands reached up and grasped Jess's shoulders with extreme urgency, gripping them tightly as determined green eyes bore into silver-blue with a steely intensity. "You promise me." The words were spoken in an unexpectedly harsh tone.

Caught off guard and shaken by the sudden and almost fierce desperation in Robin's voice, Jess stared at the resolute gray-green eyes above her own, reading them in all their undisguised guilt, then opened her mouth and simply whispered. "I promise."

Petite hands released their grip on Jess's shoulders. "Thank you." Robin visibly relaxed and settled back down beside the older woman, fully facing her. Almost hesitantly, a lone finger made its way to Jess's face and reverently traced the strong jaw and high cheekbones, then proceeded up over each dark eyebrow and across the smooth forehead, as if committing the chiseled features to memory merely by touch. "My beautiful Jess."

Jess almost lost it right then and there. It was heartbreakingly sad. Robin had extended her guilt from what had happened to David to what she imagined might happen to Jess. But worse for Robin, she had seen in her dream something that was horrible for her, borne entirely of her own perceived guilt. Finally, as Jess felt the small finger continue to trace its deliberate path, the overwhelming enormity of the situation came crashing down upon her, the intensity of it all now too much to bear. She broke down into sobs, herself, and drew the younger woman to her, letting the tears fall freely as she hugged the smaller body to her own. In her highly emotional state, Jess couldn't think of anything to say that would convey her regret at Robin's all consuming pain or to help take it away, so she just said the first thing that came to her mind. "I'm sorry, honey. I'm so, so sorry." She whispered the soft words, then kissed Robin's forehead several times, unable to stop her own tears as they fell.

They held each other for a very long time after that, neither one knowing exactly how long, although it was still dark by the time their mutual tears had dried. Robin felt suddenly awkward and very self-conscious at her overly emotional display. *All because of a dream.* Nevertheless, it was a dream that seemed so real and scared her so terribly. "Jess?"

"Yeah."

"Thanks for listening." It was an understatement, but Robin was too emotionally spent for much more.

"You're welcome, sweetheart." Jess brushed the raged blonde bangs from Robin's eyes. "Now, let's get some rest. We can talk some more later, okay? Maybe you can talk to Dr. Richmond, too."

The blonde head nodded. "Yeah."

Taking comfort in their closeness, they both finally fell into a welcome and restful sleep, neither releasing the almost possessive grip they had on each other throughout the remainder of the night and into the early light of day.

****

The office coffeemaker was a popular place, and the gossip was definitely juicy. Angie stood off to the side and spoke in hushed tones to Betty, while Paul sauntered up to check out the coffee of the day. He couldn't help but overhear their conversation, as he leaned against the wall in seeming nonchalance and poured himself a cup of the hazelnut flavor.

Angie reached for a pack of sweetener. "So, I checked out a few things, and you won't believe who has moved in with whom."

Betty's eyes went wide. "You're kidding."

"Nope. Check out the addresses on the new employee directory."

"Ooooh. Do you think that's why my boss was in her office the other day?"

A smug smile. "I'd bet on it."

"I still don't know." The other secretary became pensive. "It could be no big deal. I mean, people here have lived in the same houses together before. It's not unheard of."

Paul added a bit of creamer to his coffee, stirring it slowly as he surreptitiously listened in.

"True, but..." Angie took a long sip of her coffee. "She's sporting a new bracelet. Now, I've only ever seen her wear one other bracelet. She has exactly one bracelet, one watch and two pairs of earrings. No rings."

"You know this?"

"I've worked for her for seven years. I know what she has. Then, after Christmas she came in wearing a new bracelet. She fingers it all the time. I don't even think she realizes she does it."

Betty wasn't buying it. "It was obviously a Christmas gift. What's the big deal?"

Paul topped off his coffee. *This is getting good.*

Angie leaned in very close to her friend. "Next time you see Robin, check out her new diamond necklace."

"Wow." Betty thought about that. "You could be right. Then again, the necklace could also be from a family member."

Angie smirked. "When you see it, you'll know. Trust me, it's not from a family member."

"I don't know, Angie. I think you might be jumping to conclusions." Betty refilled her cup. "Maybe Robin's seeing someone."

"Exactly." Angie raised an eyebrow to further her point.

It happened entirely by accident. Paul nearly choked on his coffee at Angie's implication, thereby drawing attention to his presence. His own suspicions had been more along the lines of the junior partner having an ulterior motive for befriending the young associate, specifically for the junior partner's own personal and somewhat selfish case management purposes. *But this....* He lifted an eyebrow. Now, Paul knew better than to accept office gossip as the gospel truth, especially considering the source. *But still....* He'd definitely have to rethink some things. He hurriedly left the break room, heading directly for his office to do just that, as Angie and Betty likewise returned to their desks to keep an eye and an ear open for any further interesting developments.

The gossip mill was indeed juicy that morning.

****

Considerable Appeal

After a long day of mostly research, Robin emerged from her office in need of a little activity to stretch her limbs. She ducked around the copy machine and through the reception area toward the break room. Curious eyes watched and faint whispers faded as Robin approached. She snagged a can of apple juice from the refrigerator and filled a Styrofoam cup with ice before returning back out into the hallway. After she was safely out of earshot, the whispering resumed. While Robin and Jess were by no means the sole targets of office gossip that day, they did make for an interesting topic of conversation, and one that left much room for speculation.

Keith Miller met Robin in the hallway. "Hey. How's it going?" He was very charming and quite attractive.

Robin stopped to talk, pouring her apple juice into her cup. "I'm good. You?"

"Not bad." Keith hesitated just a bit before continuing. "Um...hey, Robin, if you're free Friday evening, would you like to catch a movie and maybe dinner beforehand?" He looked at her hopefully.

Oh no. The young associate shifted uncomfortably. *How do I get out of this?* In retrospect, it was not at all unexpected. After all, Robin had merely put him off before. She never really gave him any reason not to keep asking. And now, she sincerely regretted not having been straightforward with him in the first place. On the other hand, wasn't it better to keep up the charade for appearances' sake? There was really no harm in that, right? "Uh, Keith, thanks for asking. I can't make it Friday, but I appreciate the offer." *That was ambiguous enough.* She nervously took a sip of her juice. *So, how come I feel so bad?*

Keith hid his disappointment well. No one, to his knowledge, had yet been able to get Robin out on a date. "No problem. Some other time, then."

Robin smiled, belying her unease at misleading him. "Right." She turned and beat a hasty retreat back to her office, closing the door soundly and sinking down heavily into the chair behind her desk. She closed her eyes and tried to stem off an impending headache. Maybe it was the clandestine situation she found herself in, or maybe it was simply all the lying and deliberate misrepresentations she had to sustain on a daily basis, but the weight of it all suddenly fell upon her in full force, and she felt its effects in nearly suffocating intensity. The lies were present on all fronts, and they were taking a very heavy toll, indeed. From work to her family, and perhaps even to herself, the half-truths, the misrepresentations, and even the charade she was living, were all proving to be much too difficult for the associate to comfortably manage.

The evening was fast approaching, and Robin stared out at the twilight sky over the now darkened lake below, the first street lights illuminating the traffic-clogged downtown streets in the near distance. She sighed heavily. It was apparent to her that things couldn't go on like this much longer. Something had to give. *But what...and how?* Her headache became quite prominent, pounding her temples mercilessly. *What will bring relief from this burden?*

For an unknown reason, Robin's mind turned to her conversation with her parents about the unilateral scheduling of that interview with the Detroit law firm. She shook her head at the situation. *How do I make them understand?* Jess's words echoed in her mind. *The only way to make them understand is to tell them.* Robin laughed humorlessly. *Easier said than done.* Indeed, it could go badly with her parents. Very badly. She knew that. And then, what? What if they couldn't accept her relationship with Jess? Did it matter? Hadn't Robin already decided that her parents didn't control how she lived her life or with whom she decided to live it? By telling them, it certainly would eliminate one lie and perhaps stop her parents' unceasing attempts to entice her into leaving Florida. She raised an eyebrow in further thought. Telling her parents would also mean that she was serious about her relationship with Jess, and that it was not just a passing phase that she'd never need to risk anything to maintain. She thought more about that. Loving Jess was not just a phase. It was real, and it was hopefully forever. *I should tell them. At least I wouldn't have to keep up the lie to my family anymore.*

Robin checked the time. It was getting rather late. Most of the staff should have already gone home for the day. Having made what she considered a major decision, the young associate really didn't want to wait until later that evening to discuss it with Jess. She opened her e-mail program and typed in a brief message.

J,

Are you free? I need to discuss something with you.

R

Robin clicked the send button and sat back in her chair waiting for a response. She stared once again out the large window, noting that the twilight sky had now turned fully dark. The pulsing red tail lights of a small plane crossed her vision, and she let her mind absently watch as it slowly made its trek from west to east toward the executive airport only a few miles away. She was brought from her mind's idle wanderings as her computer signaled a reply to her e-mail message.

R,

Give me 30 minutes, then come by my office.

J

The young associate blew out a breath. *Okay.* From Robin's point of view, she and Jess may not be able to disclose their relationship at work, but telling Robin's parents would mean one less lie and one less charade to maintain. And that was a very good thing, wasn't it?

Green eyes closed briefly. *Or maybe it was just inviting a whole lot of trouble.*

****

Robin finished off some correspondence and kept generally busy for the next half hour. She closed out her document and checked the time, then set out for Jess's office. As she passed the darkened reception area, she noted the now empty office suite and the presence of the night cleaning crew just beginning its work. The associate rounded the corner and made her way down the hallway, approaching the partially closed door to the junior partner's office. She knocked lightly, then poked her head inside. "Hi. Am I interrupting?"

Jess glanced up from her computer, briefly checking her watch. "I didn't realize it had gotten so late. Come in."

Robin stood in the doorway. "If you need to finish something, it can wait."

"No, it's okay. I need a break anyway. It's going to be a long night for me." The junior partner smiled and waved Robin inside the office. "Now, tell me, what was it you wanted to talk about?"

The associate closed the door and took a seat in the chair next to the floor-to-ceiling window. She stared at the night sky through the reflected glass for several moments, nervously tapping her fingertips against each other and oddly wishing she had a pen to twirl. Now that she was sitting in Jess's office, she didn't quite know how to begin.

Something's going on. "Robin? Kiddo, did something happen?"

Green eyes shifted toward the closed door. "Um...I keep forgetting. We're supposed to keep that open, aren't we." She was stalling and she knew it.

"Leave it." Jess motioned toward the door. "You look tired. Is your dream from the other night still bothering you?"

"No. I'm better now." Robin was still evasive.

When she gets like this, I have to pull it out of her. Jess stood, then walked over and knelt beside Robin's chair, her voice very soft. "Then, what is it? What happened?"

"Nothing really happened. Keith asked me out again, and I misled him. Again." The associate blew out a breath. "It just got to me. He really doesn't deserve to be strung along, but I just can't seem to discourage him."

"It's not a bad thing to keep your options open for appearances." The junior partner tried to be supportive.

"Jess." The associate swallowed hard. "It's all these lies. I'm not sure I can keep on deceiving everyone." She paused momentarily. "I guess it's all just starting to get to me. I'm constantly afraid someone's going to find out about us. I have to mislead everyone all the time. I've got interviews scheduled for me that I don't want to go to. People are asking questions about things like my apartments and the necklace, and I swear people around here are talking about us."

Blue eyes closed in deep regret. Jess knew that keeping their relationship secret would eventually take an emotional toll, and now, here was the proof. She grasped Robin's hand and softly brushed the petite knuckles. "I'm sorry."

"No." Robin smiled sadly. "It's not your fault. It's just the circumstances. *A catch-22.* There are risks in telling people, but misleading everyone is hard, too." She hesitated, then got directly to her point. "I've made a decision."

"Okay." Jess braced herself. *It's not working out? She wants to move?*

"I may have to misrepresent things here at work because of the firm's concerns, but I can at least take charge of my own life when it comes to my family." The associate could see the worry in the blue eyes in front of her. She reached her free hand up to cup Jess's cheek. "I going up to Michigan to tell my parents about us, so once and for all, they won't keep on pressuring me, and I won't have to keep lying to them."

Blue eyes blinked, a bit stunned. "You're going...you want to tell them?"

"Yes. You were right. This is really the only way they're going to understand why I don't want to go back there."

"And if it goes badly?"

Robin squeezed the hand that held her own. "Then, I'll still have you." A lump formed in her throat, and her voice wavered. "Right?"

She's scared. "Yes." Jess whispered. "You will always have me." Long arms enfolded Robin in a reassuring and comforting hug.

Robin sunk into the embrace, relishing the contact and reluctant to let go. After a long moment, she pulled back slightly and rested her forehead against the older woman's, gazing into compassionate clear blue eyes. "Thank you." She whispered.

If they weren't so caught up in the moment, they would have heard the light knock at the door. A few seconds later, Michelle turned the handle and walked in, then stopped. She had assumed that no one was inside the office, having heard no response to her knocking. As it appeared, Jess and Robin were obviously having a personal discussion and seemed quite stunned at the intrusion. Somewhat shocked by the scene, Michelle quickly apologized. "I...I'm sorry. I didn't mean to interrupt. I was just going to drop off this research memo." She hastily set the document on the cherry wood desk and turned to leave.

Shit. Jess quickly stood up. "Michelle."

The senior associate paused her progress and looked toward the junior partner, but said nothing.

I feel sick. Jess was quite shaken, and one quick look at Robin's very pale features indicated that the young associate was worse off. *How do I fix this?* "Thank you for dropping that memo off." She looked candidly at Michelle. "Robin and I were having a personal conversation. Can we...count on your discretion?"

The senior associate nodded, understanding the intent of the question quite well. "Of course." With that, she left the junior partner's office, heading back to her own side of the building.

Jess just stood there. *Damn it.* She glanced over at Robin who was staring unseeingly out the large window into the night sky. *How could I have been so careless?*

Green eyes finally regarded her. "We're in trouble, aren't we?"

"I don't know."

Robin seemed amazingly calm. "Let me go talk to her." The young associate stood up. "You can finish up here, then meet me at home. All right?"

Like I can work, now. "All right." The junior partner watched as Robin opened the door and closed it behind her. *What have I gotten us into? This game is way too dangerous.*

Robin nearly ran down the hallway to catch up with Michelle, side-stepping the cleaning crew and finally meeting up with her in the senior associate's office. "Michelle." Robin stood in the doorway looking every bit as guilty as she felt.

Michelle's light brown eyes looked up, appraising Robin's unease. "Robin."

"Listen. I wanted to explain...."

Michelle put her hand up and stopped her. "It's none of my business, Robin." Her eyes softened. "Look. Whatever is between you and Jessica, it's your affair."

Robin winced at the unintentional but apt description of their relationship. "We...."

"Robin." Michelle stood up and approached the younger associate sympathetically. "I like you. You seem to be a good person. If you and Jessica want to be...close friends, then that's up to you. I will tell you one thing, though, and I hope you'll listen to me."

Robin took a deep breath. "Okay."

"You have to understand that she is a partner and you are an associate. There are rules here about that. People could get the wrong idea, especially if it's perceived that there's favoritism at play."

The younger associate felt nauseous. "There won't be any favoritism." *Jess promised.*

"That's good. I don't know whether you're aware of this, but there's already a bit of resentment here because Jessica made partner nearly two years ahead of schedule. Rightly or wrongly, many people believe she worked Harry around her finger to get it."

"No. She works hard. She deserved it."

Michelle shook her head. "See. You can't be objective, and I doubt she can either. How ever close your friendship is with her, both of you have got to watch out for that." Michelle's eyes settled on Robin's pendant necklace.

Robin followed her gaze. "You're wondering about this, aren't you?" She fingered the beveled diamonds.

"No." The senior associate tilted her head in genuine compassion. "I told both you and Jessica that I would be discreet, and I will. I don't know who gave that to you, and I don't want to know."

Robin nodded slowly. "Okay."

"Just be careful. This place is a millhouse for gossip. They'll eat you up with it, and most of it won't even be true." Michelle turned and sat back down as younger associate started to leave. "Robin?"

Green eyes peered back cautiously.

"I'm sorry for barging in like that."

Robin saw the sincere apology for what it was. "Thanks." She left

Michelle's office and rapidly headed down the hallway, ducking into the ladies' room nearby. She stood at the sink and splashed several handfuls of cool water on her face, before drying herself off with a paper towel. Weary, apprehensive green eyes stared back at her in the mirror. Aside from her birthday, the week had gone from bad to worse. First the dream, next the lie to Keith, then her decision to tell her parents, and now...this. Like a house of cards, her and Jess's carefully constructed façade was collapsing in front of them. Robin closed her eyes and swallowed hard as the contents of her stomach threatened to rebel. *What a lousy week this turned out to be.*

That, indeed, was an understatement.

Chapter 3

Jess paced, then looked up at the clock on the wall, then paced some more, nearly wearing the carpet thin. She finally stopped her useless wandering, choosing instead to sit her tall frame down on the plush sofa in the living room, waiting impatiently for Robin to return home. It was taking absolutely too long. Robin should have spoken with Michelle and have gotten back to the house long ago, well before Jess. Long fingers reached over and picked up the telephone, dialing Robin's direct line at the office. No answer. *Damn. Where is she?* The junior partner glanced at the wall clock again, watching the interminable minutes tick by, well on her way toward convincing herself that something had happened. She closed her eyes and rested her head heavily against the cushions, almost as if that action alone could make everything that was wrong suddenly just go away. Instead, a loud and very persistent internal voice echoed incessantly inside her troubled mind.

What a mess!

'Go away.' The alternate internal voice hissed, apparently in no mood for chastisement at the moment.

Not so fast. You need to quit your self-centered pity and consider things a bit more objectively here.

The alternate internal voice took offense at the remark. *'And just what's that supposed to mean?'*

You know perfectly well. Up until now, you've been looking at things only through your own eyes. Let's play a little game, shall we?

'A game?' An incredulous internal laugh. *'You're insane. This is no time for games.'*

Ah, but it's the perfect time to play this particular game. It's called

'Who am I?' This is how you play. You ask me questions, and I'll give you answers, and then you try to guess who I am.

'What the hell...? You want me to play your little game while Robin is who knows where, all alone out there?' The alternate internal voice became increasingly desperate. *'I need to find her and talk with her, not play mind games with you.'*

No. You need to play this game. Now, ask the first question. And by the way, the questions have to reflect a state of mind, not physical characteristics. Ready?

'This is unbelievable.' The alternate internal voice was exasperated beyond belief, but relented nevertheless. *'Fine. Let's get this over with. First question: Are you a friend?'*

Yes. Stick to state of mind, please.

'Fine. Next question: Are you happy?'

Yes, but I sometimes think I shouldn't be.

'Okay.' The alternate internal voice thought about that. *'Then, are you confused?'*

Yes. I want two irreconcilable things, and I don't know how to balance them.

The alternate internal voice attempted to ferret out the situation. *'Are you afraid?'*

I'm afraid of many things.

'Name one.'

I'm afraid I'll hurt the people I love.

'All right.' The alternate internal voice pondered the statement. *'What else?'*

I'm afraid people won't understand.

The alternate internal voice became sympathetic. *'What won't they understand?'*

The choices I make.

'Does it really matter if people don't understand, as long as you're happy?'

Yes, because I don't want to cause them pain.

'If you want two different things, why not weigh the pros and the cons, then decide which has the most benefit?' The alternate internal voice chose the rational approach to problem-solving.

I've done that. Someone always gets hurt.

'I see.' The alternate internal voice continued to prod. *'What if you didn't have to worry about causing them pain? Do you know what you would choose?'*

In a perfect world where no one would be hurt by my actions, yes. But this isn't a perfect world, and someone will be hurt.

'Why not just separate yourself from those whom your actions would cause the most pain?' The logical approach seemed to win out again. *'That way, you could spare them from your choices.'*

I've thought about that. They certainly wouldn't deserve to be hurt, and it might be for the best. It's just very frustrating and aggravating at the same time.

'You sound as if you're angry. Are you?'

I'm angry that I have to make a choice. It shouldn't be like this. I should be able to have both things and still be happy.

The alternate internal voice sensed a bit of desperation. *'Are you alone?'*

I'm alone at the moment, and I feel alone in my decision. There are so many pressures from many different directions. I don't think anyone understands how great the burden is for me.

The alternate internal voice, ever rational, proceeded. *'Have you talked with anyone about it?'*

Yes, but ultimately it has to be my decision. It won't be easy to do what I have to do.

'Do you know what you're going to do?' The alternate internal voice asked quietly.

I think so. Things...things have gotten so out of control, and I need to put a stop to that. I...um...give me a minute, okay? This is very upsetting for me.

The alternate internal voice became agitated, realizing something was very wrong. *'Are you crying?'*

Silence.

'Hey. Are you crying?'

I was, but I'm okay now.

The alternate internal voice was now alarmed and abruptly attempted avoidance of any further revelations. *'I don't want to play this game anymore.'*

Silence.

'Are you listening to me?' The alternate internal voice mentally called out. *'I don't want to play this game anymore.'*

Why? Is it because you know who I am?

No answer.

Finish the game. Or are you afraid?

'I'm not afraid.' The alternate internal voice lied. *'What would I be afraid of?'*

The truth. Finish the game.

An internal sigh. *'Fine.'* The alternate internal voice hesitantly continued. *'Do you know me?'*

Yes.
The alternate internal voice swallowed. *'Do you...love me?'*
Yes, very much.
'And you don't want to hurt me?'
I'd never hurt you if I could help it.
'But you might not have a choice?' The alternate internal voice asked sadly.
I suppose that's true.
'Are you far away?'
Not too far away.
The alternate internal voice internally sobbed. *'I know who you are. Are you Robin?'*
Yes.
'Are you coming home?'
I'll be there. We'll have to talk.
'I'm waiting for you, sweetheart.'
Perhaps it was due to the stress of the day, or maybe it was just the gentle ticking of the pendulum on the nearby wall clock, but Jess's internal voice immediately shut down as she shifted back against the soft sofa cushions and drifted off into a light, uneasy sleep. Her last fleeting sensation before sleep claimed her was one of being enveloped in a warm cocoon of sea-green comfort, contrasting with her last fuzzy thought that she should be the one doing the consoling.

****

Sometime later, Jess stirred, her blue eyes fluttering open to the light sensation of warm fingers stroking her cheek, leaving her momentarily confused. Robin sat curled on the sofa next to Jess and kissed the older woman's temple while lightly brushing her fingers back and forth across the smooth, soft skin. Jess tried very hard to move, but her limbs somehow wouldn't cooperate, leaving her content to melt under the tender and loving caresses. She closed her eyes again, and a small tear made its way down the side of her cheek, its path ragged and slow. She felt the tip of a small thumb gently smooth away the moisture.

"Shhh." Robin's soft voice whispered. "Why are you crying?"

Watery blue eyes opened once again. "Because I know your pain...the pressure you feel. I realized it while I was waiting for you." Jess choked back a quiet sob. "I'm sorry."

Robin drew the dark head underneath her chin. "No. I'm sorry. Every day, I put your career at risk. Every day I jeopardize all that you've worked so hard for." She held the taller woman close, speaking very softly. "I'm sorry I kept you waiting. After I talked with Michelle, I got in my car and just drove around, thinking about things. I thought about how I didn't want to hurt you. I'd never hurt you if I could help it." Soft green eyes ducked to meet saddened blue. "I have to make some choices, Jess, and they're very hard. Someone I love will be hurt, no matter what I do."

Jess was very still. "You have to separate yourself from those whom your actions would cause the most pain." Even as she said the words, she somehow knew what was coming next. Was her internal voice clairvoyant? She closed her eyes tight. She had to know. "Were you...crying?"

The blonde head nodded slowly. "Yes, briefly. I thought about my family. Even though I wish it weren't so, I know in my heart that they will never understand. It will hurt them to know about us." The younger woman swallowed. "I thought about you and the firm. Keeping the secret is so hard, and people are finding out. It's just a matter of time, and then everything you've worked for will be at risk." Petite fingers combed the dark hair, and several tears fell from regretful sea-green eyes. "All because of me."

"No. Not because of you." Jess turned and wrapped her arm around Robin's waist, burrowing her head into Robin's chest. "Never because of you. I've made this choice, Robin. I chose to assume the risk." She sunk into the embrace as the younger woman held her tightly. "There is no place I want to be other than with you, whatever the cost." Another tear traveled down the angular face as Jess became increasingly terrified that her greatest fear was about to be realized. *Please don't leave me, Robin.*

"I've made a decision." The younger woman felt the larger body tremble in her arms. She kissed the top of the dark head and rubbed her hand back and forth against the broad back. "It's all right."

No. No. No. It was happening. Jess surprised herself, as what little was left of her fragile composure completely broke down. She couldn't ever remember being so hopelessly out of control, the sense of impending loss crushing in its intensity. The trembling increased and the tears flowed freely. *Don't leave me.*

"Shhh." Robin soothed. "Jess, honey. Listen to me, okay?" The younger woman waited a few moments, as the trembling lessened and the body wrapped in her arms calmed somewhat. "I love you so much."

59

Robin whispered, then repeated. "I love you so much. Please know that. Always know that I love you."

No. The older woman's mind tried valiantly to grasp the enormity of the situation. She honestly didn't know how she was able to do it, but she gathered her voice from somewhere deep inside herself, and bravely uttered the words that cut straight through to her own heart. "You're leaving."

Leaving. Robin blinked, then placed her hand underneath Jess's chin and tilted it upward, fixing her gaze on grief-filled blue eyes. It was only then that it dawned on her. They had each been saying the words, but carrying on two entirely separate conversations. She suddenly felt sick. *Oh, Jess, no.* She rocked the older woman in her arms, then let her fingertips lightly graze Jess's face. "No, honey. That wasn't my decision. My decision was that I love you too much to give you up, no matter what the cost. I'm being selfish, I know that, but I thought about it, and I decided two things." Robin took a deep breath. "First, I'm going to go ahead as planned and tell my parents about us, and it will hurt them, I know that. But if they can't accept it, I'll be prepared to lose them, as hard as that would be for me." She clung to the larger body, now very tightly. "Second, I love you so much, and I don't want to hurt you. Please believe that." She paused, her composure nearly shot, then steadied herself and continued. "Jess, I want to stay with you. I know that sounds very selfish, because it jeopardizes everything for you. My staying with you could hurt you." She choked back a sob. "But you have to promise to tell me if it's too dangerous for you and you want to stop, or if you want me to leave now before we risk it going further than Michelle. You have to tell me. That's what I decided. I decided that I would accept your decision."

Jess sucked in a breath and half gasped in relief as she did so. She lifted a large hand and touched Robin's face, then drew herself up even with the gentle green eyes she loved more than her own life. "You want to stay?"

"Yes." The younger woman affirmed, then asked her next question in a very small voice. "Are you upset with me for being selfish?"

Jess nearly laughed, her relief so great. "Oh, sweetheart, no. You speak with your heart, and your heart is pure. It is not selfish." She lightly kissed Robin's lips. "Do you want my decision?"

The blonde head nodded cautiously.

The older woman whispered, her voice very tender. "My job, my belongings, whatever money I have, all mean nothing to me without you. I'd give all of it up in a heartbeat just to be with you. If I had you and nothing else, my life would be complete." She kissed Robin again, lingering just enough to convey everything she felt. "If it were up to me, I'd hold you forever. If it were up to me, I'd give up everything I have just to be with you. If it were up to me, I'd love you and take care of you and cherish you for the rest of your life." Jess felt she was on the verge of a commitment, and she didn't want to rush into something that was obviously so important at this overly emotional time. She steered clear of the topic just a bit. "Let me be clear. No job or career or anything else would be worth not loving you, even for one minute. That's my decision." A warm, affectionate smile slowly appeared in an attempt to break the tension. "You got that?"

The affectionate smile was returned. "Yes, I got it." A pause. "So, does that mean you want me to stay?"

Jess reclined on the sofa, pulling Robin down on top of her, and grinned for the first time that evening. "Yes. That's definitely what that means." She noted that the younger woman still wore her business suit. "You must be uncomfortable in that. How about we get ready for bed, and then we can talk some more, okay?"

Robin breathed in Jess's distinctive scent, comforted by its familiarity and the feel of the strong arms surrounding her. *This is my home.* "Yes, as long as you hold me like this."

The grin widened. "I think that can be arranged."

****

"How did it go with Michelle?" Long arms wrapped around Robin's petite body, drawing the younger woman closer as they lay snuggled together in the waterbed.

A heavy sigh. "She knows. She didn't say it in so many words, but she knows." Small fingers intertwined with larger ones. "She says she'll be discreet, and I believe her."

"Did she say anything else?"

Robin reflected on her conversation with Michelle. "She was surprisingly understanding. I didn't expect that. But she also warned me that people will talk, and that we'd have to be careful because of the perception of favoritism."

Jess nodded. "That's what Harry said."

The blonde head jerked up. "Harry knows?"

"No, not about us. Not like that. He just spoke to me about our living arrangements, and that I'd have to be careful to avoid the appearance of favoritism toward any associate."

Robin thought about the implications. "You promised, remember?" She fixed her gaze squarely on Jess in the dark. "No special treatment."

"Yes. I remember, and I told Harry that I would be completely objective."

"Can you? Be objective, I mean."

A long silence followed, longer than it should have taken Jess to answer the question outright. "I will try, and I think I'll be able to do that, but I want to tell you something. Sometimes, no matter how objective someone is, if people believe there is favoritism at play, nothing will change their minds."

The younger woman inched up so she was even with Jess. "What are you saying?"

"I'm saying that if the firm finds out about us, they absolutely will make sure you don't work directly with me anymore." *If they don't ask me to resign first.*

Robin had the same thought. "That's the best case scenario, isn't it?"

There was no reason at this point to hedge the truth. "Yes."

Jess. Robin felt her heart lurch. "This is too dangerous. I'll cost you everything."

A large hand reached up and grasped Robin's chin firmly. "You listen to me. You're not responsible for anything that may or may not happen to me. I've made this choice. I choose to be with you. I assume the risk, and if there is any backlash against you, I promise you, I will protect you."

Robin stared into the faint outline of silver-blue eyes, reading their intent, then lowered her head and tucked it in the crook of Jess's neck. "This really sucks, doesn't it."

A wry grin surfaced. Jess hadn't remembered ever hearing such language from Robin before. In context, it was oddly endearing. "Yes, sweetheart. This really sucks." They laid together for a few moments longer before Jess spoke again. "On a more positive note, Harry asked us to dinner."

"He did? How come?"

"He said he and his wife had such a good time talking with us at the Christmas party that they wanted to get together for dinner one night. This week's shot, but next week's open. Are you up to it?"

"Sure, sounds good. I like his wife." A petite finger drew idle designs on Jess's sleep shirt covered stomach. "Could we make it for sometime early in the week?" *I have a trip planned to Detroit.* The small hand came to rest across Jess's chest.

"I'll let him know." A pause, then a quiet whisper. "So, when are you planning to leave for Michigan?"

How did she know I was thinking about that? Not unexpectedly, Robin felt the larger body stiffen beneath her and the strong heart beat beneath her hand speed up slightly. "The interview is scheduled for Friday, so I'll leave Thursday. That'll give me time to explain things to my parents, and then my dad can cancel the appointment. I know it's last minute, but I've already told them I'm not interested, and they won't listen to me."

Jess looked unseeingly at the lighted digital clock. She had an uneasy feeling, and it wouldn't go away. *I don't like it.* "When are you coming back?"

The heart rate beneath the small hand now increased considerably. Robin tilted her head up and noted that Jess had focused her attention on the clock on the nightstand. The younger woman recognized the action at once as Jess's tendency to turn away from a conversation when she felt uncomfortable or threatened emotionally. *I'm not leaving for good.* "I'm coming back Friday. There'll be no reason for me to stay longer than that."

Couldn't she just call them? Damn. Jess shook her head. She knew she was thinking of herself again, and what she really needed to do was look at things from Robin's perspective. These were Robin's parents, and news like this wasn't exactly something that could easily be explained long-distance. The older woman suddenly felt ashamed at her own self-absorbed behavior. "I'm sorry for the way I overreacted before."

Light brows furrowed in the dark. "When?"

"Before, when I acted childishly, clinging to you like that. After what had happened with Michelle, I thought you had decided you didn't want to be together anymore, and that you wanted to leave permanently. I didn't consider things from your point of view, and how difficult everything was for you. I had just finished chastising myself for that very thing before you came home, and then I just lost it."

It sneaks up on me how sensitive she is to this. How do I convince her? Robin drew her hand up and stroked one of the long arms that held her. "Jess, I know how you've been hurt before, and I know how hard it's been for you to open up your heart again. That is the greatest gift to me." Soft lips pressed against the side of Jess's neck. "I promise you, Jess." She replaced her hand over the older woman's heart in a solemn vow. "I will never betray you, and I will never willingly leave you. I promise you that."

Although by now it really shouldn't have done so, the promise caught the older woman completely off-guard, and she had trouble verbalizing her next thoughts. She swallowed and responded the only way she could at the moment, tightening her hold on the smaller form and tenderly kissing the forehead resting next to her own lips.

Thank you, sweetheart.

****

The morning dawned with none of the anxiety from the previous evening. A golden white stripe of sunlight crossed the expansive bedroom, settling haphazardly over the gently sleeping forms entangled together beneath the crisp linen sheets. The taller of the two forms shifted first, blinking slowly to adjust to the increasingly bright light. She extracted her hand from around the waist beneath her companion's nightshirt and stretched her long body languidly, working out a kink in her neck as she did so. The smaller body turned over and threw an arm across a Calvin Klein clad stomach, securing its position possessively.

A dark eyebrow arched. *Trapped.* Jess attempted to remove the uncooperative arm without waking its owner. No luck. The arm, instead, tightened around her. *Uh oh. No way out.*

"You're not going anywhere." A small voice mumbled into Jess's shoulder.

A chuckle. "Well, good morning to you, too, sleepyhead."

"Mmmfph."

"Let me just say this. If you don't let me up right now, we're going to have a serious emergency here very quickly." Both dark eyebrow rose for emphasis.

Emergency? A green eye peeked up, taking note of the situation. *Oh.* The petite arm promptly removed itself from its location. "Go ahead. I'm not cruel." A happy smile. "You are coming back to bed, aren't you?"

Jess sat up. "Actually, I was going to get up and start breakfast. Want some?"

Green eyes closed again. "Um...maybe. Let me think about it."

"You're such a sleepyhead. Maybe you should go back to sleep."

"Hmmm?"

A grin. *She's adorable like this.* "Never mind." The older woman stood up, gave herself another quick stretch, then commented loudly. "Now, I just need to find my slippers."

That brought a playfully sarcastic remark from the opposite side of the bed. "You shouldn't have any problem. They practically glow in the dark."

Jess slipped on the bright yellow slippers and padded around to face Robin. "I'd be very careful if I were you, Robin. At least I can find mine." She lightly ruffled the blonde head, then beat a hasty retreat into the bathroom.

It took a minute for the sleepy woman to fully comprehend that last comment. A green eye popped open. *She better not have stolen mine again.* Robin called out loudly toward the bathroom. "When I get up, they'd better be here, Jess."

A dark head poked through the partially open door. "Did you...um...say something out there?"

"You heard me."

A knowing smirk. "Um...I plead the fifth." The bathroom door closed tight.

Green eyes, now suddenly wide awake, narrowed considerably. *She is so dead.*

****

The delicious aroma of freshly brewed coffee hit Robin as she snuggled down further into the covers. *God, that smells good.* She sniffed in the enticing scent, her nose twitching slightly, then felt a slight jiggle as a larger body settled down on the waveless waterbed beside her. She opened one sleepy eye. "Hi."

Jess grinned. "Hi, there. I brought breakfast. Are you ready to get up, now?"

Robin rolled over on her back and stretched. "It occurs to me that this is just a clever diversion to make me forget about my slippers."

"Perhaps." Jess leaned in for a kiss. "But I could think of other more interesting diversions, if that were my intent." She winked.

Robin smiled and returned the kiss. "You're incorrigible."

"Of course. That's why you love me, kiddo. Now, let's eat." Jess sat back against the headboard and waited as Robin sat up. "I made pancakes." She handed the younger woman a tray.

"Thanks." Robin added cream and sugar to her coffee, then took a sip, perusing the tray's contents. "Ooooh." A delighted grin. "And you brought strawberries, too."

"Yep. I know how much you like them." Jess reached for one very ripe strawberry and dipped it in sugar. "Here." She held it out and watched as Robin's lips took the berry from her fingers, licking them thoroughly. The dark-haired woman's mouth suddenly went dry. *God. I can't believe she has this effect on me.* "Do you remember the first time we had strawberries?"

Green eyes looked up, a bit quizzically. "Yeah, why?"

"Well, you took the strawberry from my fingers with your mouth, and I thought I would die. I was so shocked at the way I felt when you did that."

"Hmmm." Robin considered the admission. "Let me try it." She found another ripe strawberry and coated it with sugar, then held it out, observing with fascination as Jess took the berry with her teeth, then swirled her lips sensuously around Robin's fingers. *Oh, God.* Robin cleared her throat. "That was...."

Before the younger woman could finish her thought, Jess leaned over and kissed Robin soundly, whispering. "You drive me crazy."

Breathless, Robin responded. "Likewise." Green eyes then twinkled. "Now, let's finish eating breakfast. I'm starving."

Starving? A dark eyebrow arched. "Fine. But after breakfast, Robin, I have big plans for your stomach."

A shy sideways glance. "That's your job, Jess, to keep my stomach happy."

Oh boy. I do so love my job.

****

Gentle fingers grazed sensuously across the broad bare back, stroking the pliant flesh before being replaced by soft lips trailing upward toward a sensitive neck, then over behind a conveniently placed ear. The smaller body hovered over, then covered the larger one, delighting in the skin to skin contact, then extended its length as much as possible. Petite limbs stretched out, mirroring those beneath them, as small fingers entwined with larger ones.

"You did a very good job." Robin murmured.

Jess felt the whispered breath caress her ear, sending a shiver down her spine. "I'm glad you agree." A cocky grin appeared. "I take my job very seriously."

A giggle. "Lucky for me. My stomach is very happy at the moment." A pause. "In fact, all of me is very happy right now." The younger woman slowly slid off to the side and began to draw idle patterns on Jess's back. "Now, concentrate. What am I drawing?"

"Um...." Jess was almost distracted by the gentle touch. "A train?"

Another giggle. "Nope. Try again." The finger drew the imaginary image again.

"A plane?"

"Nope, but the shape is similar. Let me draw it one more time. Close your eyes and concentrate."

Azure eyes fluttered closed as Jess took in the delicious sensation. She felt the soft fingertips dip and curve into the design, which she now fully recognized. A wide smile quickly appeared. "I got it." She proclaimed proudly.

"What is it?"

The older woman flipped herself over to face Robin, twinkling blue eyes complementing her broad grin. "It's a shrimp!"

Robin kissed the lips in front of her. "You are so smart." She leaned in for several more lingering kisses, enjoying the long, slow and languid explorations, before closing her eyes and resting her head next to Jess. "I never get tired of kissing you."

"Me either." The dark-haired woman breathed. "That's the best part."

Pale eyebrows wiggled playfully. "The best part?"

"Well..." Jess drawled. "It's all very good, but there's just something about holding you and kissing you that makes me feel so connected to you. I can't explain it any better than that." And it was true, Jess really couldn't put exact words to the feeling.

"The other parts...." Shy green eyes suddenly cast downward. "Um...are they not what you expect?"

Ooooh. I think I need to explain. A slender finger hooked underneath the younger woman's chin, tilting it up so blue eyes firmly captured sea-green. "The other parts are more than I ever could have hoped for. Don't ever doubt that."

"Do you miss it?"

Miss it? "Do I miss what?" The older woman was truly perplexed.

For some reason, Robin had a hard time talking about it. It shouldn't have been so incredibly difficult, but strangely, it was. "Do you miss being with men?" There, she said it, and it was out in the open now.

Uh oh. "C'mere." Jess enfolded Robin into a strong embrace, whispering the reassurances she was sure the younger woman needed to hear. "Listen to me. You are all I need. You fill me up in the most complete way. No one has ever done that for me before. No one." *Not even James.*

"But it's different." Robin's voice was very quiet.

Jess's lips curved into a sweet smile, answering the comment honestly. "Obviously, it's different." Long fingers stroked the short blonde hair. "But loving you like this is the most wonderful thing. I'd never trade it. Never." A thought occurred to her, and she just had to ask, although to be honest, she wasn't quite sure she really wanted to know the answer. "What about you? Do you...miss it?"

The blonde head shifted upward. "Well, my...expertise in that area is not very extensive." A small smile appeared, then diminished somewhat as Robin sought to put order to her thoughts. "But, I would say that being with you surpasses everything I ever thought I could feel, or anything I've ever felt before. Sometimes, it seems as if we merge together, and I don't understand how that could be, but it's so intense that nothing else even comes close." She trailed a finger lazily across a prominent jaw. "So, to answer your question, the same as you, I'd never trade it."

"You know that I'd be happy to hold you forever. If that's all we ever did, it would be enough."

Robin contemplated that thought. "You know, I think that would be enough, too." Green eyes sparkled mischievously. "But fortunately, we don't have to limit ourselves to that." She leaned over and gave Jess an intense kiss to emphasize her point.

She's incredible. "Now, who's incorrigible?"

"I learned from the best, Jess. Remember?"

"Oh yeah." An amorous blue eye winked. "Thank you." A change of topic was in order. "Got any plans for today?"

"Nope. I'm all yours." An adorable pink blush made its way all the way to Robin's ears as she realized the context of what she'd said. *I can't believe she still has this effect on me.* "I mean, no, I don't have any plans."

"Want to take a little drive with me?"

Robin lifted slightly and braced herself up on one elbow. "A drive? Where to?"

"Well..." Jess drawled. "It's a beautiful day outside and rather warm for this time of year. How about we drive over to the east coast and do a little...." Both eyebrows lifted playfully. "Fishing."

That suggestion was unexpected. "Fishing? You fish?"

"Yep." Jess grinned happily. "Got a rod and a reel, a tackle box, and everything. How about it? It only takes an hour to get there."

Golden eyebrows knit together. "When do you have time to fish? Since I've known you, you've never mentioned it."

"Well, to be honest, I haven't had the time in a really long while, but I've always enjoyed it. C'mon, it'll be fun." Jess waited for an answer. In truth, she knew that the next week would undoubtedly be very difficult for both of them, and she figured they could use a little diversion right about now.

Robin contemplated the offer. "Hmmm." A slight pout. "But I don't have a fishing pole."

A chuckle. "I have a spare."

Why not? "Okay." Robin hopped up and headed toward the shower. "I'll make a picnic to bring with us."

Blue eyes followed the younger woman's retreating form with interest. *I love picnics.* A dark eyebrow arched ever so slowly. *And showers.* "Hey, wait up." Without another moment's hesitation, Jess sprang from the bed and quickly followed Robin into the bathroom, a picnic not the only thing on her mind as she did so.

Picnics and showers. What fun!

****

The drive to the Atlantic coast was largely uneventful. The silver Mercedes traveled the main state highway along its route, the mid-morning sun shining brightly in the late January sky. Robin had donned a pair of khaki pants and a light-blue long-sleeved cotton button-down shirt, rolled up at the cuffs. A short-brimmed floppy hat and dark sunglasses completed the ensemble. Jess, as always, thought the younger woman looked positively adorable. As for Jess, she sported blue jeans and a denim button-down shirt, complemented by silver mirrored sunglasses and a hat which held what the taller woman affectionately referred to as her fishing gear, given that several lures were affixed to the brim and sides in various positions of disarray. The resulting look was quite comical, and Robin did well to hide her amusement.

"I thought you said you hadn't been fishing in a long time." Robin held back a grin.

"Correct."

"What's with the hat, then?"

"I dug it out today. A good fisherman...or fisherperson, is always prepared." Jess gave Robin a look. "Don't you like it?"

A raised eyebrow. "Indeed. It's quite...." Robin giggled, trying fervently to come up with a suitable description for the sight. "Becoming."

Blue eyes squinted behind silver sunglasses. "Yes, it is, isn't it." A satisfied grin. "I like it. Plus, it's very versatile."

"Versatile?"

"Yes. Keeps the sun out of my eyes and holds my tackle at the same time." Jess beamed, quite pleased with herself at the practical

69

explanation.

Robin gazed as Jess in utter amazement. The older woman had such a different side to her, one which few people ever got to see. Not only was there the tough, no-nonsense, workaholic lawyer beneath Jess's admittedly striking exterior, but there was also the playful, easy-going and truly fun person inside. *Fun.* There was an enigma somewhere in there, and when Robin had a little time to herself, she'd have to think about that some more. "Did you fish a lot before?"

"Yeah, but not too much recently. When I was growing up, Peter and I would do a lot of fishing together." Jess's tone turned wistful. "We used to live on a canal, and there was a little bridge at one end. We'd go down to the bridge with our cane poles and later with our fishing rods, and we'd wait for the bait fish to come. We knew there'd be bigger fish going after the bait." She was lost in her memories. "Sometimes, we'd get our nets and walk along the seawall looking for blue crabs. We'd come back home with a bucket full of blue crabs, and my mom would make crab cakes, and crab casserole, and crab salad."

Green eyes hidden behind dark sunglasses surreptitiously watched the older woman, noting her fixated gaze on the open highway and sensing an air of nostalgia in Jess's voice as she related her story. *Are you reliving simpler times, Jess? Is your life so much more complicated now that I'm in it?* Robin shook her head of her thoughts and turned toward the side window, watching the trees and brush pass by. It was true, things had gotten completely out of control. Literally, all hell was going to break loose very soon, and the end result was anything but certain. *Will you eventually blame me, Jess, even unintentionally, for jeopardizing everything for you?*

"Hey, kiddo." The alto voice broke Robin from her musings. "We're almost there."

The younger woman noted the change in terrain. "Exactly where is it we're going?"

"First, we'll stop and get some bait, then we'll go over that long bridge over there to the other side of the Merritt Island Wildlife Sanctuary. There's a pretty good fishing hole off of one of the canals in there." A blue eye peeked above the edge of mirrored sunglasses at the younger woman, offering a ghost of a wink. "It's also very secluded."

Secluded. Robin considered that idea. *I'm starting to like this fishing stuff more and more.*

****

They parked the Mercedes alongside the narrow dirt road and dug out the rest of their fishing gear from the trunk of the car. Jess assembled the fishing rods and carried them and the bait bucket over to the canal bank. Robin took the tackle box and picnic basket, along with a throw blanket, and set up the picnic area on a surprisingly green grassy area nearby.

"Bring me that tackle box, will ya?" Jess called over to Robin.

The younger woman complied, walking over and handing the older woman the turquoise and black box. "I'm going to get the lawn chairs from the car. Do we need anything else?"

"Just the large ice chest. That's where we're going to put all the fish we catch." A broad grin. "Hope we can fit them all in there."

"You're pretty sure of yourself, aren't you?"

"Yep." Jess threaded the line through the hooks on each fishing pole. "Be prepared, Robin, to catch your weight in fish today."

"Right." Robin smirked, then went over to the car to retrieve the lawn chairs, bringing them back. "Um....Jess? You're not going to make me put the bait on, are you?"

Blue eyes twinkled unseen. "You got a problem with that?"

Robin sat down in one of the chairs. "Well..." She drawled. "You see, when I was little, my dad and I used to go fishing on the lakes, and he'd always bait the hook for me."

An eyebrow arched above the rim of the mirrored sunglasses. "I see." Jess put a live shrimp on a hook. "Did you ever catch anything?"

"Oh yeah. Bass and trout."

The taller woman handed Robin the baited fishing rod. "How'd you get the fish off the hook, once you caught them?"

"Well, my dad would help me reel them in, and then he'd unhook them for me." Petite arms cast the line into the water, sunglass-shaded green eyes watching intently as it lazily settled toward the canal bottom. Robin swallowed back an unexpectedly odd feeling. "I'd almost forgotten about that."

Jess caught the reflective tone. "Forgotten about what?" She relaxed back into her lawn chair, crossing her feet at her ankles and casting her line off toward the edge of the canal.

"The times when I was growing up, and he'd take me fishing with him on his boat. Sometimes, I think he wished he had a son to take with him."

Jess caught an underlying hint of sadness in that statement. "Why do you think that?" If truth be told, Jess was very interested in Robin's family life growing up. She had gotten the distinct impression that Robin was very protected, and the loss of David had exposed the

71

younger woman to a sudden real-life cruelty which Jess was sure Robin wasn't nearly prepared to handle. *Then, of course, who would have been prepared to handle that?*

Robin continued. "Dad and I were pretty close. He would always call me his girl. Still, I always sensed that he missed having a son to do the guy stuff with, you know, like little league games, and cub scouts, and camping trips." Dark sunglasses hid hesitant green eyes as they glanced over at the tall form in the next chair. "I couldn't help but feel that I was a bit of a disappointment to him that way."

What? Mirrored sunglasses tracked their direction from the water to Robin. *A disappointment?* Jess considered her response carefully. "I can't believe he would ever think that. I can tell how much he loves you."

A sigh. "I know. I just worry about disappointing him." *I don't want him to hate me.*

Jess focused her gaze on the water in thought and watched as the bright sunlight glinted off the tiny ripples around her fishing line. Then, it hit her...the reason why Robin had been so hesitant to tell her parents about their relationship. Jess closed her eyes and berated herself inside her mind. *Damn, Jess, you're such an idiot.* Why was it she always thought in terms of her own selfish perspective when it came to Robin? Robin wasn't reluctant to tell her parents about their relationship because she wasn't serious about it, she was reluctant to tell them because she didn't want to be a disappointment to them. *Oh, sweetheart.* The mirrored sunglasses returned their direction to Robin. "You are absolutely not a disappointment." Jess stated with conviction. "So don't even go there. You got that?"

The blonde head nodded gratefully. "Got it." Just then, the smaller woman's line went taut. "Jess, I got one."

"Well, go ahead and reel it in." The older woman watched excitedly as Robin stood up, and after a pretty good fight, reeled in a very good-sized Whiting. "There you go, kiddo! Now, go ahead and take the hook out."

"You're kidding, right?" The fish wiggled around on the line.

"Nope." Jess grinned. "Just lay the fish down on the ground, put your foot on it, and ease the hook out of its mouth. You can do it." *I know you can.*

Wary green eyes peered above dark sunglasses. "If you say so." The smaller woman took a deep breath. "Here goes." Expertly, Robin unhooked the Whiting and watched as Jess threw it into the large ice chest. *That really wasn't so hard.*

Jess sat back down and gave Robin a noticeable wink. "I think your dad would definitely be very proud."

The grinned that graced Robin's face reflected far more than merely reeling in and unhooking the fish. She considered what it all meant. The little girl inside of her had desperately wanted to please her parents, but the woman she was now was taking charge of her own life. She was in control. She decided where she lived, and where she worked, and whom she loved. Not her parents. Strangely enough, Robin had a renewed sense of self-confidence. *All from taking a hook out of a fish?* She shook her head in wonder. *Amazing.*

★★★★★★★★★★★★★★★★

Robin and Jess settled back into their lawn chairs, each with a cup of gourmet coffee they'd brought with them in a thermos, and waited for the next fish to bite. By just after mid-day, Robin had caught another Whiting, and felt inordinately pleased with herself. Jess, on the other hand, still had yet to reel in one fish. The older woman pulled up the bait bucket and peered inside.

"Jess?" Robin caught the movement. "What are you doing?"

Innocent blue eyes peeked above mirrored sunglasses. "Nothing."

She's so hopeless. "I saw you looking in that bucket. Why?"

Jess set the bucket down nonchalantly. "No reason."

Sea-green eyes narrowed behind dark sunglasses. "Jess, those shrimps are bait, not lunch. I packed a picnic, remember?"

A wounded expression. "I was merely counting them to see how many we had left for this afternoon, Robin, that's all. I certainly wasn't contemplating anything else."

A pale eyebrow arched. "Right. They're raw, Jess, and live. That is really, really disgusting."

"I have absolutely no idea what you're talking about." The dark head shook vehemently.

"You do so." Robin pointed a playful finger. "You're in withdrawal. I can see it."

"No, I'm not," Jess vigorously insisted. She glanced down at the bait bucket once again, then after an appropriate length of time, spoke. "So, what did you bring for lunch?" It was a perfectly innocent question.

A chuckle. "Ham and turkey sandwiches, carrot salad, potato chips, and chocolate chip cookies."

"Oh." A long silence. "Is that all?" Another perfectly innocent question.

Robin narrowed her eyes again. "There might be, maybe, something else."

Jess nodded thoughtfully. "Care to give me a little hint?" That made three perfectly innocent questions in a row.

Dark sunglasses hid the roll of the younger woman's green eyes. "Okay, fine. A hint. It begins with the letter 'S,' if you must know."

"Really? An excited look. "Am I going to like it?" It was official, Jess was on an innocent question roll.

The petite form set down her fishing pole and walked over to the picnic cooler, pulling out two cans. "Well, that depends on if you like...soda." Robin was teasing, and she was absolutely enjoying every minute of it.

A dejected look accompanied another quick peek inside the bait bucket. "Oh." A slight pout. *Rats.*

Robin stifled a giggle. She pulled out another item from the picnic cooler and wandered over to where Jess was sitting. "I found this in the refrigerator this morning, and I thought I'd bring it along." She handed the container to Jess. "Might you be interested in having some for lunch?"

Jess pulled her nose from the bait bucket and inspected the proffered container. The transformation was immediate. A wide smiled appeared, and she leaned over and gave Robin a quick kiss on the cheek. "You know me so well." She grinned. "Yes, of course. I'd love some for lunch." Jess was practically jumping up and down in her chair in excitement.

For her part, Robin merely stared, mouth slightly open, at Jess in disbelief. *It's amazing what a little shrimp salad can do.* She took in the taller woman's continued exuberance. *I wonder if there's a twelve-step program for this.*

For January, it was a spectacularly beautiful day outside, with plenty of sun and a gentle warm ocean breeze hovering above the secluded canal. Jess and Robin took a break from their fishing duties and ate their picnic lunch, shrimp salad and all. At least as far as lunch was concerned, the bait was safe. The remainder of the afternoon was spent fishing and chatting about various uncomplicated things, keeping things light and generally carefree. It all was very pleasant and a much-needed diversion from their more stressful daily life. Robin reflected at length on that fact while she kept a watchful eye on her fishing line. It was absolutely amazing to her how Jess just seemed to know how to make things seem better. By fishing, no less. *Who would have known?*

The blonde woman secretly observed Jess industriously casting her line in several locations, seeking out the best fishing spots. In Robin's opinion, the taller woman was captivating, and in a way, such a mystery. Jess had truly remarkable beauty, noticeable as the golden sun bathed her already bronzed skin, and her dark hair cascaded in a most appealing way about her striking features. And the woman underneath it all was amazing in every way, from the brilliant high-powered attorney to the adorably silly, fun-loving, fiercely protective, and sometimes insecure person who had given up her own heart, and captured Robin's in return. There was just so much in one package. Robin shook her head in wonder. *Who would have known?*

Furthering her thought, it was also astounding that such an incredibly complex person as Jess had spent so much of her life alone in guarded existence. That fact, Robin knew, was attributable to one person, and one person only. *James.* There wasn't any particularly rational reason for it, but all at once, the younger woman felt an uncharacteristic anger rise deep within her at the mere thought of James' betrayal. She clenched her jaw reflexively. *Damn you, James. You never deserved her love.* Deciding not to dwell on such unpleasantness, Robin mentally shook herself from her musings and returned her focus to the task at hand. After all, there were so many more fish to catch, and she was actually having fun doing it. *Who would have known?* She smiled to herself, now suddenly feeling much better.

Indeed. Who would have known?

✝ ✝ ✝ ✝ ✱ ✱ ✱ ✱ ✱ ✱ ✱ ✱ ✱ ✱ ✱

As the sun started its descent from the sky, Robin and Jess made their way back to the silver Mercedes and packed their fishing gear and picnic items. Once everything was safely stowed away, they settled into the front seat of the car and pulled out onto the narrow dirt road leading toward the main highway. Robin rolled down the passenger side window and let the waning late afternoon breeze blow freely through her hair. It had been a nice day.

"You doing okay?" Jess eased the car over some loose gravel.

"Yeah, I had a lot of fun."

The driver nodded, then glanced over at Robin. "Your nose got a little sunburned." Blue eyes inspected the damage. "But, it doesn't look too bad. In fact, it looks very cute." *Everything looks cute on her.* "Didn't you put sunscreen on?"

"Yeah." Robin touched her nose. "I guess it wasn't enough. I should have kept my hat on longer."

Jess finally pulled the car out onto the main highway. "You probably peel when you get sunburned, don't you?"

"You should see me. I'm like a lobster." Robin grimaced. "If we go to the beach in the summertime, make sure I remember to bring some heavy-duty sunscreen." She studied the terrain in front of her. "Are there any beaches around here?"

Jess nodded. "There's one just over those dunes called Playalinda Beach." She pointed, then grinned mischievously. "But I'm not sure you'd want to try that one out."

Light eyebrows furrowed. "Why not?"

A smirk. "Let's just say that particular beach is famous, or rather infamous, for its no-clothing policy."

Robin opened her mouth, then quickly shut it again. "Um...I didn't think they had any of those around here."

"Oh, yeah. It's quite a scandal from time to time. They keep trying to close it, and somehow it always gets reopened again. This whole area is a National Wildlife Refuge, and the beach is a National Seashore, so someone is always trying to preserve the natural habitat."

Robin offered a wry grin. "You can't get any more natural than that."

That drew a significantly raised eyebrow. "Good point."

Green eyes twinkled, then a light chuckle followed. "So...um...tell me, Jess, do you sometimes...frequent that particular beach?"

A shocked expression. "Why, Robin. I can't believe you'd think such a thing."

Another chuckle. "I only asked because you seemed quite...knowledgeable about the subject." A golden eyebrow arched ever so slowly to add emphasis to the implication.

"If you're saying that you'd like to try it out sometime, Robin, perhaps that could be arranged." There was an unmistakable challenge in the older woman's voice.

"No, no. That's okay." Robin backed off. "I was just curious."

Curious? Jess left that particular thought to ponder for another time and deftly changed the focus of their conversation. "So, tell me, are you a dedicated fisherman, or fisherperson, now?"

"I think I'm becoming an expert at it." Robin grinned happily.

"An expert. My, that is something." The dark-haired woman headed the silver Mercedes toward the long bridge crossing over to the mainland.

"Well, I did catch four fish, you know." Green eyes danced. "How many fish did you catch today, Jess?"

Jess mumbled something unintelligible.

"I didn't hear you, Jess. How many fish was that?"

A bored look. "One."

"One." Robin lifted both eyebrows knowingly. "And you threw it back."

"Didn't want to keep it." Jess, all of a sudden, was growing rather weary of this particular conversation, even though she had started it.

"Yes, it was rather small, wasn't it?"

Another bored look. "What's your point?"

"Nothing."

"I'll have you know, Robin, that it was a perfectly lovely fish."

Robin nodded in all seriousness. "I'm sure." A well-timed giggle. "Small...but definitely lovely."

Jess smacked her lips together in mock annoyance. "Everyone's a critic."

That sent Robin into a fit of laughter, requiring that she wipe her eyes several times. She finally calmed herself, and after a few moments of silence, turned to regard the older woman. "I really needed today, Jess. Thank you."

"You're welcome, kiddo. We'll do it again sometime, if you want."

"Okay." Robin pulled something from her pocket. "Next time, though, you can have Al for good luck."

The light dawned. "Ah, so that's why you hooked all the big fish. You had Al with you. I should have known." *It must work. She's certainly hooked me.*

"Yep. I'm a believer." Petite fingers hung Al from the Mercedes' rearview mirror. "Here, you keep him for a while." *Keep him safe for me, Jess. I'm coming back for him. And you.*

"All right." *Are you trying to tell me something? Are you leaving him with me for good?* Jess couldn't let her thoughts stray too far too soon. Robin wasn't scheduled to leave for Michigan for another five days. Besides, everything was going work out just fine. After Robin talked with her parents, much of the burden would be lifted, and a significant amount of the stress that had consumed both of them in recent weeks would be lessened. Right? Jess nodded in an attempt to convince herself of just that. *Right.* "Hey, I have an idea." Dark eyebrows waggled. "When we get home, I'll race ya to the Jacuzzi."

"Ooooh. The Jacuzzi." A delighted smile. "How can I resist an offer like that." Robin waggled an eyebrow in return. "Will you...wash my back?"

"Reciprocal back washing whilst in the Jacuzzi, Robin. That's house rule number five."

The smaller woman considered the new rule for only a half-second, then grinned. "Deal."

****

The elegant restaurant sat high above the downtown city streets, its expansive glass windows providing breathtaking views of the surrounding area in all directions with a surprisingly clear glimpse south to the Disney castle. Harry and Barbara Roberts were already seated at a table in front of one of the windows, the darkened night sky filtering in through the glass, and the cozy corner accented only by the flickering candle strategically placed on the back edge of the tabletop. Harry spotted Jess and Robin and waved them over.

"Jess, Robin, hello." Harry stood up and waited as the two other attorneys took a seat, then sat back down.

Jess nodded in greeting. "Harry, Barbara, it's a pleasure."

Barbara Roberts reached over and touched Robin lightly on the forearm. "I'm so happy you could join us tonight. I so enjoyed talking with you at the party last month."

"Thank you for inviting me." Robin watched as the waiter came over and filled their glasses with water. "This is a really nice restaurant. I've never been here before."

Barbara continued. "Harry and I love this place. We come here quite often."

The waiter proceeded to hand them their menus and recite the house specials. After a few moments of perusing the extensive selection of appetizers and entrées, they requested a bottle of fine Merlot wine, then ordered their meals. Of curious note, at least to Robin, was that Jess, in a wholly uncharacteristic move, chose not to order shrimp, neither as an appetizer nor as an entrée.

The young associate couldn't help herself. She just had to comment. "Becoming adventurous, are we?"

Blue eyes cast sideways at Robin. "Adventurous?"

"No shrimp tonight, I see." A blonde eyebrow lifted ever so slightly.

"I do eat other things, you know. Chicken Marsala is certainly one of them." A nonchalant look as Jess took a piece of bread and buttered it, ignoring the knowing smirk of her housemate.

Green eyes danced. *She's trying to act cool.* "Right. Chicken

Marsala."

The playful tone of the interaction was not lost on Barbara. From her perspective, the genuine affection between the two women was more than evident, and the easy banter, however subdued, was a dead give-away of something more than simply a casual friendship, even if her husband hadn't quite picked up on it. "How is the new year treating you, Robin?"

Robin smiled. "Very well, thanks. I just bought a new car, and I'm all settled in now over at Jess's house."

Jess's head snapped up at Robin's reference to her new place of abode. *Are we advertising this now?* She rushed to clarify. "Um...that's right. I decided it might be nice to have some company in that big house of mine."

Barbara seemed unaffected. "Oh, yes. I think Harry mentioned something about that to me last week. It must be a nice change for you, Jess."

The junior partner merely nodded. *That felt odd.* There was something about the way Barbara carried the conversation that caused Jess to wonder. Could Barbara suspect? And more importantly, was it something to worry about? *As if there wasn't already enough to worry about.* However, Barbara seemed entirely comfortable, either way, even supportive. *An ally, perhaps.* Jess considered that notion. *Perhaps.*

Harry finally chimed in, totally off-topic. "Dear, do you remember the first time we ever came to this restaurant? It has to have been more than 30 years ago now " He turned toward Jess and Robin and went on with his reminiscent musings. "This town was little more than orange groves and cow pastures at the time, and this building was one of only two high rises in the small downtown they had here at that time. It also just happened to have one of the few quality restaurants in the area."

"That's right, dear." Harry's wife continued. "We literally stumbled across it one evening, and it's been our favorite place ever since."

"Those were the days, all right." The head of the litigation department chuckled at the memory, then continued. "Back then, the firm was just starting out. We had just Gordon McDaniel and myself, and no real office staff. Barbara, here, was our bookkeeper, and Gordon's wife, Lynn, handled our administrative work."

Robin was intrigued by the story. "So, it was just the four of you?"

Barbara nodded thoughtfully. "Yes, for a while, until the firm got going. Several more lawyers eventually came on board, and the firm began to grow."

Harry glanced at his wife. "There were many times that Gordon and I didn't think we were going to last. I tell you, if it wasn't for the support of Barbara and Lynn throughout all the hard times, I'm not at all sure we would have made it. We had to work very hard to drum up business, and Barbara, here, was right out there with us helping to bring in more clients. The firm is what it is today in large part because of her perseverance, patience, and encouragement." He leaned over toward Jess and motioned back toward his wife conspiratorially. "I'll tell you a little secret. She's the boss and she never lets me forget it." He gave a quick wink.

All present caught the comment and laughed. It was a fascinating story, Jess had to admit, and even as the waiter brought their appetizers to begin their meal, the junior partner was contemplating the implications of what she'd just heard. Barbara was one of the co-founders of the firm. *Interesting.* Barbara could also turn out to be an ally of sorts. *A positive development.* So, perhaps, this new information could prove to be beneficial in the long run. *Perhaps.* The wheels were turning, as a dark eyebrow edged up ever so slowly.

Just perhaps.

****

Jess glanced up from her morning newspaper as Robin entered the living room carrying her overnight bag. "Are you ready?" It was an oddly absurd question, given the circumstances.

Unsettled green eyes caught a stripe of morning sunlight glinting off the oak coffee table before tentatively tracking up to meet cautious blue. "Not really, but I'm all set to catch my plane." Robin sat down on the sofa beside the older woman and blew out a shaky breath. "I wish it was tomorrow night, and I was back here again."

Me too. Jess acknowledged the apprehension in Robin's unsteady voice, and suddenly felt a surge of protectiveness wash over her. Her eyes hardened and she grasped the smaller woman's hand almost instinctively. "You don't have to do this."

That brought a weary smile. "Yes, I do. Delaying this serves no purpose now and will only cause more problems in the long run."

Damn it. Jess was feeling more uneasy as the moments ticked by. And guilty. *You pushed her into this, Jess, now deal with it.* She swallowed and fixed the blonde woman with an intense gaze. "I could go with you. I don't like the idea of you doing this alone."

A petite hand reached up and stroked the side of the chiseled face.

"Thank you for that." Robin bit the edge of her lip to maintain her composure, then spoke more resolutely. "But I need to do this and explain this to my parents myself." She forced a smile. "Besides, how would it look to have my boss, who just so happens to also be my roommate, suddenly show up to accompany me to a supposed job interview at another law firm in Michigan?"

Jess smiled in return. "Right. I guess that would complicate things from the beginning, huh?" She squeezed the small hand she held. "Then, I want you to promise me something, and I mean it."

"Okay." Robin's gaze never wavered from the determined blue eyes in front of her.

"You call me the moment you get there, you call me tonight after you talk with your folks, and then you call me tomorrow before you leave to come back." Jess was absolutely serious.

Robin opened her mouth as if to protest, then quickly closed it and remained silent.

"I mean this, Robin. The last time you went up there, you had a difficult time with...some things, and you didn't call me, even though I gave you my number at my mother's. You told me you'd call if things got hard for you, and then you didn't call." Jess was even more worried than she let on about the emotional toll all this would take on Robin, but there was also something else that bothered her, and she felt she needed to be honest with Robin about it. "Last time, I felt that that you didn't trust me enough to tell me what was going on with you."

Robin abruptly broke her gaze and let her eyes travel toward, then settle, on the empty fireplace, her voice very small. "I didn't know you felt that way about that."

The older woman continued. "When you were gone, I convinced myself that everything was okay because I didn't hear from you. But everything was far from okay with you. I felt it inside of me, and I ignored it." She grasped Robin's other hand and sought out unreadable green eyes with a determined focus. "I won't ignore it again. So, here's the deal. If I don't hear from you when you get there, I'm on the next plane. If I don't hear from you tonight, I'm on the next plane. And if I don't here from you before you leave to come back tomorrow, I'm on the next plane. There is no debate on this, Robin. Either I hear from you, or I'm on your Michigan doorstep. End of story."

It occurred to Robin that she should be really angry with Jess for trying to control her actions and her decisions. It was, after all, up to Robin to decide how and when to speak with her own parents about whatever she chose to speak with them about. It was also up to Robin to decide if she wanted to confide in Jess about anything. And, it was certainly up to Robin when and how often she would call Jess, if she decided to call her at all. Now, here was Jess, arrogantly trying to manipulate the situation all because she felt a bit slighted the last time Robin went to Detroit. It was totally brazen, utterly uncalled for, and absolutely intolerable. But...in spite of all that, in spite of the heavy-handed and overbearing nature of the demand, Robin simply couldn't be angry. She recognized the ultimatum for what it was...a declaration of love and concern, however over-reaching it seemed on the surface. Green eyes blinked, then a soft voice spoke, breaking the uneasy silence that had ensued. "Deal."

The dark head nodded, a small weight lifted from the broad shoulders. "We'd better get going, or you'll miss your flight."

They stood up and made their way toward the garage door. Robin stopped suddenly and looked back over her shoulder, intently studying the expansive house that had become her home. She lingered for a moment and committed the view to memory, wishing to carry the image in her mind until she returned the following evening. It was something to hold on to while she was far away from where she most wanted to be. Her home...both the residence and the person.

The action was not lost on Jess, yet her interpretation of the event was quite different. Still haunted by James' betrayal, she instinctively misinterpreted the hesitation by Robin as an indication of finality, as if Robin was taking one last look around before leaving forever and shutting the door on their relationship. It was an unfounded impression, to be sure, but Jess just couldn't help it. Although she was continually trying, she had not yet been able to completely surrender her own fears and place herself wholly into Robin's shoes. With an increasing sinking in the pit of her stomach, the taller woman turned and opened the garage door, motioning Robin toward the car.

They made their way toward the airport in near silence, each lost in their own very intense thoughts. When they finally reached the short-term parking facility, Jess pulled the silver Mercedes into a parking space and shifted to open the driver's side door. She was stopped by a gentle hand on her wrist.

Blue eyes lifted slowly. The older woman could feel the warmth of the petite fingers gently soothing her aching heart.

"Jess, I..." Robin whispered. "I love you."

Long arms gathered the smaller woman and held her in a tight embrace. "I love you, too, and I'll miss you every second you're gone." Jess finally let go and bravely straightened up, touching a hand to Robin's cheek and offering a small smile. "Now, let's get your bag and get you on that plane."

They proceeded through the main terminal and then onto the shuttle leading to the airside gates. A few idle moments were spent at Robin's assigned gate, before the gate agent finally called for the boarding of the flight. As the boarding process began, Robin grabbed her carry-on bag and stepped over into line. Purely on impulse, Jess reached inside her jacket and pulled out her recently acquired cell phone, grabbing Robin's hand and placing it firmly against the smaller woman's palm.

Light eyebrows raised in silent question.

"Just take it." Jess was very focused. "This way, you'll always have access to a phone, and it'll be convenient for you to call. Plus, I can get in touch with you." She decided it was a very good plan, all things considered.

Robin simply nodded, then gave Jess a quick hug before handing the gate attendant her boarding pass. She glanced back at the older woman and smiled reassuringly, before quickly stepping onto the jetway and making her way onto the waiting plane.

The taller woman watched the retreating form disappear from view, the urge to run through the crowd and pull Robin back into the safety of her arms almost overwhelming. With great difficulty, however, she fought the impulse. Instead, she moved over to a large window and stood there, watching the jet stoically, until it finally pushed back from the gate a few moments later and began its taxi to the runway. Unwavering azure eyes followed the jet's path as it slowly rolled forward and then drifted out of sight. Jess stared out at the empty space where Robin's plane had stood just moments before, which oddly enough, matched the empty space within her own heart, and swallowed back an unsettled feeling. In a purely reflexive motion, she brought one hand up to the window pane in front of her and lightly pressed her fingertips against the cool glass, a gentle plea voicing a silent yet considerable appeal inside the realm of her increasingly anxious mind.

Come back to me, sweetheart. I'm waiting for you.

Considerable Appeal

Chapter 4

The mid-sized jet taxied its way across the runway, then parked at its assigned gate while a flight attendant cheerfully welcomed the arriving passengers to Detroit. Once the jetway was safely secured to the forward cabin door, the flight crew began the routine process of deplaning the passengers from the aircraft and offering assistance with connecting flights.

Robin debarked the plane and briskly stepped inside the metropolitan airport, shivering slightly from the cool air that had lingered inside the jetway. Almost simultaneously, a blast of dry, heated air greeted her as she entered further into the terminal building. *What a contrast to Florida.* In truth, for early February, Robin was quite amazed at the weather difference between the spring-like climate in Central Florida and the windy and cold conditions in Michigan.

The young associate pulled out her jacket and tugged her carry-on bag behind her as she made her way through the crowded concourse toward the airport's arriving flights exit. The prearranged plan was to meet her mother curbside just outside the baggage claim area. As Robin approached the designated location, she quickly glanced at her watch and noted that the flight, surprisingly enough, had arrived a few minutes ahead of schedule. As an added bonus, she hadn't checked in any baggage, deciding instead to bring just a carry-on bag for her overnight necessities. *And a hasty exit, if the situation required.*

Robin donned her jacket, then stepped outside and scanned the waiting vehicles, finding that her mother had not yet arrived. She glanced at her watch again. *About ten minutes left to kill.* She grimaced slightly as the chilly wind went through her thin jacket. *Boy, it's cold out here.* She idly mused that the colder weather shouldn't have gotten to her like that, especially since she'd grown up in it nearly all of her life. She further considered that the warmer climate of Central Florida had done an incredibly fine job of spoiling her. With no more than a half-second's deliberation, the young associate came to the very wise conclusion that standing in the freezing cold wasn't a very attractive idea, and opted instead to go back inside the warm airport to await her ride.

A porter with a cart full of luggage edged by her as she stood just inside the automatic doorway. Since Robin now had a few moments of idle time, she took the opportunity to give Jess a quick call, just as she had promised earlier that morning. *I bet she's waiting on pins and needles.* Robin retrieved the cell phone and dialed the junior partner's direct line at the office.

After just one ring, a familiar voice answered. "Jessica Harrison."

Robin smiled, a warmth spreading within her, which the heat inside the airport couldn't begin to match. "Hi, Snoopy."

That brought a gentle chuckle. "Snoopy? Somebody sure is in a good mood." Jess was actually quite surprised at Robin's light tone of voice, considering their conversation earlier that morning.

"Well, I had a lot of time to think about things on the plane, and I decided that it's not the end of the world if my parents don't understand what I'm going to tell them. They can either accept it or not, and if they don't, I'm still going to do what I want to do." The young associate sounded entirely resolute on the matter. "It's my choice, not theirs."

"That's my girl." Jess smiled into the phone. "Where are you now?"

"Actually, I'm at the airport waiting for my mom to pick me up. She should be here any minute now."

"How was your flight? I know how the taking off part and the coming down part can get to you."

She is the sweetest person. Robin smiled at Jess's concern. "A few white knuckles, but no real harm."

"Just as long as you're okay." The junior partner swiveled her burgundy leather chair and looked out the floor-to-ceiling window at the downtown skyline, pausing for a slight moment before continuing. "I'm glad you called."

"Well..." Robin drawled. "Of course I called. I seem to remember a certain someone, who shall remain nameless but who is very hopeless, who promised to show up on my Michigan doorstep if I didn't call." Her tone of voice was playful, and held no hint of resentment at Jess's earlier ultimatum.

The older woman couldn't help but chuckle. "Glad my threats work so well." She was absolutely amazed at Robin's good mood.

Green eyes spotted a familiar vehicle outside. "My mom just pulled up. I need to go." Robin headed for the exit doors. "I'll call you later." A brief moment's silence. "I miss you."

Jess forced a cheerful tone. "Me too, kiddo." *Even though it's only been a few hours.* "Good luck today. Call me tonight, all right?"

"Right." Robin zipped up her jacket. "I promise."

"Okay. Goodbye, sweetheart."

"Bye, Jess." With that, the young associate clicked off the phone, grabbed her bag, and headed outside to her mother's waiting car. As she did so, she reflected on her brief phone conversation with Jess. All things considered, she had decided to put the best face possible on the situation and not to worry Jess any more than necessary. Robin would handle things with her parents, then return to Florida. Simple as that, or as Jess would say, "end of story."

Robin shook off a sudden wave of anxiety. *End of story.* If only she really believed that.

****

"How was your flight, dear?" Colette Wilson pulled the car out onto the main highway, driving away from the airport.

"Not too bad." Robin was not particularly in the mood for idle chit chat and decided to get to the point. "I need to speak with you and Dad about something important."

"Oh." Her mother was momentarily surprised. "All right. Your father mentioned he had a long meeting today and may not be home until late this evening."

Great. Any hopes Robin had of getting this over quickly vanished. "As soon as he comes home, Mom, I really need to talk with the both of you." She gave her mother a pointed look. "Tonight."

Colette cautiously agreed. "Okay." She stopped the car at a red light and glanced over at her daughter. "You know, he's so thrilled you decided to come back for the interview tomorrow. We really do think this is a wonderful opportunity for you."

Robin closed her eyes, the beginnings of a headache steadily pounding at her temples. She decided to remain silent on the matter. This simply was not the right time to get into that particular discussion. *Not to mention the 'other' discussion.* Unconsciously, Robin brought her hand up to the heart-shaped pendent around her neck, fingering the cut diamonds lightly. She took comfort in its texture, and oddly enough, felt Jess's presence merely by touching it. Jess's words in giving Robin the necklace filled her mind. *It's my heart. I will never ask for it back.* Petite fingers gripped the pendant tighter as Robin's own words suddenly came back to her, the ones she had spoken to Jess just days before in making her own heartfelt vow. *I will never betray you, and I will never willingly leave you.*

Her mother, oblivious to Robin's turmoil, continued. "Let's go somewhere and have a nice lunch."

Snapping out of her reverie, all Robin could do was nod and go along with the plan, deciding that she and her mother might as well have a pleasant time of it while they could. *By tomorrow, she might not be speaking to me.* In a resigned tone of voice, Robin agreed. "That sounds fine."

****

Later that evening, after dinner was finished and the dishes were washed, Robin and her mother and father retired to the living room. Thomas Wilson's meeting hadn't lasted as long as he had initially thought, allowing him to make it home in time for dinner. He settled himself back into his easy chair and pulled out the daily newspaper, glancing briefly at the front page, while Colette perused the evening television guide. Robin had considered bringing up the real purpose of her visit before dinner, but after some thought and a brief bout of nervousness, she decided to wait until a more appropriate time. That time had come.

The young associate sat on the sofa next to her mother and addressed her parents. "I have something I'd like to discuss with you both." She swallowed before continuing. "It's important."

Her father glanced up from his newspaper. "What is it, honey?"

I can do this. Green eyes closed briefly, then opened again. "It's about the interview you scheduled for me tomorrow."

"Yes, honey, it's all set up. Richard McKenzie will meet with you tomorrow afternoon at one o'clock." Thomas smiled warmly.

This is so hard. Robin looked cautiously at her father. "Dad, um...as I already mentioned to you and Mom, I don't want to move back here. I want to stay in Florida." Her eyes pleaded. "Please cancel the appointment tomorrow. I don't want to go to the interview. It would be a waste of time."

Her mother spoke up. "Robin, how could it hurt just to go meet with the man?"

"Because I will not, under any circumstances, consider moving back here. I would be wasting his time." The blonde head shook as Robin realized her parents were simply not getting the point. It really wasn't surprising, considering that her parents never got the point before.

Colette furrowed her brows. "Just what's so special it about Florida that makes you want to stay there?"

Robin spoke very softly. "Jess is there."

Colette idly turned the pages of the television guide. "Your housemate, who also works with you? Robin, you can still keep in touch with her, call her, write, and visit sometimes."

"No." Robin knew there was absolutely no way she could back out now. "That wouldn't work."

"Why is that?" Thomas chimed in.

"Because Jess and I are...close." Robin mentally berated herself for not being direct.

"I don't see the problem." Colette shook her head, somewhat perplexed. "You and she still can be friends."

I'm not doing this very well. "No, Mom." Robin took a very deep breath, trying to muster the courage to continue. "I...love Jess."

"That's very nice, Robin, but I still don't see...."

"Mom." Robin cut in mid-sentence, now speaking more confidently. "I love Jess, and Jess loves me. We want to be together." *Do you understand?*

Unfortunately, Colette still didn't seem to get it, or perhaps she intentionally didn't want to see what was becoming painfully obvious. "Robin, I understand that you're fond of your friend, but your family is here, and you have other friends here, as well."

Why must everything be so difficult? Robin looked at her mother, then at her father for a lingering moment. Taking another deep breath, she tried again. "Jess and I love each other very much. We want to be together."

There was a long moment of silence as each party contemplated that last statement. Finally, Colette spoke. "What are you saying?"

Robin swallowed hard. "I think you know."

Thomas Wilson's stern voice interrupted. "No. I don't think we do."

At that precise moment, a surge of confidence filled Robin, whether in response to the implied challenge of her father's tone of voice or simply in defense of her own life choices. She directed her gaze squarely at her father. "Let me say it to you this way so there is no misunderstanding. I moved into Jess's house. I put most of my things from my apartment into storage, but I brought over my bedroom furniture and some other items and put them into the spare room." Here, Robin shifted her gaze toward her mother. "I have my own room, but at night, I don't sleep there." She enunciated the last words very clearly.

Colette hung her head and whispered. "Oh, dear God."

Her father maintained a neutral expression, then cleared his throat. "Just so we're absolutely clear on the matter, where is it exactly that you do sleep?"

An internal sigh. *He's intent on making me say it.* Robin paused, then spoke the truth. "I sleep with Jess." She held his gaze solidly. "You may interpret the meaning of that statement in every way possible."

Colette closed her eyes, then opened them again, her face very pale. "Robin, you're...not like that."

"Like what, Mom? That I've found someone I love, who loves me and understands me? Who touches a part of my soul down deep inside of me? Who I want to be with forever? Does it really matter the exterior package if the person on the inside is the most wonderful person I could ever know?"

Her mother interrupted. "But, David...."

Robin's voice grew very firm. "I will not compare Jess to David in that way. I loved him, and a part of me always will. I will carry what happened to him with me for the rest of my life. But Jess understands that part of me, and she loves me anyway. She's helped me through some very difficult times. And I will tell you one other thing, and you may not understand it, but that doesn't make it any less true. What I feel for Jess—it's so much stronger and more intense than I ever felt for David."

Thomas Wilson leaned forward in his chair and rested the newspaper in his lap, steepling his fingers together in front of him in concentrated thought. "What I see here, Robin, is that this 'friend' of yours has obviously taken advantage of your situation. When you first left here for Florida, you were emotionally vulnerable, which was understandable considering everything that had happened. Your mother and I both knew that, but we wanted you to deal with things in your own way. We always believed that you would eventually realize you didn't want to be far away from your family, and that you'd return once you came to terms with things." His voice grew very hard. "It seems now that we have made a serious mistake. Your so-called friend, who is your immediate supervisor for all intents and purposes, has taken advantage of your vulnerable emotional state of mind in a most reprehensible way." His voice raised slightly. "She has seduced you away from your family."

"No." Robin vigorously defended. "You don't know her. She hasn't done anything I didn't want her to do. And just so you know, I was the one who took the first step in our relationship, not Jess."

"You didn't know what you were doing." Her father shook his head, then continued. "You've left the Church, Robin, and now you've taken up this type of lifestyle. Instead of dealing with what happened with David in an emotionally healthy way, you've gotten as far away from that as possible."

"Robin." Colette finally calmed herself enough to speak. "You weren't raised this way."

This reaction from her parents left Robin unexpectedly more sure of her commitment to Jess than ever before. It was a commitment, after all, even though she and Jess had never formally acknowledged it. "I'm very sorry you feel that way. If my loving someone with all my heart and soul is not the way I was raised, then that is indeed unfortunate. But it doesn't change the fact that I love Jess, and she loves me, and we want to be together." *If I say it enough, maybe they'll get the point.*

"But how can you love another woman that way?" Robin's mother asked, truly not understanding.

"I've asked myself that question many times, and it all comes down to the fact that, to me, it doesn't matter what's on the outside. It only matters what's on the inside." Robin sighed, trying to explain something which she herself didn't totally understand. "Jess is a beautiful person both inside and out. I love the person, and that person happens to be a woman." She could tell that her mother still was having a difficult time grasping the concept.

A flash of light glinted off the diamond pendant Robin wore, and Colette caught the reflection. Her mother spoke very softly, yet somberly. "Did...did she give you that?"

Robin followed her mother's gaze and brought a hand up to curl around the pendant heart. "Yes, she did. It was a Christmas gift." *Jess's heart.*

"I see." It was all Colette could say at the moment, the combination of sadness and disappointment evident in her voice.

Setting aside the newspaper, which remained mostly unread, Thomas stood up and paced the floor. He then stopped and spoke directly to Robin. "Have you and this woman made any type of commitment to each other?"

Robin's green eyes blinked. That question was entirely unexpected. "Um...we're not at a point in our relationship yet where we've formally done that, but I believe we're very close to doing so." *God, I hope I'm right about that.*

Her father arched an eyebrow, a thought occurring to him as he resumed his pacing. "I will not pretend to understand this. You have no commitment from this woman, yet you are...sleeping with her and profess your undying love for her with nothing in return but a small diamond trinket. I'm sorry, Robin, but the truth of this matter suggests that she's taking advantage of you and has preyed upon your emotional vulnerability knowing full well what happened with David. I'm sure this is hard for you to hear, but someone who would do such a thing is, and I will be charitable here, not an honorable person."

I've had enough of this. Robin stood up and looked from her father to her mother, then back again. "You are wrong. Jess is the most honorable person I know. She has always thought of my feelings before her own. She has never, even once, taken advantage of me in any way." Robin paused for a brief moment, then continued, her voice slightly shaky. "I wish you both could be happy for me, and happy that I've found someone who loves me and wants to be with me, and who makes me happier than I've ever been before. But I see that is not the case. I do want you to understand one thing, though. I love Jess. I will always love her. That will never change. Contrary to what you may think, I do know what I'm doing. I understand what it means to love her. I understand that loving her may not be an easy lifestyle, and that there are certain consequences involved. I accept all that and more. It's what I want, it's what I choose, and I will not change my mind."

Colette's saddened eyes glanced up. "We only want what's best for you, Robin."

"Jess is what's best for me."

From both Thomas' and Colette's point of view, any further discussion was futile. It was obvious to them that Robin had been completely taken in by someone who, at best, should have known better, and who at worst, preyed upon an innocent and emotionally devastated young woman.

There was an uncomfortable silence for several moments, then Robin finally spoke again. "I don't think there's anything else for me to say, except that now I think you know why I won't attend the interview tomorrow." She hesitated, unsure of her status in the family at this point, and not quite sure whether she was welcome in her parents' house anymore. "I'm going to go up to my room now. Is that all right?"

At her mother's nod, Robin proceeded up the stairs, entering her childhood room and closing the door behind her. She sat on the bed and valiantly fought the urge to cry, but was, in reality, powerless against the overwhelming emotions. It was clear that her parents were disappointed and upset. Worse, they blamed Jess, and nothing Robin could do or say was going to change their minds. Robin's tears came very fast, and she knew she needed to cry herself out before calling Jess like she'd promised. It was true, in her current state of mind, speaking with Jess at this particular moment would guarantee that the junior partner would show up on her parents' doorstep before the morning's first light, a situation that would only make matters worse. Robin wiped away her tears and reflected on what had just transpired. After all, it was a significant shock to her parents. It surely wasn't something they had ever expected to hear. *So, maybe they just need some time to get used to the idea.*

Right. And pigs can fly.

****

Jess arrived home from work, checked the answering machine for messages, and frowned upon seeing none. She had half expected Robin to have called, even though it was still rather early in the evening. It took everything she had within herself not to pick up the telephone and dial the cell phone number. *She'll call. Give her time.* Sighing, the junior partner drew a hot bath for herself, turned on the Jacuzzi jets, and let the relaxing water soothe her aching body and distract her anxious mind. It didn't work. She winced a bit as she recalled the ultimatum she'd given Robin earlier that morning, threatening to show up in Michigan if Robin didn't comply with her demand to call her at the predetermined times. The junior partner closed her eyes and mentally chastised herself for treating Robin as a child unable to handle her own affairs. *Affairs.* That was an unintended double entendre and an unfortunate choice of words. Jess had to laugh at the absurdity of it all.

Affair. Is that what she and Robin had? No. To characterize their relationship as an affair seemed so...so what? Illicit. No. That made what they had together seem tawdry. And cheap. But then again, wasn't that exactly how it would appear to anyone else looking at their relationship from a distance, including Robin's parents? An illicit affair. A tawdry liaison. Nothing more. It was, after all, quite true that she and Robin had made no formal commitment to each other, although they had promised their love to each other forever.

But an affair? Blue eyes closed tight in deep regret. The junior partner mentally cursed herself for realizing only too late that she'd pushed Robin into revealing their relationship to her parents without first making it appear more...legitimate...honest...permanent. *A commitment.* The magnitude of her own miscalculation hit her very hard, and she momentarily felt physically ill. The truth was, she had been so afraid of Robin's rejection of a commitment that she'd completely overlooked the significance of not having one. *Damn it all to hell, Jess. You're an absolute fool for not realizing this sooner. You've just set her up to be crucified.* As far as it stood right now, their relationship could be perceived as fleeting and not at all serious. *Damn.* Well, that particular misperception would absolutely have to end. Immediately. She'd remedy the situation once and for all as soon as Robin came back. *If she came back.*

Okay, fine. Remedy the situation. How? Jess would have to make a commitment, and make it real. Okay. How? *The ring, Jess. Give her the ring.* But what if Robin doesn't accept it? Or what if she accepts it but won't wear it because of the public acknowledgment it represents? *Give her the ring.* Wouldn't words or vows or promises work just as well? It would be a private declaration between them. It would mean the same thing, wouldn't it? *Give her the ring.* The junior partner leaned her dark head back against the side of the Roman tub, letting the warm bubbling waters relax her muscles for several minutes longer as she contemplated the implications of what her heart already knew, but her head was slow to recognize. A dark eyebrow arched in quiet realization. There simply was no substitute for the tangible symbol the ring represents. That was an undisputed fact.

Jess stepped out of the bath, dried herself off, then threw on her flannel boxers and one of Robin's oversized t-shirts, which although quite large on Robin, fit Jess just right. She didn't stop to consider exactly why she put the t-shirt on in the first place, but if she had thought about it, she would have realized she instinctively needed to be near the younger woman, even in the most remote way. The junior partner inhaled and caught Robin's scent as it lingered on the cotton fabric. The sense of smell proved to be a powerful catalyst. *God, I miss her.* And in that one moment of absolute and complete clarity, Jess's mind was made up. Or more correctly stated, her mind finally caught up with what her heart already knew. There were no longer any doubts, questions, fears or uncertainty. She'd give Robin the ring and take everything else as it came along. When Robin came back. *If Robin came back.*

Jess stood in front of the bathroom mirror and gazed at her own reflection, then closed her eyes and voiced once again her silent plea from earlier that day, this time with one minor, yet significant, amendment.

Come back to me, sweetheart. My ring is here waiting for you.

****

Sometime later, as Jess tried to busy herself with work she'd brought home from the office, the telephone rang. She nearly ran into the living room to pick up the cordless receiver. "Robin?"

There was a brief hesitation. "Hi, Snoopy." The younger woman put on a cheerful front.

Jess took a second to calm her racing heart, then sat down on the plush sofa. "I'm glad you called. I was getting worried."

"Of course I called. Can't have you making good on your threat to show up on my doorstep up here, now can I?" Robin was teasing, and her tone of voice was playful. Yet still, something was definitely not right.

Let's not avoid the obvious. "Um...Robin, how did it go with your folks?"

There was a lingering silence before Robin answered. "About the way I had expected. They're upset, but they didn't disown me or kick me out of the house, so I take that as a good sign."

Jess wasn't fooled and read between the lines. "So, they're upset?"

"Yes."

"But not at you."

Robin closed her eyes, realizing that Jess had picked up all too quickly on the truth. *I should have known I couldn't hide this from her.* "Right."

"I see." *It's not like this was unexpected, Jess. You knew they'd blame you.* The junior partner spoke very softly. "They...um...think I've corrupted you."

"Jess...." Robin's heart nearly broke, and her voice cracked with emotion. "It doesn't matter what they think. You and I both know the truth, right?" There was a very long silence, and Robin knew exactly what was going through the older woman's mind. "Jess, don't you dare blame yourself. You've done nothing wrong."

"But I pushed you into this." *Have I pushed our relationship too far? Here I was thinking I didn't push it far enough.*

Robin had thought she'd cried out all her tears, but now, somehow from somewhere, more tears came. "Jess, honey, please listen to me.

Just like you told me that it was your choice to be with me in spite of the risks to you, I'm telling you that it's my choice to be with you in spite of the risks to me." She wiped her eyes and steeled her resolve. "You didn't push me into anything I didn't want. It was my choice to tell my parents about us, and it's my choice to be with you. You've done nothing wrong. Even if my parents don't believe that, I do. I know the truth."

All right. This ends now. The junior partner assumed her no-nonsense persona. "I'm coming up there to get you."

Oh no. "Jess, please don't do that. It'll only make things worse." *They'll probably have her arrested for trespassing or something.* "Listen, I'm taking the early afternoon flight tomorrow, then I'll take a cab home." The younger woman's voice pleaded. "It'll be all right. Please, Jess, let me handle this."

It was against every instinct the older woman had inside her, but nonetheless, she acquiesced to Robin's plea. "Okay." *They had better let her go, or I **will** be on their doorstep. Count on it.* "Call me then, before you leave."

Robin blew out a relieved breath. "I will." She was reluctant to hang up the phone, savoring the connection she felt between them even though they were hundreds of miles apart. She laid down on the bed and snuggled up tight against a pillow. "I miss you, Snoopy."

Jess cracked a smile. "Me too. Just remember that your legal beagle loves you very much." She paused. "I'll see you tomorrow, right?"

"Right. See you tomorrow. Goodnight, Jess."

"Goodnight sweetheart." Jess clicked off the receiver and stared at it for a long moment. She was extremely close to dialing the airline and making a reservation for a redeye flight, but she had promised Robin she wouldn't interfere. A dark eyebrow raised pensively. *So I lied.* The junior partner flipped open the phone book and started dialing, then stopped, her conscience lashing out at her for going back on her word to Robin. Long fingers reached up and rubbed her forehead, then traveled down across the bridge of her nose in a futile attempt to ease the tension, as she wrestled with herself on the appropriate course of action. She paced back and forth across the expansive living room for several moments before finally coming to an all-important decision.

All right. I'll wait.

* * * * * * * * * * * * * * * * * * *

Robin opened one eye, then the other, squinting at the morning sunlight bathing her childhood bedroom. She gave herself a quick stretch, then remembered where she was and what had happened the previous evening. She hadn't slept terribly well during the night, and now apparently had made up for it by sleeping until mid-morning. Getting herself up and grabbing a quick shower, Robin finally made her way cautiously downstairs, more than a bit wary of the reaction she'd receive from her parents this morning.

Robin found her mother in the living room. "Mom?"

Colette looked up from her magazine. "Robin, you're up. You should go ahead and have some breakfast before it gets too late."

She seems okay. "Yeah, maybe I will. Um...is everything all right, you know, between us?" Robin just had to know.

"Let's not discuss that now." Colette suddenly seemed quite uncomfortable. "You should have something to eat if your flight leaves in a few hours."

Robin's blonde head nodded as she decided not to push her mother. It would take time, after all, for her parents to accept things. In a resigned tone of voice, she agreed. "All right."

"I do wish, though, that you would stay for the weekend."

She wants me to stay. That's a good sign. "I can't this time, Mom. Jess is...." Robin's voice trailed off as she caught herself at the mention of Jess's name. "Um maybe another time." She padded into the kitchen and made herself a quick breakfast of coffee and cereal, then rejoined her mother in the living room. Somehow, and for a reason she couldn't explain, Robin didn't feel quite right about leaving later that day without first discussing things again, at least with her mother. "Mom, I think we should talk about it. You're my mother. I would hope that I could talk to you."

Colette closed the magazine and set it on the coffee table, sensing that she wasn't going to be able to avoid the issue with her daughter any longer. "Your father and I want what's best for you, Robin. We don't understand this...this thing, or what hold this woman has over you. But, if you'd like to talk about it, I will listen, but I can't say that I will ever understand."

That's fair enough. "Okay. First, I want you to know that I don't want to hurt you or Dad. I came here to see you so that I could tell you about this face to face. I didn't want to do this over the phone." Robin took a breath. "I wanted you to know the truth. I didn't want to mislead you any longer."

Her mother swallowed and looked down at her hands, then asked the question that had been on her mind since the previous night. "How long has this been going on?"

Robin wasn't sure how to answer that. How long had she known Jess? How long had she loved her? How long had they been intimate? She decided to answer the only way possible. "I knew that I felt some connection to Jess from the first day I met her back in October. I didn't understand it, and I tried to deny it, and so did she. After almost a month of working together and becoming friends outside of work, I finally realized that I couldn't fight the feelings that I had for her any longer. They were too strong. There was just something about Jess that called to me down deep inside, almost as if I had known her forever. It was then that we finally acknowledged what we both knew to be true." Robin glanced at her mother to gauge her reaction, but the expression was neutral, so she continued. "If you're asking when I first knew that I loved her, I can't give you a precise date. It seems as though I've loved her forever. If you're asking when we became...serious, I can say that for a long time, we both weren't ready for that. It was shortly before Christmas when I realized with absolute certainty that I wanted to be with Jess forever, and then I knew I was ready for a serious relationship."

Colette finally looked at her daughter. "At Christmas, when we were there, you never said anything to us. We even had brunch together with her."

Robin regretted the deception, but still defended her actions. "I didn't want to upset you, and I was nervous about people knowing about Jess and me. It seems kind of immature now, when I look back at it, but I wasn't ready for anyone to know."

Colette had one more question, still unsure if she should ask, but finally giving in to her own curiosity. "Is this her normal lifestyle?"

What is she asking? It took a moment for Robin to finally understand what her mother was getting at. "No. This is new for Jess, too. There was someone, a man, who had broken her heart a long time ago. It still haunts her to this day, and she hasn't let anyone get close to her again, until me. Sometimes I'm amazed that she trusts me so much, considering the pain he caused her."

"I see." But the truth of the matter was, Colette really did not see.

Robin saw the quizzical look on her mother's face. "You still don't understand, do you?"

"I'm sorry, Robin." Colette shook her head. "I don't. I can understand how you would want to be friends, even good friends, but I do not understand the romantic part of this."

"We want to share our whole selves with each other. Not hold anything back. It really doesn't seem all that strange, does it?"

Her mother held a blank look, but was otherwise silent.

The younger woman sighed, realizing any further explanations she might give would be useless. "At least you've listened, and I appreciate that." Robin checked the time. "I need to get ready to go. I'd like to give Dad a call at work, at least before I leave. I didn't like the way we left things last night."

Colette shook her head. "He's not there. He's...out of town."

Out of town? "I didn't know he had to go out of town. Where did he go?"

The silence that ensued was deafening.

"Mom?" Robin felt a wave of apprehension grab her. "Where did Dad go?"

Colette decided there was no use in hiding it. "Florida."

Robin's green eyes closed tight reflexively as she felt physically sick. *Jess.* "Where exactly in Florida?"

"Now, Robin, your father is very worried about you. He just wants to talk with this woman face to face."

This woman. "No!" Robin was very agitated. "Without telling me? I can't believe he did that." She was shaking. "I have to call Jess and...." She started to head for the stairs and the cell phone in her room.

"He took the first plane out this morning, Robin. I'm sure he's already there by now."

Robin was beyond upset. "I don't care. I've got to call her." She raced upstairs, pulled the cell phone from her bag, and dialed Jess's direct line at the office, her fingers shaking as she did so.

After two rings, Angie answered. "Good morning. Jessica Harrison's office."

"Angie, it's Robin. Could I speak with Jess, please?"

"I'm sorry, Robin. She's been on a conference call all morning and left instructions for me to take all her messages."

Stay calm. She hasn't seen him yet. "Okay. Angie, could you give her a message as soon as she gets of her conference call? Please tell her to call me on the cell phone right away? It's urgent."

Ooooh. I wonder what's going on in paradise. "All right, Robin. As soon as she hangs up, I'll give her your message."

"Thanks." Robin clicked off the phone and sucked in a deep breath in a vain attempt to calm her nerves. The next number she dialed was for a taxi cab to take her to the airport. Packing her bag and then rushing downstairs, she paused just long enough to look at her mother still sitting on the sofa. "I'm leaving for the airport now. I've called a cab and will wait outside for it." Her voice was more of dismay than anger. "I can't believe you kept this from me, and I can't believe Dad did this."

"We're worried about you, Robin. I'm sorry you can't see that. He just wants to talk with this woman."

This woman. Robin stopped in her tracks and gazed squarely at her mother. "Her name is Jess. That is the third time this morning you've referred to her as 'this woman.' I love her, and I'm sorry you can't see that." She echoed her mother's words back at her. "I had hoped...." Robin shook her head, the sting of the betrayal by her parents hitting her hard, as she fought the tears welling up in her eyes. "Never mind. I need to go." Without a backward glance, she stepped outside the front door, not sure if she'd ever be able to return to this place again.

During the cab ride to the municipal airport, she tried again to reach Jess, but the junior partner was still tied up on her conference call. Upon arrival at the airport, Robin attempted to obtain an earlier flight, unfortunately to no avail. It seems that Friday flights into Orlando are a rarity, considering the fact that the Central Florida area is the number one vacation destination. How her father managed to secure an airline seat on such short notice was quite a mystery. *He probably paid someone for their ticket.* Resigned that she'd have to await her scheduled flight, Robin took a seat at the gate, clutched the cell phone in her hand, and hoped and prayed that Jess would call before it was too late.

****

Jess had no sooner hung up the phone after her two and a half hour conference call when Angie knocked and poked her head inside the office door. "I have your messages, and there's someone waiting in the lobby to see you."

The junior partner glanced at her organizer. "I don't have anyone down on my calendar for this morning."

Angie set the messages on the corner of the cherry wood desk. "He said he didn't have an appointment but was hoping you would agree to meet with him."

Strange. "Who is it?"

"He said his name is Thomas Wilson."

Jess's head snapped up. *Uh oh. Something's wrong.* Her pulse started racing, and for a long moment, she was entirely speechless. *Damn. This can't be good.*

Angie apparently had not made the connection between Thomas

Wilson and Robin. She waited patiently, and upon not hearing any instruction, prompted Jess. "What do you want me to tell him?"

I could refuse to see him. Blue eyes closed, then opened. *But what if something's happened with Robin.* "All right. Go ahead and bring him in here. There's no need for a conference room."

The junior partner stood up and waited as her secretary escorted Robin's father into the office. "Thank you, Angie. Please hold my calls." Once her office door was safely shut, Jess turned her attention toward her unexpected guest. "Mr. Wilson, is everything all right? Is Robin here, or…."

Thomas interrupted. "Robin's not with me. She presumably will be on whatever flight she's scheduled to take back here later today. I need to speak with you separately. And no, everything is not all right."

Shit. "Okay. Please have a seat. What did you want to speak with me about?"

Robin's father settled into the chair by the floor-to-ceiling window and focused his gaze squarely on Jess. "I'll be blunt. Robin has told her mother and me that you apparently have a relationship with my daughter which is more than platonic. Is that correct?"

Here it comes. "Yes. That is correct."

Thomas grew increasingly agitated. "She seems to believe that, as she so consistently put it, she loves you and you love her and you both want to be together. Would that also be correct?"

Jess tilted her head to one side. "I would say that is accurate, yes."

"All right." Thomas stood up. "Here's the way I see this. Aside from the moral implications of this matter, which I won't get into right now, Robin is in no emotional condition to know what she really wants. She's had a difficult year, and was emotionally devastated prior to coming down here to Florida."

Jess just listened, even though she was becoming increasingly annoyed at the tenor of the conversation. The man had flown all the way from Michigan and apparently had a lot to get off his chest.

Thomas continued. "It seems that while Robin was trying to come to terms with what happened with David, for whatever reason, she filled the emotional void created by his loss with you. I won't mince words here. It appears to me that you have taken advantage of her fragile emotional state of mind."

The junior partner flexed her hands unconsciously, utterly offended at his statement, then responded, her voice terse. "Number one, Robin is perfectly capable of knowing what she wants, and number two, I have never taken advantage of Robin, emotionally or otherwise. And you are absolutely correct, we will not get into the supposed moral implications of this matter."

"Is Robin seeing a psychologist?"

Jess blinked. "You know that she is."

"Then you would admit that she's having trouble dealing, at a minimum, with David's death."

He's good at this game. "It's normal and healthy for Robin to want to come to terms with what happened. It doesn't mean that she's incapable of knowing what she wants."

Placing the tips of his fingers on the edge of the cherry wood desk, Thomas glared directly at Jess. "Do not imply to me that what you're doing with my daughter is normal and healthy."

A dark eyebrow arched at his attempted intimidation. "I am implying, sir, that Robin is perfectly capable of knowing what she wants."

"And that would be you?" It was a rhetorical question that required no response. "I don't think so. Eventually, she will realize her mistake, and I don't want her to be destroyed emotionally again."

In spite of the obvious arrogance of his statement, Jess had to admit that he had a point. One of her greatest fears was that Robin would eventually realize that their relationship was a mistake, and that Jess was merely an emotional substitute for David.

Thomas stared out the large window at the view at the downtown skyline. "Let me ask you this. What are your intentions?"

"Excuse me?"

"What are your intentions toward my daughter. It seems like a simple enough question."

Jess had to stop and consider her response carefully. "If it were up to me, I'd devote my entire life to making sure that Robin was loved to the fullest. But it is not entirely up to me. A lot has to do with what Robin wants."

"It's convenient for you, isn't it?" Thomas continued to stare out the window.

The junior partner was perplexed. "What's convenient?"

"I know of your reputation in the legal community. I can be very resourceful. You're not an easy person to work with, as I understand it. Robin's convenient for you. She'll do your work. She idolizes you. Some sort of hero worship thing. It seems to be a pretty good deal. You get someone to help manage your caseload as long as you keep her happy, give her little diamond trinkets, claim you love her."

Hold it, buddy. Jess stood up. "I don't like that implication."

"Why?" Thomas turned to face Jess. "Hits a little too close to home?" He focused his attention back out the window. "This is a nice view."

"What's your point?"

"I'm willing to bet your managing partner and litigation department chair haven't a clue about your relationship with my daughter. And I'm also willing to bet that your firm has a policy against personal relationships between supervisors and subordinates."

Shit! I will not be blackmailed. "I will say this only once, and because you are Robin's father, I will afford you that respect, but you are way off base. You come into my place of business, unannounced, demand to see me, and imply that my personal life is somehow tied to some ulterior motives on my part. That is not the way it is." Jess enunciated the last sentence very succinctly.

In a blink of an eye, Thomas whirled around. "You're carrying on a clandestine, not to mention illicit, affair with my daughter right underneath your law firm's nose. From what I understand, you've made no commitment to my daughter, as if such a commitment would make what you're doing any less reprehensible."

Illicit Affair. Jess mentally cringed at the reference to what she, herself, had only realized the night before. *Nothing escapes you, Tom.* "For your information, I love Robin. To me, that is most certainly not reprehensible. If and when Robin and I make any type of commitment to each other, that is entirely up to us."

"I can see I have not made my point." Thomas sat down. "I would encourage you to end your relationship with my daughter immediately."

"And why would I do that?"

Thomas' eyes hardened. "If you insist that I spell it out for you, so be it. I can not allow my daughter to be abused in this manner. As her father, I have an obligation to protect her. Therefore, should you continue with your inappropriate conduct toward Robin, I will have no choice but to take this matter to the firm's upper management. You should consider your options carefully, then make the appropriate decision. End it now." He sat back in his chair, confident he held all the cards. He had one more ace to play, should he need it.

Son of a bitch. I refuse to be blackmailed. "And if I reveal my relationship with Robin to the firm, and accept the consequences of doing so...."

"Well..." Robin's father stroked his chin, as if in considerable thought. "Then that would be extremely unfortunate."

Spit it out. "How so?"

He played his ace. "I believe that Robin is emotionally incapable at the moment of realizing the precarious position she is in while working with you. She's seeing a psychologist, and has yet to come to terms with David's death, along with the guilt she feels as a result of it. Because of her emotional disability, she doesn't understand that her job may be tied to certain, shall we say, favors she affords you. Personal favors. After all, considering that Robin works almost exclusively for you, you do prepare her performance evaluations, do you not?"

The weight of the implication landed on Jess like twelve tons of bricks. *My God.* How could she have been so blind? She was so worried about the favoritism perils of their relationship that she completely missed this. *Sexual harassment.* She directed her attention back toward Thomas. "All performance evaluations are completely objective and subject to the review of the Management Committee." The junior partner paused just long enough to refrain from saying something clearly unfortunate, then continued "And any 'personal favors' as you say, number one, are none of your business, and number two, would be completely consensual."

"So says you."

"And Robin." Jess was more worried than she let on.

"Robin, who is emotionally fragile. One might even say she has an emotional disability at the moment. I think we both know what we're talking about here."

Damn it. How could I have misjudged this? "You'd have a very hard time proving any such allegations."

Thomas felt victory within his reach. "I don't need to prove them. I merely need to make the charge and file a complaint with the State Bar Association. There'd be an investigation. It's mandatory. You'd never recover from the scandal, and neither would this firm. To think that a firm of this reputation had partners who preyed on vulnerable young associates in such a detestable way...." He left the thought deliberately unfinished. "Well, let's just say I'm sure any such investigation would be devastating to this firm."

Jess felt sick, a thought occurring to her that truly made her ill as she addressed Robin's father again. "You'd put Robin though an investigation of such a nature?"

The corners of Thomas's mouth curled ever so slightly. "The real question is...would you?" He stood up to leave, his point clearly made. "End it now. You have the weekend."

Jess watched as Thomas Wilson left her office, then sank back into her leather chair. She closed her eyes in genuine anguish before opening them again. *I will not be blackmailed.* Idly, she glanced over at the messages Angie had left for her on her desk, noting that the top one was from Robin marked "Urgent". *Oh, sweetheart.* There was absolutely no way Jess could speak with Robin right now. *I need time to think.*

Just then, Angie knocked and opened the door. "I have a few more messages for you. Robin's called three times. She said it's urgent and for you to call her on the cell phone." Her secretary placed the additional messages on the desk, noting Jess's pale features as she did so. Then, Angie put two and two together, and it all suddenly became absolutely clear. Thomas Wilson is Robin's father. Robin's called three times, all urgent. *Oh boy. There is definitely trouble in paradise. Just wait until Betty hears this.*

"Angie, I'd like you to hold my calls and take messages for the rest of the day. Also, cancel my appointment this afternoon with Ted Riley on the Williams case. Go ahead and reschedule it for sometime next week." The junior partner stood up, grabbed her briefcase and headed out the door, her nausea at what had transpired overwhelming.

I need some air. Now.

****

Robin hailed a taxi cab outside the airport's main terminal upon returning to Orlando. It was already after five o'clock, and her attempts to reach Jess all day long had been unsuccessful. Her frustration was further complicated by the fact that she was unable to use the cell phone at all during her flight, and the plane wasn't equipped with an airphone. After situating herself in the cab's backseat, she picked up the cell phone and tried the junior partner again at the office, dialing her direct line only to reach the voicemail. Robin briefly considered trying to reach Angie, but then realized that, given the late hour, the staff had already gone home for the day. *Maybe Jess is at home.* Robin gave the cab driver directions to The Ranch and then called the home number. The answering machine picked up. *Not there or screening calls?* Robin chose not to leave a message at either location, opting instead to go home and search out Jess for herself.

Upon arrival at The Ranch, Robin found that Jess was nowhere to be found and her car was nowhere in sight. Sighing, the young associate decided to check the firm again just in case Jess had stepped out for a bite to eat before returning to get some more work done. Robin scribbled out a note to Jess and left it on the dining room table, then hopped into her metallic blue BMW and headed downtown toward the firm.

Twilight had started to settle upon the city when the young associate finally pulled her BMW into the building's parking garage. She breathed a sigh of relief when she spotted Jess's silver Mercedes parked in its usual spot. *She's here.* Robin quickly entered the lobby, gave the guard her usual greeting, and stopped to sign in the after-hours log. Perhaps it was because she was so anxious, but a wave of panic started to set in. *What if she's upset with me? Maybe that's why she didn't return my calls.* The elevator car arrived and Robin punched in the night code, riding up to the sixteenth floor law offices of Roberts & McDaniel. Gathering her resolve, she passed through the darkened reception area and then down around the corner toward Jess's office.

Robin stopped at the familiar wood door, sighing inwardly. Even though the door was partially closed, she could see that the lights were off. *She's not here.* Dejected, the associate opened the door wider and scanned the office, debating with herself whether to leave Jess a note. She had just decided against the idea when she saw the darkened silhouette sitting in the chair by the large window.

"Jess?" Robin hesitantly called out.

The silhouetted figure turned slightly. "Robin." The voice was familiar, yet oddly somber.

The associate entered the office, closing the door behind her. "I've been searching for you. I tried to call, but...." Something about the situation struck Robin. Jess didn't get up to greet her, or inquire about her flight, or sound in any way happy to see her. Robin raced over to the chair. "Why are you in the dark?"

There was nothing but silence.

"Jess." Robin knelt on the floor next to the chair and tried unsuccessfully to capture the junior partner's gaze. Her heart sped up. "He...was here, wasn't he?" *Does she blame me?*

There was more silence.

She won't talk to me. Robin became very worried. "Jess, I didn't know he was coming. When I found out, I tried to call." Her voice became shaky. "Jess, I swear, I didn't...."

"Shhh." The junior partner turned and brought a hand up to the side of Robin's face. "I know." Long fingers stroked the soft cheek almost hypnotically.

The younger woman inched around to the front of the chair. "What did he say to you?"

Her only response was Jess lowering her head.

"Please talk to me."

Jess finally spoke, her voice hoarse. "I thought I had everything all figured out. If the firm found out about us, I'd take the penalty, whatever that was."

Robin's tone became hard. "He threatened to go to Harry and Gordon?" The associate steeled herself. "He had no right to do that...to threaten you." She was finally able to capture Jess's gaze. "We'll figure something out. If I have to work with someone else, I'll do that."

The junior partner smiled a very sad smile, then ran her fingers slowly through Robin's bangs. "If it was only that simple."

What's going on? Something was very wrong. Robin felt her stomach clench. "Jess? You're scaring me. What happened?"

Jess refused to look at Robin, instead fixing her gaze out the window into the night sky. "I'm such a fool." Her voice was soft. "I arrogantly thought I had everything under control. It never occurred to me that...." She couldn't even say it, the mere thought making her ill.

Robin's stomach clenched further. "What?"

"I was so focused on the perception of favoritism. Remaining objective. I should have seen it, but I didn't."

A petite hand reached up and turned Jess's face to look into silver-blue eyes. "What didn't you see? Please, Jess, tell me."

"That our relationship could be seen as abusive. That since I evaluate your job performance, you could perceive your job as being tied to...." Jess's voice was barely a whisper, as she swallowed reflexively. "Providing certain favors to me." It was all Jess could do to maintain her composure. Breaking down right now would only make matters worse.

Providing certain favors. Robin mulled that phrase around in her mind, until it suddenly hit her with a sickening clarity. *Sexual harassment.* "No!" Then another thought came to her, and Robin nearly doubled over in real pain. "He threatened you with that?"

All there was now was silence. Jess was simply unable to speak.

"Jess, he can't prove it. He doesn't have standing. He doesn't know how it is with us."

The junior partner found her voice again. "He doesn't have to prove it, just make the charge. He's right. The Bar will investigate. It's mandatory. The firm, me and...you will be subjected to an investigation. He believes that you are emotionally fragile, and that gives him grounds to file such a charge." Jess paused, and then had to ask. It was something that had been on her mind for the better part of the day. "Robin..." She looked at the younger woman hesitantly, her voice very soft. "Did you ever think...that your job was tied to...."

Robin's eyes grew wide, and she rushed up and hugged Jess to her, realizing the enormity of junior partner's torment. "No!" She hugged tighter. "No. I never once thought that. It's consensual. You know that." She pulled back, her eyes now glistening. "I love you. What we do, I choose freely to do. If you fired me tomorrow, I would still love you." *Have you been tormenting yourself all day over this? Is that why you didn't call me back?* It somehow cheapened everything they had together to put it into such a perverse context as tying job retention to providing 'certain favors.' "Jess, what we have together is very special to me. Never doubt that."

The junior partner merely nodded, then stood up and walked around Robin's kneeling form, stepping closer to the window and gazing out at some unseen object in the night sky. Without turning around, she spoke. "I will not allow an investigation to taint you. You're just starting out, and believe me when I say that a reputation follows you in this business where ever you go. I will not permit an investigation to damage your reputation, not to mention what a scandal of this nature would do to this firm."

"What are you saying?" *Is she resigning?*

"I've thought all day of all the options. If I choose to leave the firm, that may save the firm from a scandal, but it wouldn't prevent an investigation from going forward." Jess was unable to look at Robin. "Your father gave me an ultimatum, and although I've tried, and believe me, I've tried very hard, I can't think of any other way to remedy this situation. It was my lapse in judgment that brought us to this point, so I have to take responsibility for what happened, and how best to resolve it with the least bit of harm to all involved."

Robin stood up and went over to the window where Jess stood. She rested her hand on the older woman's forearm and looked up as the junior partner continued to gaze out at points unseen. "What ultimatum?"

"If I...ended our relationship, he wouldn't file a complaint with the State Bar or reveal our relationship to the firm."

Blackmail. "You're not going to let him get away with that." Robin suddenly had a very ominous feeling. "Are you?"

Silence.

"Jess? Are you?"

Up until this point, and for as long as Robin had known her, Jess had always turned away and distracted her gaze when she felt uncomfortable or emotionally threatened. But now, Jess focused her gaze squarely on Robin, blinked once, and then delivered her answer. "Yes."

Robin reacted as expected. "No! You can't. What about us?"

"Now listen to me, Robin. I won't let you or anyone else pay for my mistakes."

"Is that what you think our relationship is? A mistake?" Robin was beside herself.

Damn it. I'm not going to get through this. "No." Silver-blue eyes softened. "No. But this is the only way out of this."

"But I love you." Robin began crying. "I love you."

"And I love you, sweetheart. And that's why I can't let this scandal taint you." Although Jess seemed relatively calm on the outside, inside she was absolutely shattered. After all, she'd had all afternoon to perfect her brave front, and it took all of her willpower just to make it this far. Robin's crying was nearly her undoing.

"You can't let him win. We love each other."

The junior partner saw Robin approach, and took a step backward to maintain a distance. Otherwise, Jess was silent.

"Please, Jess." Robin pleaded as she reached up and grasped the diamond heart pendant she wore around her neck.

It was actually a good thing that the lights were off in the office, as Jess's eyes were surely glistening. "I promised you that if there was a backlash against you, I would protect you. This is the only way I know to protect you."

"And I promised you that I would never leave you."

Jess's heart broke into a million pieces. "I release you from that promise."

"Well, I don't. I take my promises seriously.

"You told me that I had to tell you if it became too dangerous and I wanted you to leave. You told me that you would accept my decision." Silver-blue eyes closed, then opened again. "Robin, it's too dangerous." Jess never thought she'd say these next few words. "I want you to leave me." She swallowed back a sob. "I want you to accept my decision."

"Jess...." Robin tried to approach again, but Jess once more backed away.

"I need for you to go on home now, Robin."

More tears fell. "No."

"Don't argue with me on this."

Robin shook her head. *This can't be happening.* "This isn't over."

"Go on home now. Don't wait up for me." Silver-blue eyes watched as Robin's form slowly turned toward the door. "And Robin."

The young associate looked back.

"Go ahead and sleep in your own room tonight."

Robin let go a strangled sob, and then in resigned fashion, made her way out of the office and into the hallway, closing the door behind her. She stood there, bracing herself against the wall, then slowly sank to the floor. What Robin didn't know was that inside the office, Jess had done much the same thing, collapsing to the floor in front of the large window and letting go of all the pent up emotion she'd held inside, as waves and waves of tears overcame her, and just wouldn't stop.

Outside the door, Robin wiped the tears from her eyes and stood up. *What just happened?* This whole thing seemed surreal. How could it end like this? It was at that one moment that Robin made a decision that would define who she was and everything she believed in. Some things are worth fighting for, and this was certainly one of them. She turned and opened the office door, intent on arguing her point one more time. "Jess, I...." What she saw inside tore at her very soul. In dim silhouette, Jess was curled up on the floor, rocking herself and sobbing uncontrollably. Robin quickly closed the door behind her and rushed over to the older woman, gathering her in her arms and holding her tightly. "No." She clung tighter. "No, Jess. I will not leave you."

Jess had lost all control. She couldn't form a single word, let alone speak to Robin. She relaxed her body, lost in the comforting presence that surrounded her and provided her safe haven from the storm within.

Robin clutched Jess's head to her chest, letting her tears fall onto the dark head. "You are so brave." She whispered, now realizing exactly what Jess had done. "You are the bravest person I know. You'd crush your own heart to protect me." The significance grabbed at the younger woman in the most profound way. If there was one thing Robin was absolutely certain about, it was that Jess's greatest fear was that she'd give her heart away again, only to have it torn apart by betrayal or abandonment. To have Jess shatter her own heart to spare Robin was the greatest sacrifice the older woman could ever have made. More tears fell on the dark head as Robin reflected on that. "I love you so much. I will never, ever leave you." She continued to rock Jess in her arms. "You gave me your heart, remember? And I promised I'd take good care of it. I won't give it up now. It's safe with me."

It was completely dark outside, the downtown city lights twinkling through the night sky. While safely enveloped within Robin's embrace, Jess took comfort in the quiet peace the nighttime afforded, trying to gather herself into some semblance of composure. In truth, she had no willpower to turn Robin away again, even though she knew what failing to do so meant. Still, she couldn't speak her acceptance of what the younger woman offered.

Robin held on tightly, gazing likewise out the large window into the night sky. Finally, she placed the tips of her fingers underneath Jess's chin and lifted it upward, whispering softly. "You and I are meant to be together. We're a part of each other. Even apart, you're with me and I'm with you." She shifted so the older woman could sit up facing her. "Can you feel it, Jess?" Robin raised up her hand and cupped the older woman's cheek, then brought Jess's larger hand up to her own face in similar fashion. "Can you feel it? When I touch you and you touch me?" She trailed her hand down and lightly stroked her fingers against Jess's neck, then back up to her cheek again, repeating the motion continuously. "It's like magic, this energy between us. I've felt it since the very first time you touched me." Robin brought her other hand up to rest against Jess's opposite cheek, smoothing away a few strands of hair. She locked her gaze with silver-blue eyes in the darkness and whispered again. "Can you feel it?"

Since Robin had come back into the office, Jess hadn't said a word. She was completely lost in Robin's soft touch. Finally, she spoke, her voice barely a whisper. "I feel it. I thought it was just me."

"No. We both feel it. We have a connection. We're meant to be together."

"But your father..." The junior partner started to protest.

"Shhh." Petite fingers pressed against Jess's lips. "We'll figure something out. Together, Jess. Together. We're meant to be together, and we'll figure something out together." Robin kissed the palm of Jess's hand, brushing her lips against the blue and white sapphire bracelet Jess wore around her wrist. "Forever, remember?" She fingered the bracelet she'd given Jess, recalling the inscription. "Do you understand what I'm saying?"

The older woman wasn't sure, but she sensed hints of a commitment in Robin's words. "Yes. Together forever."

"Yes." Robin smiled. "You can't get rid of me." She tilted her head slightly to the side, a thought occurring to her. "I'm like crazy glue."

Crazy glue. The memory came back at Jess. "Crazy glue?"

"Yes. And I'm very sticky."

"I see."

Robin's smile widened. "And you're stuck with me. You got that?"

Jess returned the smile. "That's my line."

A small, yet relieved chuckle came from Robin. "So, we're clear, right?"

"Yes."

"So...any slipping out the back, Jack?" Petite fingers laced with larger ones.

"No."

"Or making a new plan, Stan?"

The irony of the role reversal was not lost on Jess. "No."

Robin brought their joined hands to her lips. "You're not going to be coy, Roy?"

"No."

"How about hopping on the bus, Gus?"

Silver-blue eyes captured gray-green. "Never."

Robin kissed the knuckles of their joined hands reverently. "Will you ever drop off the key, Lee?"

It was sudden, and it was strong. Jess engulfed the younger woman in a heartfelt hug. "No, sweetheart. I won't ever drop off the key." *We're meant to be together.*

Robin pulled back and rested her forehead against Jess's. "No one leaves."

Jess nodded in agreement. "No one leaves."

"Good." Robin grinned. "Glad we got that settled." She arched a pale eyebrow. "Even if you do steal my slippers and have a very strange fetish for a certain seafood-related item."

Silver-blue eyes narrowed. "Are you accusing me of slipper-napping?"

Slipper-napping? "Well, if the shoe fits...."

"Ooooh." Jess chuckled for the first time all day. "That was really, really bad." She stood up, bringing Robin along with her. "And by the way, it's not a fetish."

Robin patted Jess's arm indulgently. "Whatever you say, Jess. Now, let's go home."

Home. The truth of the matter was, they were already home, and they both knew it.

Chapter 5

Emotions were still quite raw by the time Jess and Robin made their way back to The Ranch. To say it had been a stressful day would have been an understatement. They prepared a simple dinner of pasta with marinara sauce and ate quickly and quietly together as the full weight of the day's events settled heavily and uneasily upon them. Although there wasn't much by way of dinner conversation, neither Robin nor Jess minded the silence, instead taking a familiar comfort in each other's presence. It wasn't lost on either of them, as they silently reflected on what had transpired, that the day could have ended much differently, and quite unhappily. The more each of them considered that fact, the more disturbing it all seemed. Was their relationship so fragile and tenuous that someone determined to break it apart could succeed so easily? It was a frightening thought, and a question that, for better or for worse, preoccupied both of their minds as they finished their meal. As much as they might not have wanted to admit it to themselves, it was now becoming abundantly clear that while their bond and connection seemed quite strong, their commitment to each other was still a relative uncertainty. And that was something that would simply have to change, and change fast.

Once the dinner dishes were cleared away and washed, both women felt the effects of emotional exhaustion begin to claim them. Rather than watching TV or reading the daily newspaper, they instead decided to turn in early that evening. They performed their nightly rituals and readied themselves for bed, finally turning out the lights and slipping quietly underneath the crisp cotton sheets of the queen-sized waterbed.

After what seemed like an eternity of uneasy silence, Robin

shifted toward Jess and broached the topic that was in the forefront of both of their minds. "We should talk."

Jess didn't move. "I know."

The smaller body inched closer, Robin's voice barely a whisper. "What are you thinking about?"

"I...um...." The older woman suddenly turned her head and focused her gaze on the dim light of the digital clock on the nightstand. "I owe you an apology."

Pale eyebrows furrowed slightly. "For what?"

There was a very long silence as Jess continued to look in the opposite direction.

"Jess?" A petite hand reached up and turned Jess's face toward her own, feeling a bit of moisture in the process. "You're crying. What is it?"

The older woman took a breath to steady her voice. "I asked you a question earlier that was out of line. I should have had faith in you. I'm sorry."

Robin still wasn't sure what it was Jess was referring to. "What question?" She curled herself around the larger body and rested her cheek against the top of the dark head.

Even though it had been several hours, Jess's emotions were still very near the surface, and she found it difficult to speak. "I asked you if...um...you ever felt your job was tied to..." She hesitated, then continued. "Providing me certain favors." She closed her eyes tightly in regret. "That was way out of line of me."

Robin felt the moisture increase. "Shhh, honey. It's all right." Petite fingers wiped away the tears, as Robin hugged Jess close to her. "I will admit to you that for a split-second I didn't understand how you could ask me that, considering everything we've had together." She stroked Jess's cheek with her fingertips. "But then I realized that you probably had been tormenting yourself for most of the day over that. I knew you didn't really think it was true. You just needed me to say so."

"Yeah, but that was no reason for me to insult you like that." The older woman finally turned her head and looked up at Robin. "I am very sorry."

"It's all right. I understand." Robin continued to brush her fingers back and forth against Jess's cheek, then spoke very softly. "Do you know how much I love you?" She kissed Jess's forehead. "I know what you were prepared to sacrifice to protect me. I know how hard that was for you." Tears formed in Robin's eyes. "I didn't think it was possible, but I love you more now than I did before."

Jess felt small arms encircle her and hold her very close, and she sunk almost desperately into the embrace. "Can I ask you something?"

"Of course."

"What made you come back into my office?"

It really wasn't an easy thing to explain. Robin, nevertheless, attempted to put words to what she felt. "I just couldn't give up on us. I wanted to talk to you some more to try to convince you that we could work through this. I didn't think that everything we had together could just end like that." She caressed Jess's cheek, running her fingers down along her neck, then back up again in continuous motion. "But then I saw you, curled up on the floor, and I felt this horrible pain inside of me. I can't explain it, but it hurt worse than anything I've ever felt before."

The older woman was quite embarrassed to have been caught in such a moment of weakness. "I didn't mean for you to see me like that."

"I know." Petite fingers brushed across the dark eyebrows soothingly. "But the moment I saw you, I knew what you had done. I knew that you had given up the one thing you were most afraid to lose." Robin couldn't help herself. She let her tears flow freely. "You shattered your own heart to protect me."

"I'd do anything to protect you." Jess's voice was sincere, but then grew more somber. "But I'm not doing a very good job of that right now. Your father...."

Robin stopped her. "No. You protect me. You've always protected me, even from the very beginning." She took hold of one of Jess's hands. "I figured it out, Jess." She placed the larger hand on her own stomach underneath her nightshirt. "I figured it out. When you put your hand here, I feel it. I feel that you're protecting me. It's the safest feeling I know."

Subconsciously, maybe that's what Jess was doing, although she'd be hard pressed to explain it. "It just feels right to do that."

"Yeah." The younger woman smiled, a memory now coming back to her. "The first time you put your hand on my stomach was when we were in New Orleans on the riverboat, remember?" She grinned in the dark, recalling the moment. "For some very strange reason, which I really don't understand, you thought I was going to fall overboard."

Jess felt a little tension ease. "You were leaning half-way over the edge of the railing. How was I suppose to explain to Harry how I'd lost the new associate in the middle of the Mississippi River?"

A quiet chuckle. "I wasn't going to fall in, silly." A petite hand covered the larger one resting on her stomach. "But you put your arms around my waist, and your hand was on my stomach, and at that moment, I felt very protected." Another thought occurred to her. "Maybe that's why my stomach is my favorite place for you to touch me."

Jess cocked her head to one side. "Your favorite place?"

That brought another grin and a slight blush unseen in the dark. "No, not like that. It's more of a comfortable feeling. I feel a warmth inside of me because I know you're there."

It must be true, Jess decided. "I have a confession to make."

Confession? "Spill it." Robin combed her fingers through the dark hair.

"One time, right after we first knew each other, we were sleeping and I woke up before you. I realized that my hand was on your stomach underneath your nightshirt. I practically had a coronary when I thought of what I had done to get it there."

"That was before we...."

The dark head nodded. "Way before. I tried to take my hand away, but you grabbed it and held it in place."

The younger woman reflected on that. "See, even though I was sleeping, I still knew I wanted your hand there."

Jess became very quiet, and several minutes passed before she spoke again. "Your father gave me the weekend to...."

"I don't want to talk about him." Robin cut her off, her voice hard. It made her both angry and sick to think about what he had done. "He hurt you and threatened you, even though he knew that I loved you." Up until this point, she actually hadn't allowed herself to consider the ramifications of what had happened. Not only had her father hurt Jess, but he had hurt Robin in a most despicable way, disguising it as protecting her. She sniffled quietly and wiped away a few stray tears, then repeated her statement. "I don't want to talk about him."

"It's okay, sweetheart. We won't talk about him right now." Jess brushed the hand resting on Robin's stomach back and forth in a soothing motion. "But you know I'll have to go to Harry first thing Monday morning. You know that, right?"

"I know." Robin replied simply. "I'm going with you."

The dark head shook. "No, I'll handle it."

"Jess...." Robin inched herself down to look the older woman directly in the eye. "We're in this together. Remember?"

Even though Jess knew Robin was right, it just hurt so much to involve her in this mess any more than necessary. Finally, the older woman accepted Robin's wish and acquiesced. "Yes, I remember." She leaned in and gave Robin a soft kiss. "Together forever."

We're going to make it through this. Robin curled herself back around the taller body and resumed stroking the chiseled face. She felt the large hand still resting on her stomach likewise stroke her soft skin. For some reason, she became very melancholy. *I almost lost this.* "I almost lost you tonight."

"I know." Blue eyes closed again, trying to shake off the sadness. "I'm sorry for sending you away. At the time, I thought it was the right thing to do. I was wrong." The older woman was overcome with emotion again, finally unable to talk anymore. *I almost lost everything. Our relationship should have been stronger than that.*

It was one of Jess's character traits, Robin decided, to take the blame for something that hurt someone she loved. But at this particular moment that blame was misplaced. Robin slid down and raised herself up on one arm, looking at the older woman with a softening gaze. "Honey, you're not to blame for this. You're not to blame for loving me and wanting to protect me." She trailed soft, gentle kisses over the beautiful face, placing several more on Jess's lips in a gesture meant to offer comfort. "You always do the protecting." She bestowed another loving kiss on the older woman's lips. "Let me protect you tonight." She laid back and hugged older woman close to her, combing her fingers slowly through the dark hair. "You're heart is with me, Jess, and it's safe. I'm protecting it. We're together, and that's all that matters."

Jess breathed in Robin's scent, one which she always thought smelled like fresh raindrops, and let the soft touch relax her as she slowly succumbed to sleep's embrace. Her last thought was that although their relationship was certainly stronger after the emotional events of the day, it was still far too delicate to withstand the storm that was yet to come. And that was something that had to be resolved soon, one way or the other.

Swim or tread water. Fish or cut bait. Deal or shuffle the deck. Any way you looked at it, it still meant the same thing. As the petite fingers gently and lovingly stroked Jess's face, and her mind drifted toward slumber, the choice became obvious.

Quit procrastinating and make the commitment. Now.

****

Jess woke and blinked several times, adjusting her eyes to the early morning light. She had slept surprisingly well, better than she should have considering everything that had happened and everything that was yet to come. Perhaps her sound sleeping was due to the comforting presence that had surrounded her throughout the night, the same presence that surrounded her still with the start of the new day. Blue eyes subtly surveyed her companion's slumbering form. Tousled short blonde hair fell haphazardly just above closed green eyes, with a portion of the petite body draped casually over her larger one. It was a position her companion had occupied countless times before, except now, there was a new and interesting development. One petite hand was placed underneath Jess's Calvin Klein sleep shirt so that it rested protectively on the older woman's bare stomach. A gentle smile twitched at the corners of Jess's mouth. *She's right. It does feel good.* A large hand securely covered the smaller one.

Suddenly, her companion stirred, sea-green eyes fluttering open, only to squint in the relative brightness of the early morning sunlight. "It's too early to wake up." Robin's voice was rough from sleep. "You can't leave. You're my pillow." She closed her eyes again.

A deep chuckle. "Is that what I've been relegated to, your pillow?"

"Yes. Now don't talk. I'm still sleeping. It's practically the middle of the night."

Middle of the night? "Um...Robin, I hate to tell you this, but it's most definitely not the middle of the night. The sun is shining, and the birds are singing."

"Mmmfph. That's lovely, Jess, but if you start quoting poetry right now, you're going to seriously regret it."

"Ooooh, I think I'm afraid."

"You should be. Now, shhh. I'm sleeping."

Another deep chuckle. "Okay, no poetry, but how about a song?" Jess began singing the familiar tune, her voice performing the rendition with a certain degree of gusto. "Zip a dee do dah, zip a dee ay. My, oh my, what a wonderful day. Plenty of sunshine heading my way. Zip a dee do dah, zip a dee ay. Mister bluebird's on my shoulder...."

That's it! "Jess." Sleepy green eyes opened, then narrowed. "You are so dead."

"What? You don't like the song or my singing?" Jess was goofing around, and it felt really, really good.

"Let me put it to you this way. The song is fine. The singing is fine. It's the hour of the song and the singing that is not fine. Are we clear?"

"Absolutely." Jess grinned, then after an appropriate amount of time, started humming.

Green eyes glared.

"What?"

"Let me amend my previous statement. The song is fine. The singing is fine. The humming is fine. It's the hour of the song and the singing and the humming that is not fine. Now, are we clear?"

"Perfectly." It was really too good of an opportunity to pass up. Jess started whistling.

Robin lifted herself up on one arm and smacked her lips together, seemingly perturbed. "Must I clarify my previous statement yet again?"

"Only if you want to." Jess replied innocently.

"Fine. Let me make this abundantly clear. The only thing that is acceptable at this particular hour of the morning is quiet. Are there any questions?"

"Nope."

"Good." Robin laid back down and drew the covers around her. After a moment, she felt a rhythmic tapping against her back, decidedly in time to the tune of the previous song. A clearly unhappy groan followed. "You really are determined to drive me crazy this morning, aren't you?"

The dark head shook vehemently. "No, I'm not."

"You are so. Is there some particular reason you felt compelled to play the drums on my back?"

"Um...I have absolutely no idea what you're talking about."

Robin narrowed her eyes. "I think you do." It was useless at this point to try to sleep. The younger woman sat up against the headboard and looked pointedly at Jess. "Okay. Let's try this again. Is there something you want?"

Jess grinned. "Well, now that you're up...." Before she could finish her statement, a pillow came flying out of nowhere and landed directly on top of her. A large hand promptly removed said pillow in mock indignation. "Hey! Watch it there."

A petite finger wagged purposefully in Jess's direction. "That's what you get for waking me up." Fully awake green eyes then rolled playfully. "All right. Come on over here, Snoopy."

The older woman happily complied, scooting over and placing her head on Robin's lap. She stretched her tall body to the full length of the queen-sized waterbed, then rested her chin on her hands and looked up, her clear blue eyes sparkling. "Hi."

She's so hopeless. "Hi to you, too." Robin grinned and brushed the dark bangs. "To what do I owe this good mood of yours?"

Jess cocked her head slightly. "I'll have you know, Robin, that this is my usual pleasant self."

119

Robin chuckled lightly. "I see." It was absolutely amazing that all of the anguish and tension of the previous evening had somehow dissipated. Of course, the reason for that could have been the fact that they were safely tucked away in their own little corner of the universe far from the problems of the world. "Okay, then to what do I owe this usual pleasant self of yours?"

A long finger flicked the edge of Robin's nightshirt. "Well...." Jess drawled. "I slept really, really well, and when I woke up, you had your hand on my stomach, and I've now decided that my stomach is my favorite place for you to touch me."

A blonde eyebrow arched. "Is that so?"

"Yes." Jess had what only could be described as a terribly sexy grin on her face. "Of course, there are other places, too." She pulled Robin down underneath her in one swift motion, then waggled an eyebrow suggestively. "Wanna try them all out?"

Robin countered with a terribly sexy grin herself. "You're impossible."

"I'm incorrigible."

Green eyes locked onto sparkling blue. "That too. And yes, I intend to try out all of your favorite places, one by one." Petite hands lifted Jess's Calvin sleep shirt over her head. "Starting right...here." Robin rained kisses down the older woman's neck and bare chest.

"Um...." Jess suddenly lost her train of thought. "Those are...really good places." She sat Robin up and gripped the edges of her nightshirt, lifting it off of the younger woman easily. "So, tell me Robin, aside from your stomach, which I know is your favorite place and which is my job to keep happy, do you have any other favorite place you'd like me to try out?" Jess lowered Robin back to the bed. "Or should I just surprise you?"

"Um...." It was Robin's turn to lose her train of thought as Jess's hands glided along the smooth skin of her stomach and chest, trailing goose bumps in its wake. "Surprise me."

The taller woman slowly leaned down and gave Robin an extraordinarily soft and tender kiss. She pulled back just a bit and gazed adoringly into beautiful green eyes. "I love you, my sweet Robin. I'm so very grateful that I woke up this morning and you were here. If I seem especially happy today, that's the reason why." She gave Robin another tender kiss. "What I'd like to do now is show you how much I love you, if that's okay."

Sea-green eyes focused on crystal blue in quiet understanding. They both needed this intense connection after everything that had happened. "Yes." Petite hands entangled in the long, dark hair. "And let me do the same for you."

The gentle and reverent touches and kisses that followed served to strengthen even further their bond in the most intimate way. For both of them, every touch and every kiss was a treasure to be held dear, never to be lost or taken away again.

****

"Ooooh, something smells really good." Robin padded into the kitchen and peered curiously around Jess as she fixed breakfast. "What're you making?"

"Pancakes and bacon." The older woman threw back a look at Robin. "Hungry?"

"I'm starving."

"Me too." Jess mixed the pancake batter. "I seem to have quite an appetite this morning."

A petite hand patted Jess's stomach. "Yes, you were rather frisky earlier, weren't you?"

"Frisky?" The taller woman snaked an arm around Robin's waist and whispered seductively into a perfectly shaped ear. "Let me assure you, Robin, you most definitely have not seen frisky."

Robin couldn't help herself. A bright pick blush crept up her face. *How does she do that?* "You're incorrigible."

"Yep." Jess poured some pancake batter onto the griddle. "You bring out the best in me, kiddo."

The blonde woman grabbed a cup of coffee, then sat down at the kitchen table. "So, is there anything on your agenda today?"

Jess sighed internally. She'd been debating with herself all morning about whether to phone Harry and request a meeting with him right away regarding her situation with Robin. *And about Robin's father's threats.* She considered the matter a bit further. Of course, then again, nothing was really going to change over the weekend. Robin's father wouldn't have a chance to do anything until Monday, at best. So, why let it spoil the entire weekend?

"Jess?" Robin looked curiously at the older woman. "Did you have anything you wanted to do?"

Jess skillfully flipped a pancake. "Nope, not today. Was there something in particular you had in mind?"

"Well..." Green eyes glanced idly at the morning newspaper. "I was thinking perhaps, if you wanted to, we could go back to that beach we went to before and watch the sunset again."

That could work. In truth, watching a sunset together might have a relaxing effect, serving as a kind of calm before the storm that was almost certain to come. "Sounds like a plan, Stan."

"Great." Robin grinned, then snagged a piece of bacon. "I'll pack a picnic."

Smiling blue eyes cast Robin a sideways look. "What is it with you and picnics, anyway?"

A green eye winked in return. "Wouldn't you just like to know." Robin poured herself another cup of coffee, then sat back down as Jess set a plate of pancakes in front of her. "Um...Jess?" The smaller woman stared at her plate. "What are these?"

Perfectly innocent blue eyes glanced up. "What are what?"

A small finger pointed down at the pancakes. "These."

"They're pancakes, Robin." Dark eyebrows lifted almost comically. "Why? Don't you...like them?"

"I'm sure they're delicious. I was just wondering why they happen to look like that."

The older woman bent down and scrutinized the pancakes in question. "Um...like what?"

Robin continued to stare at her plate in utter bewilderment, then narrowed her eyes considerably. "Jess, they look suspiciously like a particular seafood-related item." A frank look. "And we both know what I'm talking about."

Jess, unaffected, sat down with her own plate of pancakes. "I just thought, Robin, that it would be nice to have a little variety instead of the same old boring round ones." She poured syrup on her pancakes, then jabbed a piece of a tail and waved it in front of Robin, intent on making her point. "Wouldn't you agree?"

Robin couldn't help but stare open-mouthed. *This is even more serious than I had originally thought, if that's even possible.* "Jess, honey, listen to me. Pancakes are supposed to be round. They're not supposed to be shaped like shrimp." The younger woman looked Jess directly in the eye. "Do you understand what I'm saying?"

"Yep." Jess took bite. "Pancakes, round, not shaped like shrimp. Got it."

"Good." Robin put butter and syrup on her shrimp-shaped pancakes. "Glad we're clear on that."

"Perfectly." Jess continued eating, then after an appropriate length of time, commented further. "I don't know what it is, Robin, but don't you think the pancakes taste especially...good today?" She grinned happily.

Robin took a bite. "They taste like pancakes."

"Yes, but there's just something about them this morning that makes them taste...better than usual, wouldn't you say?"

"They taste like pancakes."

The older woman, oblivious, continued further. "I think they taste very good."

A golden eyebrow lifted slightly. "Jess, there's nothing different about these pancakes other than the shape, right?"

"Right."

"So you know that they can't possibly taste different. You understand that, right?"

Silent contemplation.

It's not a hard question. "Jess?"

More silent contemplation.

Robin prodded further. "The shape of the pancake has nothing whatsoever to do with the taste. You do understand that, right?"

Contemplation now concluded, Jess finally answered. "What I understand, Robin, is that plain old round pancakes taste much more boring than my shrimp-shaped pancakes, which taste very good."

Robin shook her head in complete exasperation. "You are so hopeless."

An all-knowing sigh. "You just won't admit, Robin, that I'm right."

Good grief! A quick roll of the younger woman's green eyes. "Okay, Jess." A petite hand reached over and patted a larger hand sympathetically. "You're absolutely right. Shrimp-shaped pancakes taste much, much better than plain old boring round ones." Another eye roll. "Happy now?"

"Yes." A wide grin. "See, I knew I was right all along."

Robin threw up her hands. *Oh brother. I see I definitely I have my work cut out for me, here.*

****

The early afternoon sun shone brightly, tracking its way steadily toward the western horizon. Jess and Robin rode in near silence in the silver Mercedes toward the Gulf of Mexico beaches, both deep in their own thoughts. They had attempted their usual playfulness earlier on in the day, trying to recapture some semblance of normalcy, but as the daytime wore on, the weight of their situation settled increasingly heavier upon them.

Robin's eye caught the small good luck charm hanging from the rearview mirror, recalling when she'd put it there the previous weekend. "I see you kept Al up there."

Jess glanced at the plastic monkey, then focused back on the road. "Well, I knew you'd come back for him."

"Did you? Know that, I mean?"

"I hoped so." Azure eyes closed briefly, then reopened. "But then everything changed with your father."

The younger woman watched the passing trees. "I'm glad you kept Al hanging there. I still think he's good luck. I mean, he's still there and we're still together." Green eyes tracked over to settle on Jess's taller form. "Right?"

A large hand reached over and grasped Robin's smaller one. "Yes, sweetheart. We're still together."

"So, as long as he's hanging there, I think things will be okay."

It took a moment for the complete implication of that comment to sink in. It was something Jess really hadn't considered before, but it was certainly worth thinking about in a serious manner. Robin's putting her faith in a small plastic monkey was a bit worrisome. After all, Robin had given up her faith in God and now seemed to have replaced that faith with her belief in a tiny good luck charm. *We're going to have to talk about this.* "Sweetheart, things will be okay because we'll make them okay. It certainly won't hurt to have Al around, but we'll work things out ourselves, together. You told me that, remember?"

"Yes." Robin grew pensive. "I just feel that we need everything on our side." She let go of Jess's hand and reached up for the good luck charm, pulling it down and studying it intently. "Sometimes, it seems no matter what we do, some things just can't be helped. They're out of our control."

Jess decided to take a chance and say something she wasn't sure Robin would take well, but nevertheless, she said it anyway. "You could say a prayer."

The blonde head jerked around, as green eyes locked onto cool blue for the tiniest of seconds before darting away again. "No, Jess." Her voice had a hard edge to it. "I don't think I could do that." *Don't push me on this.*

The older woman cringed inwardly. Maybe things weren't going well with Dr. Richmond. After all, Robin hadn't discussed her sessions, and Jess hadn't asked, wanting instead to give her all the privacy she needed in order to come to terms with things. *But still....* Blue eyes watched as Robin hung the plastic monkey back in its place on the rearview mirror. *We need to talk about this seriously...sooner rather than later.*

"Hey, Jess." Robin changed the subject. "When we get to the beach can we go looking for seashells?"

Let's just let it go for now. "Sure, if you want to." Jess turned off the main highway onto the Gulfside Boulevard." Any particular reason?"

"I was just thinking of making a collection, and maybe filling some glass jars with them to use as decorations."

The older woman arched an eyebrow. *Not a bad idea.* "Did you ever hear the story about putting a large conch shell to your ear and listening to the sound?"

"Um...no, I don't think so." Robin glanced over at Jess. "What do you hear when you do that?"

Jess threw Robin a sly smile and then shook her head. "I'm not telling."

Green eyes narrowed slightly. "You are very mean to me. C'mon, Jess." Robin whined. "Just tell me. Please."

"Nope. Sorry." The older woman grinned playfully. "Here's the deal, kiddo. When we get to the beach, you go find one and then you can hear it for yourself."

Wary blonde eyebrows knit together. "You're putting me on."

A wounded look. "Would I do that?"

"Yes."

"Well..." Jess drawled, stringing out the sentence. "Fine, if you'd rather not know...." She tapped her fingertips lightly against the steering wheel.

"Okay." Robin jumped in, then pointed her finger purposefully. "But that's the first thing we're doing when we get there, and all I can say, Jess, is it had better be worth it."

Jess gave Robin her most sultry look. "Oh I can guarantee, Robin, it will definitely be worth it."

All Robin could do was close her eyes and swallow hard. *It's amazes me that she can do this to me with just one look.*

"By the way Robin, I was just wondering, how am I doing in the point department?" Jess glanced at the smaller woman expectantly.

"Well..." It was Robin's turn to drawl out the words. "You were doing really, really well up until this morning, when you deliberately woke me up with your frisky self." An exaggerated sigh. "Regrettably, I was forced to deduct points for that."

A playfully dejected look. "I see."

"Yes." The younger woman continued. "Fortunately for you,

though, you do have an opportunity to redeem yourself today."

"Really now." A now more hopeful look. "So tell me then, Robin, just what is it I have to do in order to 'redeem' myself, as you say?"

A petite hand reached over and grasped a larger one, lacing their fingers together in a contact that meant more than the appearance offered. "Anything you want."

I'm counting on that, sweetheart.

****

"Take a walk with me?" Jess got up from the beach blanket once she and Robin had finished their picnic lunch.

"Sure." Robin stowed the picnic items, then stood up. "We still have to find one of those conch shells so I can listen to it." She peered up at Jess cautiously. "I'm gonna like this, right?"

"Trust me." Jess winked. "You'll like it." The taller woman gave herself a quick stretch, then grabbed her sweatshirt and tied it around her waist.

"It's amazing that there's hardly anyone else around." A petite hand reached over and grasped Jess's larger one, intertwining their fingers. "I kind of like that because I want to have you all to myself." It was true. Although it was a spectacularly sunny and mild day, there was absolutely no one out on their more secluded portion of the beach.

The older woman led them both down to the water's edge. "So, how are you doing?" They proceeded along the shoreline hand in hand.

"Good." Robin answered a bit too quickly.

Jess slowed and then stopped walking, her blue eyes gauging Robin's demeanor. "How are you really doing?"

Green eyes regarded her taller companion. "How can you always tell?"

Jess thought about that. "I just can." It was the truth, and there was no way she could even begin to explain it. "So, what are you thinking about?" She resumed walking.

Robin breathed in the slightly salty air, delighting in the sights, sounds and smell of the Gulf waters lapping gently just beyond their footsteps. "Do you sometimes think that things happen for a reason, and nothing really happens by chance?"

Jess contemplated that question for a moment, then answered. "I've thought that way sometimes, yes." She spotted a pelican perched on a piling from a washed out pier. "Why do you ask?"

It was curiously difficult to explain. "Sometimes, I feel that I was destined to know you." The sun was steadily tracking toward the horizon casting long shadows along the sand as they walked. "I've thought about this a lot, and so many things just seemed to fall into place the moment I met you."

"I think I understand." The older woman watched the waning sunlight dance off the calm salt water as a small wave lapped perilously close to their feet. "I've always loved the beach and the color of the water. It fascinated me, even when I was a kid." She stopped again and gazed into Robin's sea-green eyes. "I think it finally makes sense to me."

For her part, Robin looked up, her eyes locking onto the crystal blue ones beside her. "On a clear day, when I'd look up at the sky, I'd think how beautiful the color was. Sometimes, I couldn't stop looking at it." She turned fully and faced Jess, grasping both of the larger hands within her own. The feelings at that particular moment were very strong and defied all reasonable explanation. "I really, really love you."

The taller woman leaned in very close to Robin. "And I really, really love you." She brushed her lips softly against Robin's in a tender kiss, then pulled back and murmured. "Are you ready to find that seashell now?"

"Yes." Robin quickly scanned the shoreline, spying a large conch shell half submerged in the sand up ahead. She ran over and dug it out, then held it up for Jess to see. "Is this what you were talking about?"

"Yep. Now, put the opening up against your ear and listen."

The younger woman did as instructed, listening intently to the amplified sound. As she listened, her eyes grew very wide. "It sounds like waves crashing." She cast a questioning gaze. "But the waves here are too small to make that sound."

She's adorable. A very wide grin appeared. "It's amazing, huh?"

"Yeah." Robin was completely fascinated by the discovery. "I think we should bring this back with us. Would you mind if I gathered up a few other shells, too?"

"Nope. Let me help you find some really nice ones." As they scoured the beach for intact shells, Jess decided that it was really quite fun just to spend a carefree day together with no worries other than finding the perfect seashells. *Fun.* She mulled that thought around in her mind. *Robin makes everything fun.* It was something Jess hadn't even realized she was missing until Robin came into her life. She smiled to herself in true amazement. Whether it was Christmas trees or ice cream, grocery shopping or picnics, fishing or hunting for seashells, everything about life with Robin was fun. *Absolutely amazing.*

In a relatively short while, they had succeeded in gathering up a healthy assortment of varied and colorful seashells. Upon determining that they had collected enough, they used the bottom portions of their over-sized t-shirts to haul them back to their picnic area. The day was nearing its end, and after a leisurely stroll along the shoreline to watch the seagulls dip and circle the waves, Robin and Jess decided to head back to their beach blanket and sit and watch the sun slowly set into the sea. They both donned their sweatshirts to ward off the chill from the early evening's sea breeze, then sat together to await the day's main event.

After smoothing out the beach blanket, Jess positioned herself directly behind Robin's smaller form and snuggled in closely. "You doing okay?"

"Perfect." The younger woman nestled back against Jess's chest as long legs enveloped her in a cocoon of warmth. "This is really nice."

Long arms wrapped around the petite waist from behind. "Yes, it is." The older woman rested her chin on Robin's shoulder, then felt smaller hands come to rest directly on top of her own. "It's going to be a pretty sunset. I can already see the red sky."

Robin sighed in contentment. This was the perfect moment. *Why can't everything be this simple?* She looked back over her shoulder. "Thank you."

Jess cast a quizzical look. "You're welcome, but for what?"

"For everything you are and everything you do."

It was, indeed the perfect moment, Jess decided, as she smiled back at Robin. She closed her eyes and reveled in the warmth of simply being together. And it was good. Really, really good. It was exactly the moment she felt she'd been waiting for, it seemed, all her life.

Green eyes focused steadily on the horizon and admired the beauty over the sea in all its quiet majesty. As Robin sat and gazed at the orange, mauve and hints of purple painting the early evening sky, she felt a warm hand gently lift one of her fingers and slowly place something upon it. She swallowed hard and then looked down, now seeing the beautiful diamond solitaire ring gracing her left hand. Her heart sped up.

"I love you, my sweet Robin." Jess's low alto voice spoke softly into a nearby ear. "I want you to know that you're the best thing that's ever happened to me. You've brought so much happiness into my life." She hesitated for a brief second, then continued. "I know I'm not the easiest person to get along with, but if you'll let me, sweetheart, I'd like to spend the rest of my life with you, loving you." Her voice became raspy with emotion as she spoke her heartfelt appeal. "I commit myself and my love to you forever. I commit my mind, my heart, my body, and my soul to you, to take care of you, to cherish you, and to love you as long as we live, and beyond." She took a breath. "If you'll let me."

Robin took a moment to steady herself, trying desperately to calm her racing heart. She slowly turned to face Jess, her watery eyes glistening as she lifted a hand to reverently cup the older woman's cheek. "Yes." It was barely a whisper, and all she could get out before the tears spilled out onto her face.

"Sweetheart." Long fingers gently wiped away the fallen tears, then grasped the smaller hand and kissed the knuckles tenderly. "I love you so much."

Robin swallowed again, finally regaining her composure, then shifted slightly and reached for her bag lying nearby on the beach blanket. After a brief moment, she returned to her previous position and once again faced Jess, her voice soft, yet sincere. "I love you, Jess, very much." She held the older woman's left hand and slowly and deliberately slid a diamond cluster ring onto her finger, then voiced her own considerable appeal. "I want to be with you forever. I commit my mind, my heart, my body, and my soul to you, to take care of you, to cherish you, and to love you as long as we live, and beyond." Green eyes locked fervently onto blue. "If you'll let me."

Jess heard herself gasp. She truly hadn't expected a ring from Robin in return, and the fact that it now rested upon her finger was something she was still trying to comprehend. Suddenly, tears of her own welled up in her eyes, then fell onto her cheeks. "Yes." She gathered Robin tightly in her arms as they clung to each other in an embrace that seemed as though they couldn't get close enough. "Yes, sweetheart."

After a long while, Robin pulled back and rested her forehead against the older woman's. "I knew it all along."

"Knew what?"

The smaller woman closed her eyes, taking in the entirety of the moment. "That we're meant to be together." She smiled, then shifted herself back around to face the setting sun, grasping Jess's hands in the process and replacing them around her waist. "It's setting now. Let's watch."

For her part, Jess simply held Robin close to her, again resting her chin on the younger woman's shoulder. The sun slowly dipped below the horizon, creating a myriad of dazzling colors in the western sky. *We're meant to be together. No one's ever going to keep us apart.* Finally, once the sun had all but disappeared, and the sky had darkened its hue, Jess laid gently back against the beach blanket, bringing Robin alongside her.

It was absolutely magical and something more intense than either of them could ever have imagined. They belonged, not just together, but also to each other, joined and bound in every imaginable way. They laid side by side, staring silently into each other's eyes, carrying on a complete conversation entirely without words. Neither knew how long they stayed that way, but dusk finally settled upon them as the twilight slowly turned into the darkness of night. Wary of breaking the spell, they quietly gathered up their beach and picnic items and walked directly to the car, loading it silently and heading back in the direction from which they had come. If anyone had been watching, that person would have no doubt seen that neither woman lost physical contact with the other during the entire length of the two-hour drive home.

Upon arriving at the house, the intensity of the evening hadn't diminished or waned, but instead increased in strength, as the significance of their mutual commitment flooded their senses and filled their hearts. The fact of the matter was, they couldn't get close enough to each other, and any separation, no matter how brief, was almost painful in wake of the perceived loss. They spent the remainder of that evening whispering quiet words of love to each other and declaring once again their undying and unyielding commitment. Robin, at one time, likened the sensation to their merging together, and for all intents and purposes, that's exactly what it was.

It was very welcome, very intense, and very good.

****

The soft light from several candles strategically spaced throughout the living room, along with the gentle flickering flames of the fire in the fireplace, cast an ethereal glow upon the two figures as they lay entwined on the plush sofa. Soft jazz music emanated from the stereo in the far corner of the room, providing a relaxing ambiance to bring to a close their magical, and yes, mystical weekend. It was almost difficult to imagine that the weekend had ended the way it did, considering what had come perilously close to happening just days before.

Jess kissed Robin's blonde hair and held her close. "How are you?"

"Good." A petite finger drew tiny circles on Jess's cotton shirt sleeve, then trailed down and lingered on the soft fabric covering her stomach. "I don't want this weekend to end."

The older woman smiled. "Me either." She looked directly into green eyes. "But we do need to talk about some things."

Robin cast her eyes downward. "I know."

Jess really didn't want to spoil the mood, but they'd been avoiding the subject all weekend long, and understandably so considering their deepening relationship, but the matter simply couldn't wait any longer. The fact was, they now had to focus their minds on reality and deal with the issues that confronted them. While they had been at the beach, Robin's father had called and left a message on their answering machine indicating that he'd be in town Monday evening and asking to see Robin. Jess sighed inwardly, then cautiously broached the topic. "Have you decided if you're going to see your father?"

It took a moment for Robin to respond, her emotions warring between hurt and anger at his betrayal. Finally, she lifted herself up on one arm and brought her free hand up to stroke Jess's cheek. "Yes. I will see him, but he'll have to come here if he has anything to say to me." Her jaw clenched reflexively, the fine muscles twitching slightly. "I can't forgive him. He hurt you, and by hurting you, he also hurt me."

"I'm sorry." Blue eyes closed in regret, sensing the pain Robin felt.

She's not responsible. The smaller woman's voice was very soft and very gentle. "You know, you always do that." She brushed a finger across Jess's lips. "You always take the blame upon yourself."

"I just don't like to see you hurting." It was the absolute truth, but there was also something else about the situation that seemed to cut very deep. Jess thought about that for a long moment, then suddenly it became clear. What Robin was feeling, and what Jess knew was causing the deepest pain, was the betrayal, something the older woman was intimately familiar with. "I know what it's like to hurt like that, and I wish I could take the pain away, but I can't."

The blonde head merely nodded. "What my father did to you is unacceptable to me, and I'm going to tell him that. If he follows through with his threats, I'll make it clear to him that I will never, ever see him again."

The taller woman let out a heavy sigh. "I don't want to come between you and your family." That fact bothered her more than she let on.

"Jess, no matter what happens, you're my family now." A small thumb lightly brushed across the ring she'd placed on Jess's finger. "He'll have to accept that."

Long arms gathered Robin to her and settled the smaller body at eye level. "You are very brave, yourself, do you know that?" Jess watched the play of flickering light dance across Robin's fair features.

131

"You'd risk your family for me."

"Because I love you." Robin leaned in and placed a soft kiss on Jess's lips. "Because we're meant to be together." She gave Jess another loving kiss. "Because you're my family now." Her lips met those in front of her own, bestowing another more lingering kiss, before settling her head back against the plush sofa cushion.

"Sweetheart..." Jess hesitated, resting her gaze on the ring on Robin's finger. "There's something else we need to talk about." She wasn't sure how to bring up the subject, and she wasn't quite sure how it would be received. "When we talk with Harry, we're going to have to see how he wants to handle the situation."

Perplexed green eyes followed Jess's gaze. "What do you mean?"

"Because of the uncertainty with respect to your father's intentions, and the delicate nature of the situation, I think it's very likely that Harry will want to keep this entire matter confidential." Jess never took her eyes from the ring. "Do you understand what I'm saying?"

Entire matter. Robin considered that phrase. *Confidential.* Sea-green eyes fluttered closed in understanding. In fact, she understood all too well what Jess was saying. "We can't wear them."

It was a cruel irony, Jess realized, for them both to have taken such a step toward deepening their relationship only to have that step secreted away by perpetuating the existing deception. It was also not lost on Jess that it was extremely unfair of her to have given Robin the ring in the first place, only to realize later that it would be ill-advised to wear it. *Damn it, Jess. You screwed up.* Her remorse now became very intense. "I apologize to you, Robin. I didn't think this through. It was unfair of me." Suddenly, her eyes welled up. "I wanted so much to show you that I was committed to you, that I knew you were right that we're meant to be together. I didn't...." She couldn't finish her sentence.

"Honey, shhh. I understand." Robin hugged Jess close to her. "It means so much to me to know that you love me enough to make that commitment." A petite finger wiped a bit of moisture from the older woman's eye. "You know that I feel the same way about you. You know that, right?"

"Yes." The dark head nodded solemnly. "I know."

"That's all that matters then."

Jess was quiet for a moment, then continued. "Um....Robin, there's something else." *Might as well get it all out in the open.* "My guess is that Harry will take some action against me for putting the firm in this situation."

The smaller woman blinked, processing that information, then spoke very slowly and very somberly. "Will you have to resign?"

"I don't know. I might be able to convince Harry that I should take a leave of absence until this matter is resolved, or at least until we know what your father intends to do."

Robin closed her eyes, her own remorse beginning to take hold. "I feel like I'm hurting you." The blonde head fell forward on to Jess's shoulder. "I feel like I brought this on."

A long finger reached beneath the younger woman's chin, tilting it upward. "Robin, honey, listen to me. We both want to be together. We both assume certain risks so that we can do that." Jess knew it was a long-shot, but nevertheless, she tried to ease Robin's mind with the best possible outcome. "It could still work out okay. I've known Harry for a long time. He's a fair man."

Robin nodded, understanding exactly what Jess was trying to do, then glanced at the ring on her finger for a long moment. "It's all right if we wear them at home, right?"

That brought a gentle smile. "Yes, sweetheart. It's all right if we wear them at home."

The music in the background served to soothe and comfort them, allowing the anxiety of the moment to drift away on the harmonic notes of the light jazz melody. Robin nestled her body further between the sofa cushions and her larger companion, tucking her head underneath the strong jaw. She felt the loving touch of the long, slender fingers as they brushed the side of her face and combed through her short, blonde hair. And all at once, everything seemed to be all right. They were together, and they had each other. Whatever was yet to happen, that fact would forever remain true.

"I have a question for you." The low voice finally spoke again, a lighter quality coming through in its tone. "I was just curious about something."

Pale eyebrows furrowed slightly. "Okay. What?"

"At the beach, you had the ring with you. Did you always carry it wherever you went?"

"Um..." A small smile twitched at the corner of Robin's mouth. "I have a confession to make about that."

A broad grin appeared. "Spill it, kiddo."

"Well, it's like this. When I suggested that we go watch the sunset, I was kind of thinking that, if the timing was right, I'd give it to you then. That's why I brought it with me."

"I see."

"Yes." Robin shift herself up even with Jess, her green eyes now twinkling. "But somebody, who shall remain nameless but who is also very hopeless, beat me to it."

"Is that so?" The older woman placed a tender kiss on Robin's sweet lips.

"Yes. That means, of course, that you have effectively earned enough points to make up for the ones I, sadly, had to deduct from you because of your frisky self waking me up."

Jess was thoroughly enchanted. "I thought I assured you, Robin, that you most definitely have not seen frisky."

The smaller woman gave Jess a very sly wink, then whispered into a conveniently placed ear. "Neither have you."

That caught Jess's attention. *Oh boy.* The tables had effectively been turned. "Why Robin! You...." She was quickly silenced by a petite hand covering her mouth.

"Shhh." There was an unmistakable gleam in Robin's eyes. "You talk too much." She then slowly and very deliberately bestowed dozens of gentle and loving kisses over every inch of the older woman's beautiful face.

Jess, as usual, melted in the wake of the soft contact. It was amazing. It was as if Robin knew her better than she knew herself, and knew exactly what she needed in advance of the turmoil that lay ahead.

Finally, the blonde woman looked up and gazed into magnificent blue eyes, a question now presenting itself in her mind, but curiously difficult to voice. She wrestled with herself in an attempt to find the right phrasing for what she wanted to ask, then leaned in closer and softly whispered her gentle plea. "Jess, will you let me take care of your heart forever?"

Cerulean eyes fixed on sea-green as Jess considered the question. Hadn't they made their commitments clear? Then, what was it Robin was really asking? The older woman thought some more about that, until finally it registered with an absolute and complete certainty. Robin's question was a reaffirmation. It was declaration by Robin of her willingness to endure whatever lay ahead, and asking Jess in return to once again declare her commitment to do the same. Jess's answer was simple, but held more meaning than its simplicity revealed. "Yes." She brought her left hand up and stroked Robin's face, then grasped a smaller hand and entwined their fingers together, both rings now prominently displayed in front of each of them. "Yes." Jess repeated the commitment and gave Robin a heartfelt kiss, followed by several more, and several more after that, to reinforce her solemn vow.

Chapter 6

In the dim shadow of the dawn's first light, Jess glanced at the digital clock on the nightstand and noted the time. Just past 6:00. She had been awake for the past several hours thinking about the confrontations the day was certain to bring. Robin was still sleeping, and in an effort to get herself up without disturbing her companion's slumbering form, Jess slowly and carefully extracted her tall frame from the waveless waterbed. She ventured out into the living room and stood over by the sliding glass doors, staring out at the tiny ripples in the heated swimming pool. As she let her mind wander, the familiar echo of her internal voice became louder, until it was finally too strong to ignore.

You must be very proud of yourself.

'*What the...?*' The alternate internal voice was extraordinarily annoyed. '*Why are you back again?*'

Must we resort to the same old tired routine? Point of fact, I wouldn't be here if something wasn't bothering you. So, now that we've established that, let cut the crap and proceed, shall we?

'*I'm not in the mood.*' The alternate internal voice sighed wearily. '*Just go away.*'

Sorry. No can do. Come on, now. Spill it. What seems to be the problem this chipper morning?

As usual, the alternate internal voice grew belligerent. '*Listen, I'm not into trick questions. You know full well what the problem is. Therefore, as you very eloquently put it, let's cut the crap.*'

My, we are a bit testy, aren't we? Fine. Then, let's begin. It seems there are several things on your mind, one of which involves that very special ring on your finger. Am I correct?

The alternate internal voice hesitated for a split second. *'Yeah, and what of it?'*

Well, number one, you're going to have to take it off, and number two, you seem to have a bit of a doubt about the whole thing.

'Listen buddy, as to number one, Robin and I have discussed it, and we've determined that taking the rings off outside of home is the prudent thing to do' The alternate internal voice attempted a convincing argument. *'And as to number two, your assumption is absolutely and totally incorrect.'*

Is that so?

'Absolutely, positively.' The alternate internal voice responded assuredly.

Wrong answer. Let's get to the heart of the matter, no pun intended. Isn't there just the tiniest bit of doubt in your mind that Robin's commitment to you, and your commitment to her, were more circumstance driven rather than truly sincere?

'What?' The alternate internal voice bordered between incredulous and extremely offended. *'I absolutely think no such thing.'*

Once again, you refuse to admit it. By the way, do you have a problem discerning the difference between illusion and reality?

'You're really starting to annoy me, buddy. I'm not psychotic.' All things considered, it was a questionable statement. *Is there a point to this conversation?'*

Only that you and Robin should probably have a little talk and make sure you're both clear as to each other's motivations. Surely, you wouldn't want her or her father to infer that the ring that is so prominently displayed on her finger is the result of his insinuations to you regarding your lack of commitment. And again, surely you would want to know beyond any doubt that Robin's ring to you is given sincerely and is not merely an 'in your face' move meant to prove something to her parents.

The alternate internal voice, refusing to see the obvious, blew off the reasoning. *'For your information, not that I have to explain anything to you, I'm sincere and she's sincere. End of story.'*

Fine. Have it your way. Just don't come whining to me later on when the questions start surfacing in ways you least expected.

'Like that would happen.' The alternate internal voice sniped, then became even more sarcastic. *'Can we move on and finish up this little tete-a-tete sometime before I start collecting Social Security?'*

If you insist. What's your game plan for today?

'Simple. Robin and I talk with Harry. I convince him that the firm isn't in jeopardy. Then, I either continue on as before, or take a small leave of absence until we know what her father intends to do.'

Is that all?

An exasperated sigh. 'What do you mean, is that all? Isn't that enough?'

Perhaps. What if he asks you to resign?

'He won't.' The alternative internal voice treaded perilously close to denying the severity of the situation.

You seem quite confident about that. If he doesn't, Gordon or the Management Committee might do so.

The alternate internal voice continued, now in full-blown denial. 'They won't, and besides, I'll worry about that later. Right now, we're just dealing with today.'

What about Robin's father?

'What about him?' The alternative internal voice innocently asked.

Don't play coy. Do you plan on being present when he shows up at your house?

'I don't know. Robin and I haven't discussed that.'

Don't you think you should discuss it? After all, you don't know what his reaction will be. If you're present, it may be wind up being a free for all. Then again, if you leave them to their privacy, you can't keep your eye on things to make sure they don't get out of hand.

'I'll defer to what Robin wants.' It was a simplistic and noncommittal response.

Don't be foolish. Decide together what is the best thing to do. She'll need your support, not your placating her.

You think you know everything, don't you? You think you have all the answers. You think that I'm incapable of making any correct decisions on this matter, and that I need you, the all knowing voice of whatever, to tell me even when to breathe.'

Apparently so.

'I don't need this.' The alternate internal voice had now had quite enough. 'I have to go out there and put my job on the line, then I have to worry about Robin's talk with her father, and on top of it all, I have to wonder whether it's all sincere or contrived.'

So, you finally admit the problem. It all comes down to your doubts. Isn't this exactly where we came in? You'll never be one hundred percent sure about both of your motivations until you deal with it head on.

The alternate internal voice would hear none of it. 'I will never insult Robin by questioning her sincerity. Never.'

All right. Be that way. Stick your head in the sand and maybe it will all just magically go away.

'Damn right.' The alternate internal voice was once again in full sarcastic mode. *'Now, why don't you make like a tree and leave. Or, make like the wind and blow. Pick one.'*

Funny. It seems, though, that you once again refuse to deal with the obvious. Denial does not suit you. Just remember one thing.

'And what would that be?' The alternate internal voice waited with false curiosity.

You've got a lot more to lose than just your job, and the sooner you come to realize that, the better off you'll be.

Ignoring the implicit warning, the alternate internal voice effectively shut down the conversation. *'I think I'm finished, here.'*

Exactly.

****

The sun was now in full morning brightness, its rays streaking through the sliding glass doors and casting yellow-white hues upon the tiled floor. Jess continued her gaze at the pool, watching nearly mesmerized as the automatic pool sweeper performed its daily ritual, the tail occasionally flinging itself wildly above the water's surface. As a stream of water squirted haphazardly across the shallow end, the motorized sweeper dipped far below the now shimmering ripples, temporarily out of sight.

Small arms surrounded the taller woman from behind, the petite body pressing close against her back. Jess closed her eyes and enjoyed the warming sensation. *This is the only thing I ever want.*

"Been up long?" A voice still rough with sleep softly murmured between rigid shoulder blades.

"A little while." Came the preoccupied reply.

Robin stepped around Jess's larger frame and peered up into worried blue eyes. "Thinking about today?"

Jess looked at Robin for a moment, then refocused her attention back upon the pool waters. "Yeah. We need to talk about something."

Pale eyebrows knit together. "Okay."

"Um...." Jess grasped Robin's hand and led them over to the plush sofa, sitting them both down. "Tonight, when you talk with your father, I want you to know that I can stay away or be here, whatever is the best thing. I don't want to be in your way if you want to have a private conversation, and yet, I don't want to leave you alone if you'd rather

I'd be here."

Robin swallowed, considering all the options. "To be honest, I've been thinking about that, too. This is your house, and I don't want to tell you to go someplace else."

The older woman sensed something more. "But...."

"But, I really think I need to speak with him alone. I want him to know how I feel, and I don't want him to have the impression that what I say is somehow...."

"Influenced by me." Jess finished for her.

"Yeah." An apologetic smile. "What do you think?"

"I agree." The dark head nodded. "I think that's the best way to handle it. I'll give you as much time as you need."

Robin ran her fingers through her short blonde hair in slight frustration. "I just feel bad that you have to leave your own house while I talk with him."

"Sweetheart, this is your house, too." Blue eyes stared pensively at the darkened fireplace. "This is what we'll do. Tonight, I'll go and pick us up something to eat for dinner, and then I'll wait until I see his rental car gone before I come back inside. Will that be okay?"

"I think so." The blonde head bowed slightly. "Um...I don't want you to be gone too long, though. I mean, I don't think I'm up to arguing with him over and over again."

What exactly is she worried about? Jess mulled that statement around in her mind until it finally made sense. What if her father refuses to leave until he convinces her he's right? *You're such an idiot, Jess.* "Okay. What about this? I'll give you an hour with him. I'll knock on the door, and if you need more time, don't open it. If you're ready to end your conversation, open the door and that'll be his cue to leave." She looked directly at Robin to gauge her reaction. "Will that work?"

That could work. "Yeah." A small, yet warm smile. "Thank you."

"You bet, kiddo. Everything's going to be fine, so don't worry." Jess pressed her forehead lightly against Robin's. "You got that?"

That brought an even wider smile and a small chuckle. "Yes, I got it." Then another thought came to Robin, and she looked at Jess out of the corner of her eye. "Um...Jess. What exactly did you have in mind for dinner tonight?"

"I don't know." It was a perfectly innocent answer.

Right. Green eyes narrowed suspiciously. "Yes, you do. Just spill it."

The older woman knew she'd been caught. "Okay, okay. Chinese."

I knew it. Robin smiled and shook her head in subtle amazement. "Jess, just make sure you get something else, too, besides 'you know what.'"

Jess stood up and gave her a wounded look. "You have absolutely no faith in me." She entered the kitchen and poured herself a cup of coffee.

"Sure I do." Robin followed along. "I have total faith that you're going to get a certain Chinese dish which we know you always get." She retrieved the half and half and Florida orange juice from the refrigerator.

"For your information, Robin, I do like other Chinese food, too." Jess's expression was totally serious.

"Right, Jess." The younger woman reached over and patted Jess's arm. "You like other Chinese food, too." A subtle eye roll. "Get whatever 'other Chinese food' you want, then."

"Fine, I will."

A knowing smile was Robin's only response. *I could bet money on this.*

****

Robin sat in the corner chair in Harry Roberts' office, drumming her fingers impatiently upon the upholstered arm. She stopped briefly, glanced over at Jess in the next chair, then resumed her nervous finger tapping as they waited for the litigation department chairman to return. Without much additional delay, Harry finally entered his office, followed closely by his secretary, Betty. She dutifully placed a cup of fresh coffee on his desk and waited for further instructions. Harry took a moment to peruse some paperwork, than handed it to her with directions for distribution. Now that this pressing matter was adequately taken care of, he stepped behind his desk and settled himself into his navy blue leather chair, giving Betty a last minute instruction to close his door and hold all his calls.

Harry took a sip of his coffee, then looked across the desk at Robin and Jess. "Sorry for the delay. Now, what can I do for you both?"

Jess flexed her hands slowly, then decided to get straight to the point. "A situation has come up which we need to discuss with you." That sounded innocuous enough.

"A problem with a case?" Harry shifted and got comfortable in his chair.

"No." The junior partner continued. "It's a situation involving

Robin and myself." It was still a fairly innocuous sounding statement.

"All right." The head of litigation took another sip of his coffee. "What's up?"

Here goes. Jess blew out a breath. "Robin and I have developed a...personal relationship that we feel has the potential of impacting the firm."

That drew a raised eyebrow from Harry. "Well, I know that you're both sharing a house, and I'm not surprised that in living and working together, you've become good friends."

Robin spoke for the first time. "No, Harry. It's more than that."

"More?" He took his half-empty coffee cup and deliberately placed off to the side, then focused his gaze squarely on Jess. "Why don't you tell me exactly what's going on?"

Jess paused slightly, then proceeded. "Over the course of our working together, Robin and I have become close." She glanced over and gave Robin a warm smile. "After a while, we decided that we wanted a more personal relationship." It was extremely difficult, Jess now realized, to put the nature of their relationship in terminology suitable for the business environment. "We've decided that we want to be with each other for the rest of our lives."

Harry leaned forward in his chair, his eyes very wide and his mouth slightly open. "Are you saying what I think you're saying?"

"Yes." The young associate spoke again. "Jess and I are together."

There was a very long silence as Harry stared at both attorneys, completely stunned. Not only was he old school in his law practice, but he was old school in other matters, as well. He cleared his throat uncomfortably, then spoke again. "I see."

"Now, Harry." The junior partner attempted to rescue the discussion. "We've been completely professional in all our business dealings. We've kept this very quiet in the office."

His face grim, Harry asked the next question. "You're aware of the firm's policy on personal relationships between supervisory personnel and subordinates, are you not?"

Jess held her chin up. "I am."

He stared at his hands, deep in thought, and without looking up, continued. "How long has this...relationship been going on?"

At this point, Robin saw no need not to be completely honest about the situation. "Almost since the beginning."

The head of the litigation department closed his eyes and brought his hand to his forehead, rubbing the bridge of his nose in an effort to absorb what he was hearing. "You've been involved together for months, and now you've suddenly decided to disclose this information. Why?"

The junior partner started to explain. "Because, Harry...."

Robin interrupted. "Jess, let me." Her eyes captured azure, pleading to allow her be the one to answer the question. Upon seeing no resistance, she began. "Last week, I told my parents about my relationship with Jess. It didn't go well with them." That, indeed, was an understatement. "I didn't know it at the time, but last Friday my father flew down here and spoke directly with Jess."

The junior partner jumped back in. "Harry, let me tell you exactly what happened. Robin's father paid me a visit last Friday and wanted me to end my relationship with his daughter. I wasn't going to do that, for reasons I'm not going to discuss, and I told him so. In response, he insisted that if I refused to end our relationship, he would inform you and Gordon about this matter himself."

Harry gazed at Jess pensively. "So, let me see if I understand this. You kept your relationship concealed, and you never would have disclosed it to the firm but for the fact that Robin's father threatened to reveal it. Do I have that correct?"

Jess flinched at the way he put it, but his statement was entirely accurate. "Yes." She softly confirmed. "That is correct."

At this admission, Harry sat back in his chair, not hiding his disappointment. "All right. The first thing that's going to happen is that I'm reassigning you, Robin. Clay Taylor needs some associate assistance on several of his cases. Go meet with him sometime this morning and find out what he needs. I'll let him know you'll be helping him."

"Okay." The young associate responded quietly, then gave Jess a questioning look.

Harry caught the glances passing between the two attorneys. "Am I missing something?"

Jess squared her shoulders. "There's more."

"More?" The look of disbelief on Harry's face would have been comical if it wasn't so serious.

Robin closed her eyes, then proceeded once again. "Yes. During the past year, I've had some upsetting things happen, and I didn't deal with them very well. I lost someone very close to me. I've started seeing a psychologist to try to deal better with what happened." She looked from Harry to Jess. "My father believes that because of these things, I'm 'emotionally fragile,' as he put it, and that Jess has somehow...taken advantage of my situation." She winced as she said the last part.

At this point, the head of the litigation department simply stared at Jess across his desk, entirely dumbstruck, not saying a word, not moving, and not begging for a further explanation.

Jess swallowed hard, then broke the uncomfortable silence. "Harry, I haven't done the things Robin's father thinks I have. I would never do that. Nevertheless, when he was here on Friday, in addition to stating that he would reveal our relationship to you and Gordon, he also stated that he would..." She took a deep breath, then held her chin up. "File a complaint with the State Bar Association against me and the firm for improper conduct if I didn't end my relationship with Robin." *Damn it. This is hard.*

Harry edged forward in his chair again, his jaw clenched visibly. "Exactly what improper conduct would he allege?"

"He believes that Robin is emotionally vulnerable. Since I prepare Robin's performance evaluations, he believes that she could perceive that her job is tied to continuing our relationship...in a way that is satisfactory to me, personally." *God, I can't even say the words.*

The young associate couldn't let that statement stand as implied . "Harry, it's not true. I never believed that. Never."

He held up his hand in front of him, his face expressionless. "Are both of you telling me that, Robin, your father intends to file a complaint with the State Bar Association implicating this law firm and Jess, who is one of our partners, in allegations of improper conduct, the nature of which is sexual harassment?"

The junior partner closed her eyes, the distaste in her mouth now threatening to overwhelm her. Nevertheless, she stated her answer calmly and succinctly. "Yes."

If the atmosphere inside the office was tense before, it was now strained beyond all measure. Harry hung his head and rested his forehead on the tips of his fingers for several moments, again not uttering a word.

Robin, realizing that Jess was in jeopardy, sought to explain further. "Harry, none of what my father thinks is true. Jess has never, even once, acted improperly toward me." Despite her efforts, the young associate saw that the situation was, at best, grave. "I've agreed to meet with my father tonight, and I'm going to make it clear to him that I won't end my relationship with Jess. In light of that fact, I'm also going find out from him whether he still intends to follow through with his threat to file a complaint with the Bar Association."

Harry folded his hands on top of the desk in front of him and spoke again, clearly displeased. "All right. Here's what's going to happen. I'm going to discuss this matter with Gordon this morning and then with the full Management Committee. It's likely that the firm will hire outside counsel to represent us. Robin, regardless of what your father does or does not do, either someone from the Management Committee or our outside counsel will need to contact him regarding his intentions as it relates to this law firm." He emphasized the last several words. "For now, Robin, I want you to go meet with Clay Taylor and see what he needs by way of assistance. Furthermore, this entire matter is to remain strictly confidential, regardless of the ultimate outcome. Is that clear?"

Robin mulled that statement in her mind, not at all liking the implication. Having the entire matter remain confidential was one thing, but having it remain confidential indefinitely was most certainly a problem. Still, now was not the time to debate that issue. "I understand."

"Good. Now, Robin, if you'll excuse us, Jess and I have some partnership matters to attend to." The head of the litigation department gave them both a look that indicated there would be no argument.

This can't be good. Seeing a nod from Jess, the young associate rose and left the office, closing the door quietly behind her.

Once the door was safely shut, Harry looked pointedly at Jess. "What I want to know is why you didn't come to me with this when it first started. Haven't I always been supportive of you, given you whatever help you needed? Hell, I even stuck my neck out for you and pushed through your partnership well in advance of the normal track. I sat right there in your office not too long ago and reminded you of the perils of becoming too close to someone whose performance you evaluate. So, tell me, Jess, how could this have happened?"

His words, although quite understandable, stung. And the truth was, he was absolutely correct. "You've always been supportive, Harry, and I have greatly appreciated that, but to answer your question, all I can say is that there were many complications. I wasn't sure that my relationship with Robin would last very long, for reasons that I don't want to get into, and I saw no need to create a problem if one didn't exist." A slight pause ensued, mercifully disrupted by the faint whistle of the mid-morning freight train passing below. "I also wanted to continue working with Robin. I knew that you'd have to reassign her if you knew about our relationship. The fact is, and we both know it, I can be somewhat difficult at times to get along with. Robin does an excellent job, and for some reason, we seem to work very well together. I wanted that to continue. The bottom line, though, is that it was selfish of me to do that, and I realize it now. I put my own interests ahead of the interests of this firm, and for that, I'm very sorry." Jess bowed her head and stared at her hands. "I was also...worried about what you might think of me if you knew about the true nature of my relationship with Robin. I was uneasy about that, and Robin and I weren't ready to disclose it to anyone."

The disappointment slowly left Harry's face, replaced now with genuine sadness. "Jess, I would have hoped that you would have been able to talk to me. I was there for you when all that mess with James happened, wasn't I? I won't deny that I'm surprised to learn of your relationship with Robin, and I certainly won't say that I understand it. I absolutely would never have guessed in a million years that either one of you were...." He left the thought unfinished. "The fact is, now we have a situation that is a real danger to both this law firm and you. If you had just come to me earlier, even when I sat in your office and discussed keeping a line between your professional and personal relationships, we could have reassigned Robin. If we'd done that, her father would have absolutely nothing to base his allegations on. You would no longer be her supervisor, and therefore, she couldn't possibly perceive that her job might be tied to keeping your relationship satisfactory to you, personally."

Jess couldn't deny his logic. Looking back on it, it all seems so mishandled now, but at the time, her thinking on the matter appeared perfectly reasonable, or so she led herself to believe. *What a difference perspective makes.* "You're right, Harry. I made a serious mistake. I'll accept whatever action you decide to take against me, but I want to say that Robin has done nothing wrong here, and I'd ask that she not be penalized because of my poor judgment."

Harry nodded, considering the request. "Okay. I agree, Robin's not the responsible party here, and I foresee no formal action being taken against her in connection with this matter. My best guess, however, is that the Management Committee will want to speak with both you and Robin separately, probably this week, and then make its final decision. I'm sure you understand the gravity of this situation, as it stands. Most likely, if Robin's father follows through with filing a complaint with the State Bar, our first duty will be to protect the firm. Unfortunately, in that case, the Management Committee will most certainly ask that you sever your partnership here."

Not a surprise. "I understand."

"If Robin's father chooses not to file a complaint, the Management Committee may consider the risk you took to be unacceptable to this firm's well being, and then still ask that you sever your partnership." The litigation department chairman stroked his chin thoughtfully. "Then again, it may opt to take a more lenient approach. Honestly, right now, I just don't know."

Jess decided to try her best shot at brokering a deal. "I'd like to propose an offer to the Management Committee. I'll be willing to take a leave of absence until this matter is resolved or until the Management Committee makes its final decision. If they later decide to ask that I sever my partnership, I'll do so retroactively as of today. If they take a more lenient action, I'll accept whatever that is, and then return to work after fulfilling such requirements."

The older attorney sighed heavily, then nodded. "All right. I'll take your offer to them. For now, prepare for me a list of all your cases and their status so that I can redistribute them for supervision among the other litigation partners. I'll ask that you begin your leave of absence immediately thereafter. In addition, I'd like to see both you and Robin in my office first thing tomorrow morning to discuss her meeting with her father, and also to discuss any further requests of the Management Committee."

"I understand." The junior partner stood up from her chair and glanced over at Harry, her expression one of true remorse. "For what it's worth, Harry, I am very sorry."

Harry merely nodded as Jess left his office, then sank slowly back into his chair as the full weight of the matter settled upon him. He picked up the phone and dialed Gordon McDaniel, requesting an urgent meeting with him. Under the watchful eye of his secretary, he slipped out of his office and gloomily made his way in the direction of the Managing Partner's office. *What a fine way to start out a Monday morning.*

Indeed.

****

Paul sauntered down the hallway and turned into the break room, the aroma of freshly brewed coffee capturing his attention and leading him directly to the coffee of the day. *Irish Crème.* He poured himself a cup, then poked his head inside the refrigerator, hunting for some half and half. Not locating any, he was mentally preoccupied as Angie and Betty made their way toward the coffeemaker, their low-key conversation now attracting his attention now far more than his flavored coffee.

"You should have seen it, Angie. They were all in his office with the door closed for a really long time. Then suddenly, Robin left alone, and she didn't look very happy. Both of our bosses stayed in there a little while longer, before your boss finally left. She was certainly looking grim, as well."

"Wow." Angie was definitely enjoying the gossip. "What do you think that was all about?"

Betty grabbed a cup of the decaffeinated blend and sat down at one of the tables. "I don't really know, except that my boss suddenly announced that he had a meeting with Mr. McDaniel, and that he would be tied up with the Management Committee all afternoon."

Paul, in an attempt to appear disinterested, added powdered creamer to his coffee and continued to listen to the hushed voices.

"So, that explains it." Angie joined her friend at the table and considered all of the information. "My boss told me that she had some administrative work to finish this morning, and then she'd be taking an indefinite leave of absence."

Betty's eyes grew wide. "Really? So, what do you think happened?"

"Well...." Angie leaned in conspiratorially, putting the events of the last several days together. "Figure it out. Robin's father came to see my boss last Friday, and right after that, she left for the day and told me to cancel her afternoon appointment." The secretary took a sip of her coffee. "Then, today she and Robin met with your boss, and suddenly, now he's having meetings with Mr. McDaniel and the Management Committee, and my boss is taking a leave of absence."

"Yeah, but what would be serious enough for all that?"

Paul's ears perked up, and he leaned in a bit closer, but otherwise was silent.

"Oh come on, Betty. Like I told you before, there's definitely a little trouble in paradise. I'm guessing that Robin's father made some kind of demand on either my boss or the firm, or maybe even both."

Betty refilled her coffee cup. "Ooooh, I'd love to know what that was."

"Yeah, me too." Angie knit her brows together in thought. "You know, if there's some sort of relationship going on between them, and I think there is, my boss is in the position of supervising a subordinate with whom she's somehow involved." The secretary smiled, very proud of her deductive reasoning. "That's it, Betty. Don't you see? We've got a little favoritism at play."

"Yeah, but how does that involve Robin's father?"

"Yeah, you're right." Angie looked up pensively. "I haven't figured that part out yet. But whatever it is, it's really big."

Having heard enough of the conversation to get the general idea,

Paul left the break room and rounded the corner, heading straight for Robin's office. From his perspective, she'd definitely gotten herself into something that she wasn't prepared to handle. He stopped in front of the closed door, then knocked.

Robin immediately perked up. *Jess.* "Come in." She watched as the door opened and Paul poked his head inside her office. With an inaudible sigh, she picked up her pen in order to appear busy and waved him in. "Paul, what's up?"

"Can I talk with you for a moment?"

Now what? The young associate had been on pins and needles waiting for Jess and really didn't want to spend her time chitchatting with Paul. *Let's get this over with.* "Sure, come in." She watched him close the door and settle into the chair opposite her desk. "Do you need some help with something?"

"Uh...no. Actually, I thought I should mention something to you, as a friend. There's apparently some talk going on among the staff about Jessica Harrison and you. It sounds serious." It was surprisingly difficult to discuss this matter in a way that didn't appear gossip oriented, which in fact it was.

Robin's eyes grew wide, and she nervously started to twirl her pen. *How much does he know?* Harry's words of admonishment about keeping the matter confidential came rushing back to her. "I really can't discuss anything with you, Paul."

The senior associate leaned forward in his chair. "Listen, Robin, whatever's going on, if you need someone to talk to, I want you to know that I'll be happy to help in any way that I can. I've been with the firm a while now, and I know how things operate around here."

Is he serious? More like providing a sympathetic ear to catch me on the rebound. In light of everything that was going on, his offer seemed more like an absurd joke. "As I said, I can't really discuss anything with you. I'm sorry."

"All right." Paul stood up. "For what it's worth, and you don't have to say anything, just listen. Becoming involved in any way with Jessica is a definite career killer. You can't possibly win. She'll either cut you down professionally, or if she's taken down, she'll take you down with her." He stepped over to the door and rested his hand on the doorknob. "It's sounds as though she's into something big, and things may not go well for her. You'd do well to be very careful." With that rather ominous thought, he left the office, closing the door behind him.

A dull, constant headache pounded at Robin's temples. She brought her fingers to either side of her head, slowly rubbing the areas in a futile effort to ease the tension. Predictably, it didn't work. Barely another minute passed before another short knock sounded at her door. *I'm so not in the mood for this. Maybe they'll just go away.* The knock sounded again, followed by a muffled, yet familiar voice from the other side. *It's Jess.* The associate's heart sped up. "Come in."

The door opened. "Hey." Dark eyebrows raised in a bit of uncertainty. "Bad time?"

"No." Anxious green eyes met blue. "It's okay."

"Good." The junior partner stepped inside the office and closed the door. "I wanted to let you know what's happening." She decided to put a positive spin on the morning's developments. "After you left Harry's office, I spoke with him about my taking a leave of absence, beginning today, until this matter is resolved. He has agreed to take the proposal to the Management Committee."

The same anxious green eyes studied Jess carefully. *There's more.* "What's the likelihood they'll consent to that?"

Damn. I'm too transparent. The older woman sighed. "Well, it really depends on what your father decides to do. If he goes forward and files the complaint with the State Bar Association, then the Management Committee will have no choice but to cut me loose. Keeping me on would be too much of a risk for the firm in light of the allegations. Then again, even if your father decides not to file the complaint, they could still cut me loose for jeopardizing the firm's well-being." Seeing Robin's grimace, Jess hastened to focus on the more positive news. "Robin, listen to me." She paused for emphasis. "Should your father decide to forego filing the complaint, the Management Committee could still just as easily determine that there was basically no harm, no foul. You'll already be working with someone else, and therefore, retaining my partnership would provide no substantive risk to the firm."

Robin's voice was very soft. "Do you really believe they would go for that?"

The junior partner didn't want to misrepresent the seriousness of what could happen, but worrying Robin was unnecessary, considering that nothing, as yet, was definite. "I honestly think there's a good chance of a favorable outcome." *Although there'd likely be a reprimand.* "They're going to want to talk with both you and me this week, and then before they make any concrete decision, either the Management Committee or the firm's counsel will probably want to speak with your father regarding his intentions."

The young associate closed her eyes, desperately wishing that her headache would simply disappear. "So, what you're saying, basically, is that my father holds your future in his hands."

149

Jess stepped over to Robin's chair and knelt down beside it. "No, that's not what I'm saying. It doesn't matter what your father does or doesn't do. I'm going to be okay, regardless. Harry's also assured me that there will be no repercussions against you. So you see, we're both going to be okay, here." Blue eyes fixed steadily on green, intent on conveying absolute confidence. "You got that?" A small, hesitant nod was the only response. "All right." The older woman stood up and walked back around to the front of the desk. "Now, I've just given Harry a list of my active cases and their status. As soon as he reassigns them, you can discuss with the supervising partners whether your continued assistance will be required. Otherwise, take your direction from either Harry or Clay Taylor. Are you okay with that?"

"Yes." There really wasn't much else to say.

Jess offered a small reassuring smile. "Don't worry. Everything's going to be fine. You go back to work now, and I'll see you at home later tonight." She stepped over toward the door. "So, I'll give you an hour with your father, and then I'll knock on the front door. Is that system still okay?"

As a matter of fact, Robin had just confirmed the time of her meeting with her father. "It's fine. He'll be at the house at seven."

"All right, kiddo." The junior partner winked, then turned the door handle. "I'll see you back at home." Without a backward glance, she closed the door behind her and headed directly toward the elevator lobby.

Jess punched the button and waited for the next elevator car to arrive. If only she really felt as positive as her previous words tried to convey. For that matter, if only she had handled everything differently right from the start. Then, too, if only she had acquiesced to Robin's father's demands and dealt with the consequences later on. If only this. If only that. She could beat herself up with second-guessing. The problem was, right from the very beginning, nothing was ever going to be easy. That was an absolute and inescapable fact. From the very first moment she saw Robin and noticed, however inappropriately, those beautiful sea-green eyes capturing her in their verdant gaze, nothing was ever going to be easy again. It was a truism she'd come to accept, and gladly so, but still, she could have handled things so much better from the outset. If only she had done that, then none of this entire mess would have occurred, and the pain they were now both experiencing wouldn't exist at all. If only. With a disgusted sigh, she boarded the now waiting elevator and watched as the doors slowly closed, and perhaps most fittingly so, closed with them her continued partnership with the firm.

If only. She certainly could beat herself up over that.

****

Robin paced the floor nervously, gauging the time on the clock as she awaited her father's arrival. She glanced out the large living room window and watched as a pair of headlights pulled into the driveway. *It's time.* She'd known all day long what she wanted to say to him, but now that he was actually here, she stood at the window nearly frozen in place. Internally, her mind raced from one emotion to the other, warring between anger and sadness, and then back again. In truth, she was both, and everything in between. As the doorbell rang, she straightened her shoulders and calmly walked over to let her father inside.

"Hi, Robin." Thomas Wilson took in his daughter's appearance. "You're looking well."

That's a matter of opinion. Her voice was detached and carried no emotion. "Come in." She motioned him inside, then led him into the living room. "Have a seat."

Her father settled into the chair opposite the plush sofa and glanced around the room curiously. "Is...um...are we alone?"

"Jess is out right now." *I'm not telling him when she's coming back.*

He nodded. "So, tell me, how are you doing, honey?"

All things considered, Robin didn't know whether to laugh or cry at his absurdly paternal demeanor, one which seemed completely oblivious to the turmoil he'd so recently caused. "I've been better." Absolutely in no mood for idle chit-chat, she sat down on the sofa and decided to get right to the point. "So, what was it you wanted to see me about?"

Her father steepled his fingers together, placing them to his chin for a brief moment, then responded. "You've no doubt heard about my conversation last week with Ms. Harrison."

Green eyes grew very cold. "I'd hardly call your threats and your ultimatum a conversation."

"Now, Robin, I only asked her to view the situation from another perspective. Things rarely are as they appear, and I pointed out to her the obvious appearance problems of her continued relationship with you. I only asked that she do the right thing for herself, for you, and for her law firm. That's all."

That's all? Now, Robin wasn't often prone to displays of anger, but she nearly lost her composure at his self-serving statement. "You didn't ask anything. You blackmailed her and you threatened her. And what's worse, you did this even though you knew I loved her."

Thomas leaned forward in his chair. He knew he'd have a hard sell with Robin, but he truly believed he could prevail if his daughter would just give him the chance to explain why he did what he did. "It's because I love you and because I'm aware of the pain you've been through during this past year that I felt the need to look out for you. I didn't want to see you emotionally devastated again."

"And just how did you think I would react emotionally to having Jess end our relationship? Did you think I'd just get over it, and that there'd be no emotional devastation involved with that?"

He rested his elbows on his knees and steepled his fingers together once again. "I knew it would be difficult for you at first, but I also knew that eventually you would come to see that it wasn't the lifestyle you wanted, and then you'd realize that it was the right decision in the long run."

Robin shot up angrily. "Let's get one thing straight. You decided to go behind my back to Jess and force her into ending our relationship because it was what you wanted, not because it was what I wanted. How could you possibly decide for me what's best for me? The last time I checked, I was an adult capable of making my own decisions."

"But you've had some emotionally difficult times recently, and it's only natural that you'd need some comfort. That's exactly why your mother and I wanted you to come home. We wanted you to have your family nearby to turn to, not this woman who you've barely known but a few months."

This is insane. Robin felt her anger build even further. "You interfered in a relationship that you knew was important to me. You can try to justify it all you want, but the fact remains that you hurt Jess, and because you hurt Jess, you also hurt me."

"Honey, your mother and I only want what's best for you. We've always wanted what's best for you. You need to know that. We don't want to see you hurt again, as you ultimately would have been in this circumstance." Thomas Wilson now got to what he considered to be the main point of his visit. "Did...did she end it with you?"

"You mean, did Jess break off our relationship?" Robin let go a disgusted laugh. "Yes, she did exactly what you thought she'd do. She told me she was acceding to your ultimatum so that she could protect me against a scandal, one that you said you would create." Robin approached the darkened fireplace and closed her eyes tight, unable to look at him any longer.

Her father sat back in the chair, satisfied. "It's for the best this way, honey. I know it doesn't seem like it now, but you'll realize it someday. That lifestyle wasn't the right thing for you."

Robin whirled around. "Whatever lifestyle I live is for me to choose, not you. You have no right to make that decision for me. You don't get to pick who I love." As she said this, her hand moved and a flash of light reflected off the diamond ring she wore.

Thomas knit his brows together and pointed at his daughter's finger, confused. "What is that you're wearing?"

"This?" A petite hand lifted slightly to give him a closer look. "Jess gave it to me."

"What?" This made absolutely no sense. "She gave that to you? When? You didn't have it on last week when we saw you."

Robin now got an almost perverse satisfaction at his inquiry. "This past weekend, Jess and I exchanged rings."

What? Thomas stood up and faced Robin. "Why did she give you that? I thought you said she ended it with you."

"She did end it with me, just like I told you she did." Robin fingered the gold band, then focused her attention squarely on her father, noting his stunned gaze at her ring. "Contrary to what you profess to believe, Jess is a very honorable person, and you knew that. In fact, when you tried to 'persuade' her into ending our relationship, you counted on her doing the honorable thing. You counted on her breaking it off with me. But what you didn't count on in your blackmail scheme was that I wouldn't let her go through with it."

Her father couldn't believe what he was hearing, and his utter incredulity registered plainly on his face. "Robin, listen...."

"No. You listen." His daughter was trembling in barely controlled anger. "You have no right to interfere in my personal or professional relationships with anyone. I'm an adult capable of knowing what I want. I want Jess in my life, and you'll just have to accept that. If you believe that somehow I don't know what I want, or that I'm making some supposedly horrible mistake, then whatever happens, I'll accept the consequences of my own actions. I don't need you to rescue me from myself."

Thomas shook his head. It was clear that his daughter had been completely taken in by this woman. "I presume this exchange of rings means something."

You better believe it. "We've committed ourselves to each other forever, and nothing you do is going to change that. Also, you should know that I stand by Jess. I can issue ultimatums, too. If you insist on filing your complaint with the State Bar Association, I don't ever want to see you again."

"Now, Robin, isn't that just a little extreme?"

Green eyes flared. "Don't you think that filing a complaint with the Bar Association against Jess for alleged sexual harassment, which I absolutely deny, is just as extreme?"

It was true, Thomas hadn't counted on his daughter's determination to continue this relationship. And although it stared him in the face, he absolutely refused to accept the subtle irony that his own actions had actually caused his daughter to become closer to this woman. "All right, Robin. You've made your point."

But Robin wasn't quite finished. "You should know that Jess and I have revealed our relationship to the chairman of our litigation department. He has informed the firm's Management Committee of the situation. Thanks to you, Jess is on an indefinite leave of absence and may ultimately lose her partnership over this."

"I think your blame, Robin, predictably is misplaced. This woman should have thought about the consequences of her actions before she broke the rules."

Not wanting to argue law firm etiquette with him, Robin chose to ignore the comment. "Are you or are you not going to file a complaint with the Bar Association? I want you to know that no matter what you do, I will always love Jess, and we will stay together. If you file that complaint, when all is said and done, Jess and I will still be together, and the only thing you will have accomplished is that you won't ever see me again."

Perhaps her firm's Management Committee will take care of this problem. It appeared that punitive action was already underway, and that being the case, his objective wasn't to alienate his daughter forever, even though he knew he was right about the situation. "No, Robin, I won't file it. I don't want to put you through an investigation of that nature."

Robin closed her eyes in visible relief. *At least that's something.* "You need to understand one more thing. I'm very angry with you for what you've done and the impact it might have on Jess's career. What you did is unacceptable to me. It's going to take a lot of effort for me to get past this, if I ever do. I'm not a child any longer. You'll have to accept that. You'll also have to accept that I'm doing what I want to do, and I'm with who I want to be with."

Thomas simply could not leave the issue where it stood and proceeded further. "Robin, it's clear that you don't always know what's best for you. Even David had the good sense to ultimately realize that."

What? The blonde head snapped up. "David had the good sense to realize what?"

"David finally understood that it was his obligation to take care of you, and that the financial burden of running a household should properly fall on him." Thomas stepped a little closer to Robin, trying to gauge the look of confusion on her face.

I never told him what David and I argued about that night. The emotional blow of his statement nearly knocked Robin over. "Are you saying that you spoke with David about that? Is that the reason he changed his mind?"

"He changed his mind because he became aware of his responsibilities."

"No!" Robin nearly doubled over in anguish. "You didn't. You didn't do that."

Thomas really didn't understand his daughter's reaction. "Honey, all any of us ever wanted was to do what was best for you."

Robin looked at her father with tear-filled eyes. "You interfered, and now David is dead." There was more significance to that statement than first appeared.

If she wasn't so occupied with that woman, she'd understand. He sighed audibly. "David's accident was a terrible tragedy, and I can see that you're still trying to get past the grief over what happened. That's exactly why your mother and I were hoping that you'd come home, so that we could deal with this as a family."

The green eyes that stared back at him held something so profoundly deep that it was entirely unreadable. "Jess is my family, now." Again, there was more significance to that statement than first appeared.

Thomas turned wearily toward the door, realizing that he'd gotten about as far with his daughter as he could for the moment. *Let's give this just a little more time.* "All right, Robin. You've made your point, here. I'll not file anything with the State Bar Association. I'm presuming your firm will handle things from now on. Please, though, think about what we've discussed. Your mother and I care about you, and we want to help you through the pain you're experiencing."

It was all too clear to Robin that her father had missed the point of their conversation entirely. Or perhaps he was just refusing to acknowledge it. "Can I ask you one more thing?" At his slightly surprised nod, Robin continued, her anguish still apparent. "Why did you help me through law school and assist me with my student loans if I wasn't supposed to bear part of the 'financial burden' of running the household?" *I'm sure the reason isn't because you care about me.*

To Thomas, the answer was truly obvious, and he couldn't understand why Robin would even have to ask. Nevertheless, he indulged her question. "You met David in law school, honey. We were hoping you'd find someone suitable for yourself."

It was all Robin could do not to fall to pieces, the full impact and implication of what he said hitting her with a devastating force. Stunned beyond all measure, she led the way toward the front door and peered cautiously outside, hoping that Jess wasn't already waiting. With as much strength as her voice would allow, she managed a weak goodbye, then watched as her father got into his rental car and pulled out of the driveway. She was relieved, even grateful, that he was gone, and even more relieved that Jess hadn't yet arrived home. The obvious reason for her temporary, but welcome, comfort was that she didn't want her father and Jess to run into each other. But the far more significant reason, and one which was yet to be fully realized, was that she couldn't bear to have Jess see her in such an obvious state of distress. With one look, the junior partner would not only immediately tear out of the house in frantic search of Robin's father, but probably make matters much worse in doing so. In Robin's anguished mind, the simple fact of the matter was that Jess was dealing with losing her partnership in the firm, and Robin, for better or for worse, just couldn't add her own problems to the already heavy burden. *I need to calm down before Jess gets home.*

The petite form slowly retreated back into the living room and sat down on the sofa, repeatedly rocking back and forth in an effort to dispel the heartache and to gain some semblance of composure. Finally, she wiped her eyes and took several deep breaths to calm her anxious heart, then sat very still on the sofa cushions as she waited for Jess to come home.

Somewhere between the Chinese restaurant and The Ranch, a taller figure stopped on the side of the roadway, got out of a silver Mercedes, and doubled over in an intense pain that had no rational or explainable origin.

****

Jess pulled into the driveway, and upon seeing that the rental car was gone, walked up to the front porch, Chinese take-out food in hand. She wasn't sure exactly what to expect, so she lightly knocked on the door and waited for Robin to answer. Barely a minute passed before the younger woman appeared in the doorway.

"Is it safe?" Jess strode inside, cautiously checking out the surroundings as she placed the take-out cuisine on the dining room table.

"Yeah." Robin put on her brave front. "He's gone."

"So, did it go all right?"

"Let's eat dinner and I can fill you in." In truth, food was the absolute last thing Robin wanted to think about.

"Okay." The taller woman stood silently for a moment, instinct telling her something wasn't quite right. "How long ago did he leave?" She pulled some plates down from the cabinet and stepped into the dining room.

I just need to get through dinner. "I guess it's been about twenty minutes or so." Green eyes peered curiously into the take-out bags. "So, did you get it?"

"Get what?"

A frank look.

Jess sat down. "What if I didn't?"

The frank look persisted, this time with a slightly raised eyebrow.

The older woman sighed dramatically, resigned that she'd been pegged. "Okay, fine. Yes, I did." An innocent look now appeared. "Want some?"

Robin took a seat, appearing somewhat preoccupied. "Maybe."

Hmmm. She doesn't want to play. Jess dished the shrimp with lobster sauce onto her plate. *Okay, fine. Let's not dance around this, then.* "Tell me, how did it go?"

The answer came very quickly. "He said he wasn't going to file anything with the Bar, so I think that's good news." *It's the only positive thing that happened.*

A crease formed in the center of Jess's slightly narrowed eyebrows as she studied Robin's demeanor. "Yeah, that is good news. I'm glad he backed off." *Something's going on here.* "Are you sure everything's okay?"

"Yeah." The blonde head nodded. "I...um...also told him about our commitment." Robin glanced at the ring on her finger.

"I see." Jess took a bite of her food as she pondered the information. "And how did he take that?" *She's not eating.*

"Well, he was surprised." Robin pushed the food around on her plate. "He thought you would have ended it between us."

"Did he give you a hard time about the fact that we're still together?"

Don't play twenty questions now with me, Jess. Please. "It's pretty much the same story. He wants me to move back there. I told him for the millionth time that I'm not going to do that. He said I need my family to help me deal with things. I told him that you're my family, now."

At Robin's matter-of-fact tone, Jess raised an eyebrow. *Well, that was succinct. Maybe she doesn't want to talk about the details.* "All right." The older woman sighed internally, then dished another spoonful of Chinese food onto her plate, taking particular notice that Robin hadn't eaten a bite. *Don't pry, Jess. If she doesn't want to discuss it, let it go.* "I forgot to mention earlier that Harry wants to see us first thing in the morning. He'll want to know what your father intends to do, and then he'll relay to us any further requests of the Management Committee."

Robin nodded, but was otherwise silent as she continued pushing the food around on her plate. *I can't do this anymore. I need space.* "Jess, I think I'm going to go lie down for a little while. I need some time alone." She reached over and placed her hand on top of the larger one next to her. "It's not you. It's just been a long, stressful day for me all the way around."

Reflexively, Jess gave her a warm smile. "Sure, kiddo. Go on. I'll clean up here." Unseen, questioning blue eyes watched as Robin left the table and headed down the long hallway. It was almost as if she couldn't get away fast enough. *Stay out of it, Jess. She'll tell you what's going on if she wants you to know.*

****

It was well over an hour later, after the dishes had been cleared and washed, after the daily newspaper had been thoroughly read, and after several game shows on television had concluded, that Jess stood up from her position on the sofa and began pacing the floor. Robin hadn't come back out, and although Jess's mind was telling her to let Robin deal with things in her own way, her instinct was telling her to do just the opposite. *Damn. What the hell is going on here?* Robin's behavior made absolutely no sense. It was understandable that she'd be angry, or even upset, after seeing her father, but this type of withdrawal was very strange.

With a single-minded purpose, Jess ambled down the long hallway and then into the master bedroom, somewhat surprised at seeing it empty. *Well, she did say she wanted to be alone.* The older woman felt a twinge of disappointment strike her at the apparent rejection, then turned around, intent on heading back into the living room. And she would have made it, too, if she hadn't felt another stab of intense pain come and go just as mysteriously as it had done earlier that evening. She braced her hand against the wall until the feeling passed, and then purely on instinct, turned back and proceeded further down the long hallway toward Robin's room.

Upon reaching her destination, she noticed that the door was slightly ajar and the room was dark. She flipped on the hallway light, then knocked lightly on the wood frame. "Robin?" Concerned blue eyes peered inside.

No answer.

Jess pushed the door open wider, bathing the bedroom in the dim light from the hallway. "Sweetheart? Is everything okay?" At the continuing silence, she entered the room, now seeing the petite form curled up on the bed. *Sleeping?* Surveying the situation, she stepped over and knelt on the floor beside the metal frame, then gently rested her hand on Robin's shoulder. It was at that moment, as her eyes gained greater focus in the faint reflected light, that she saw the trails of tears streaming from Robin's closed eyes. "Robin?" Jess now became very worried and moved her hand to the younger woman's face, stroking it gently. "What's wrong, honey?"

Robin couldn't answer. *Jess, I don't want to involve you.*

Damn it! What did he do to her? "Please tell me what's wrong, sweetheart."

After another lengthy silence, a small voice finally answered. "I can't. I'm not sure you'll understand."

Jess knew beyond all doubt that whenever Robin said those words, it was like a code, one which over the course of time, Jess had finally been able to decipher. It meant that whatever was wrong somehow involved David. *David. Why the hell can't he ever leave us alone?* Jess stopped herself. This was certainly not the time for irrational jealousy, and she had to push those petty feelings aside. *You'll just have to accept that this is a part of her, Jess, and that it will likely always be there.* Long fingers gently combed through disheveled blonde bangs. "Honey, you can tell me anything. Nothing will ever change the way I feel about you. You know that."

Should I? Robin wasn't sure she was doing the right thing, but she needed a life preserver right now, and Jess was it. She drew in a breath. "All right. Will you lie down here next to me?"

"Of course." Relieved that Robin was at least talking, Jess climbed onto the bed and settled herself next her. "How's this?"

Almost instinctively, the smaller woman snuggled close to the larger body. "Good." And, it was true. It was good. Very good. And very safe.

As gently as she could, Jess attempted to prod Robin into talking about what was upsetting her. "Tell me what's wrong, sweetheart." A long finger brushed back and forth against Robin's cheek.

I hope you'll understand, Jess. Robin took a moment to consider how she wanted to phrase what had happened, then began. "All this time, since the accident, I never understood why David changed his mind so suddenly about my having a career." Her voice was shaky as she spoke, and noticeably rough. "I blamed myself because we fought that night, and because I said some horrible things to him." Tears now came quickly. "And I never got to take them back, and tell him I didn't mean them."

"Shhh." Jess kissed Robin's forehead. "He knew you didn't mean what you said."

Robin's voice turned very somber. "I found out why David did what he did." The petite body began trembling. "My father went and talked to him, and told him that he expected David to assume certain responsibilities. He told him that it was David's obligation to take care of me, and that the financial burden of running the household should properly fall on him, and only him."

Well, that definitely explains a lot. The larger body wrapped around Robin tighter. "And after that, is that when David came to see you?"

"Yeah." More tears fell. "And we fought about it, and then he left." Robin looked at Jess with pain filled eyes. "I didn't know that my father had interfered." She struggled with the next words. "He interfered, and now David is dead."

It all began to come together for Jess. David wasn't upset solely with Robin that night. He was upset because he was put in a no-win situation by Robin's father. *That son of a bitch.* "Sweetheart, no one can change the past. At least you know the whole truth, now. You know that there were many things that led up to the accident. It wasn't your fault."

It was clear that Jess wasn't comprehending the obvious parallels. Robin inched higher and looked into compassionate silver-blue eyes, her voice immeasurably sad. "You don't understand."

I'm trying, here. The older woman patiently prodded further, her tone very gentle. "What don't I understand, honey?"

"When my father interfered before, David died." A visceral shudder traveled all the way from Robin to Jess. "Now, my father's interfered again." The tears, once more, fell.

It took Jess longer than it probably should have to finally grasp what Robin was saying, primarily because she never saw it coming. But now that she'd make the connection, it was with extreme heartache that she realized it really wasn't so surprising, after all. *Dear God. She's afraid history will repeat itself.* "No, Robin, sweetheart. Listen to me." She wiped away a tear from the younger woman's face. "That was an accident. Nothing else. You have to believe that."

It was true that Robin knew on a purely intellectual level that Jess was absolutely right. But her heart held the fear, nonetheless. She snuggled further into the warm embrace, until her body stopped rebelling against the tidal wave of emotion that had overtaken her just moments before. There was still something, though, that her heart needed her to do. She wrestled internally with how to best phrase her intent, then finally looked up, and gave voice to her heart's appeal. "Jess?"

"I'm here."

Robin barely whispered the next words. "Could I feel you?"

Well, this was a strange request. Weren't they already snuggled together? Surely Robin could feel that. The older woman considered the unusual request further, and although still not quite understanding it, nevertheless agreed. "Of course. You can do whatever you want."

Slowly, and with infinite deliberateness, Robin began her journey. She took a larger hand into her own and stroked the length of each slender finger in reverent acknowledgement, then brought her lips down and kissed each finger softly, one by one. Lingering further, she caressed the palm, earnestly tracing its crisscrossing creases with her fingertips, then covered its tender skin with several tiny kisses. After many moments of devout attention to the one hand, Robin repeated the gesture in a stunningly similar fashion on the opposite hand. She then proceeded onward to the right wrist, feeling the pulse beat, almost as if counting the cadence, then bestowed several gentle and venerating kisses there, as well.

For her part, Jess was totally transfixed. The touches and kisses were in no way sensual. They were more reverent. Still, she couldn't put her finger on what, exactly, she was experiencing or even what Robin's mission was.

Next, a petite hand moved to Jess's stomach beneath the faded red t-shirt and rested against the smooth skin, while Robin laid her head down on the older woman's chest. She listened to the strong, living heartbeat beneath her ear, taking comfort in its rhythmic harmony, then kissed both areas several times in a solemn benediction just as she'd done before. As her journey progressed, she methodically worked her way up to Jess's neck, breathing in the distinctive and nourishing scent, providing healing comfort to her wounded soul. With a feather light touch, the small fingers traced the broad shoulders, then moved along the collarbone, before stopping at the next beating pulse point. Her fingers lingered for many moments, feeling its living and pulsating rhythm, then, just as before, Robin placed several small kisses along her fingers' pathway in continued homage.

Jess laid prone on the bed, unable to move, enraptured by what was happening. It was almost as if Robin was mapping and memorizing her. She considered that for several moments, as she felt the gentle fingers tracing the contours of her upper body, then nearly cried as the realization finally hit her. It was unmistakable that Robin was committing Jess's entire being to memory, imprinting it firmly in her consciousness, as if one day it would be all she had left. *No! This isn't right.* Jess's mind practically screamed that Robin should stop, that history wouldn't repeat itself, that everything would be okay, but her voice curiously remained silent.

Robin's gentle fingers moved up to the angular face, mapping and tracing the strong jaw and high cheekbones with more tenderness than Jess had ever experienced. Silver-blue eyes closed, as the delicate touch of the petite fingers glided over every part of her face, capturing her essence in an intimate connection. Small kisses followed in the fingers' wake, until each and every area had been duly sanctified.

Her journey finally complete, Robin laid on the pillow very close to Jess, but did not speak. She stared at the dim profile for a very long time, then the streams of tears returned.

Jess remained still, processing in her mind the significance of what had just happened. It was readily apparent that whatever Thomas Wilson had done, it had sent Robin spiraling into a place of intense pain. *Intense pain.* Jess had to forcibly reign in her anger. A part of her wanted to find him and tear him apart limb from limb, and another part of her just simply wanted to cry at Robin's anguish. She fought both impulses, and instead, focused all her energy on consoling the one who held her heart. Glancing over at Robin, she saw that the tears had now appeared once more. "Don't cry." It was a desperate plea.

Instead, the tears came faster. "But I don't want you to die."

Jess finally broke, her own eyes now releasing all the pent up emotion she's tried so hard to suppress. "No. No, sweetheart." She gathered Robin into her arms, and gently rocked her, whispering through her tears with as much reassurance as she possibly could convey. "I'm here. It's all right. You've got me forever, remember? I promise you, honey, I'm not going anywhere." Those last words were a promise she knew she ultimately could not control. *I hope Matt Singleton's finished preparing my will.* Jess slowly combed her fingers through Robin's blonde hair, offering her gentle words of comfort, then began to quietly hum a soft and soothing melody.

The tender stroking of her hair, combined with the low vibrations of the gentle tune, did in fact, ease Robin's weary soul. It wasn't long before she began to slip into sleep's embrace, surrounded within the safety of her heart's protector. As she drifted off, her mind offered up a fervent appeal, pleading that no one, not her father, not the firm, not the highest power in the universe, take this love from her. Even though she didn't realize it at the time, she had just given thought to a silent prayer.

Jess heard Robin's breathing deepen in sleep as the anxiety finally lifted, then reflected on the events of the day. Guided by instinct, Jess felt certain that there was more to this story, but until Robin opened up to her, all she could do was pick up the pieces of a profoundly battered soul. She shifted slightly, then noticed that a portion of her faded red t-shirt was gripped within a petite fist held tightly against Robin's slumbering body, as if she was desperately clinging to something that was slowly being taken away. For Jess, it was the first time in a very long while that she felt entirely and undeniably helpless in the face of such deep and intense anguish.

And it literally tore at her heart.

Considerable Appeal

Chapter 7

The sun had set long ago. A cool night breeze blew in lightly throughout the spacious living room, occasionally rattling the vertical blinds at the bay window. A tall figure sat on the plush sofa, posture relaxed, as a pair of petite bare feet rested comfortably in a denim clad lap. Long fingers gently and skillfully massaged each tired foot from heel to toe, focusing briefly on the tender insoles, before stroking and caressing the arches and ankles once again. After many moments of thorough attention to each foot, the smaller form lifted up and shifted completely around, so that now, the golden blonde head was situated squarely upon the aforementioned lap. Smiling green eyes met crystal blue.

"Thank you." Robin sighed deeply in contentment.

"You're welcome." Jess combed her fingers through Robin's short blonde hair. "Feel better now?"

"Yes. You know, you do that very well."

"Well, not to brag or anything, because you know I'm very modest, but foot massages are my specialty."

That brought a light giggle. "Is that so?"

"Yep." A dark eyebrow arched expectantly. "So...?"

"Um...." Pale eyebrows furrowed slightly in question. "So what?"

"You know." Jess nodded confidently.

"Um...nope. What?"

An exaggerated sigh. "Well, if you're going to make me say it...." The low voice held a playful tone. "Okay, fine. So, tell me Robin, do I get any points for my excellent foot massaging skills?"

"My. We are modest, aren't we?" Robin grinned. "Let's see, do you think you should get some points?"

"Yes. In fact, Robin, I think I should not only get regular points, but I should also get bonus points."

The younger woman raised both eyebrows above her golden bangs, then put on a serious face. "Bonus points?"

"Yes. This is because I have to make up for those points you erroneously deducted from me last weekend."

An outraged expression. "You woke me up, as I recall, practically in the middle of the night, with your zip a dee do whatever song."

A very bored look, but otherwise no response.

"And then..." A petite finger wagged purposefully in Jess's direction. "Your frisky self started singing, very loudly I might add, about Mr. Blackbird sitting on your shoulder."

The very bored look continued.

"And then, as if that wasn't already bad enough, you proceeded to start humming and whistling, and thumping your fingers all over my back."

Jess waited with infinite patience. "Are you finished?"

"Yes."

"Good, because number one, Robin, it most certainly was not the middle of the night. Number two, that is a perfectly lovely song. And number three, it's Mr. Bluebird, not Mr. Blackbird, just so you know."

Green eyes narrowed considerably. "The point is not whether it was Mr. Bluebird, Mr. Blackbird, or any other bird. The point is that you woke me up."

"Maybe." A blue eye winked. "But it turned out okay, didn't it?"

"Yeah, it did." Petite fingers grasped larger ones.

"So..." A mischievous grin appeared. "Wanna hear the song again?"

Robin crinkled up her nose. "Don't push it, Jess." She brought their joined hands to her lips and gave the knuckles a light kiss. "Here's the deal. You restrain yourself from singing that zip a dee do whatever song, and I'll give you regular points plus bonus points for your foot massaging skills."

Jess grinned, pleased that her subtle blackmailing skills had served her well, then bent down and kissed Robin soft lips. "It's a deal, kiddo." She spent the next several moments slowly combing her fingers through the younger woman's short blonde hair before finally setting all playfulness aside and bringing the conversation back to more serious matters. "How was your day today?"

"I guess it was all right. Clay Taylor's not too bad to work with." The smaller woman let go an audible sigh. "But I'd much rather be working with you."

"Well, sweetheart, I think we need to be honest about that. Whichever way this thing goes, I don't think they'll allow us to work together again." Jess found that thought unexpectedly painful, much more so than she'd first considered.

Robin's voice became noticeably shaky. "I'm so sorry that my father did this to you...to us."

"Shhh." The taller woman soothed. "No matter what the firm does, and no matter what your father does, it doesn't matter, because we have each other. You just keep on thinking about that, and everything else will sort itself out just fine." Jess closed her eyes, then sighed to herself. They had carefully tip-toed around the subject up until now, but considering Robin's state of mind after her father's visit the previous evening, it was clear that they really needed to talk more about what had happened. Wounds tend to fester unless they're given the chance to properly heal, as Jess herself knew well from first-hand experience. Whatever had happened with Robin's father, it was quite clear that Robin's wounds ran very deep. "You were very upset last night after your father left. How are you doing now?"

Green eyes focused on some point in the distance, but otherwise, there was no response.

She won't talk about it "I'm very sorry he hurt you." Long fingers stroked Robin's face. "I want to help you, if I can. Will you let me?"

A small tear made it's way down the side of Robin's face, but there was still no response.

Damn it, Jess. You've upset her. "I'm sorry. I'm sorry, sweetheart." Long arms gathered Robin up into a gentle hug. "I didn't mean to upset you." If truth be told, Jess was very distressed at the younger woman's inability to talk about everything that had happened. It seemed instead as if Robin was retreating further into herself over this matter. *Let it go, Jess. How do you think you'd feel if you'd just found out that someone close to you had interfered not once, but twice in your life, with disastrous consequences?* Resigned that Robin didn't want to talk about it, Jess carefully laid the blonde head back upon her lap. "When you're ready, honey, I'm here."

There was another prolonged silence, then the smaller woman finally spoke. "Jess?"

"I'm here."

Robin's voice was rough. "Do you think I'm a good attorney?"

What? Well, that was certainly an unexpected question. "Absolutely. I'm very proud to have worked with you."

At least that's something. "Thank you." The words were barely a whisper, but nevertheless a sincere acknowledgment of the validation.

What's this all about? Dark eyebrows furrowed in concentrated thought.

"Jess?"

"I'm here."

She's here. With everything that was happening, the simple fact that Jess was still with her was immeasurably comforting. Robin tried to force her mind into believing that it would always be this way. "Thanks for being with me last night. I guess finding out about what my father did really shook me up." She hesitated, then asked a question that had been on her mind since the previous evening. "What made you come to my room?"

In truth, it was still an unexamined question. Just what was it, exactly, that caused Jess to go into Robin's room the previous evening? Instinct? Or maybe concern? Or...*pain.* Yes, that was it. It was the pain. A large hand pressed against Robin's cheek. "I was worried about you. I wanted to see how you were doing, so I checked our room, but you weren't there. I thought that you must've wanted to be alone for the rest of the night, so I started to go back into the living room, but before I got very far, I felt a pain inside of me. I can't describe it, but it was really intense." Blue eyes looked up for a brief moment, then refocused on Robin. "It was strange, but I felt the same thing on the way back from picking up the Chinese food last night, but I haven't felt it again. I don't know why, but after I felt it the second time, there was something...I don't know. I just had to go find you."

"Are you sick?" Robin's voice held an almost urgent concern.

"No. I feel fine."

The younger woman's mind recalled that she had doubled over in anguish after her father had revealed his role in the events leading up to David's accident. Upon further reflection, she also recalled the horrible pain she'd felt as she entered the junior partner's office the night Jess tried to break things off between them, her own startled green eyes catching sight of the crumpled form curled up on the floor in the wake of a shattered heart. *We're connected.* "Jess?"

"I'm here." Jess tried to reinforce that concept.

"I felt it, too, or something like it, that night when I came back into your office." Robin thought about the events some more. "I think we just know when each other's hurting."

It could be true. "Do you think that's it?"

"Yeah." Something else then came to mind. "Remember when I was gone during Thanksgiving, and you told me that you felt it inside of you that I was upset?"

Jess grew contemplative. "Yes, I remember. I could feel that something just wasn't right, even though you were hundreds of miles away." The older woman grew increasingly annoyed at herself, yet again, for not relying more on her instincts back then.

But what if I'm wrong? "Will you still go see a doctor and have it checked out?" The tone of urgency returned to Robin's voice.

Attempting to dismiss the matter, Jess protested. "I don't think that's necessary. I feel fine. I think you're right. We just know when each other's hurting."

Apparently, it was the exact wrong thing to say. Robin sat straight up, a look of near terror in her eyes. "No. What if I'm wrong? What if it's something else?"

Jess couldn't have been more insensitive if she'd tried. "But, Robin, there's nothing to worry about. I'm fine."

After a second, pleading green eyes focused intently on confused blue. "Please, Jess." It was a desperate appeal, although barely audible. "I don't want you to be sick." *I don't want to lose you, too.*

After a long moment of processing the perceived fear, Jess closed her eyes and hung her head as the realization finally sank in. *But I can't have her worry every time I get a damn hangnail.* Not quite sure either of them was up to that particular conversation, and certainly not wanting to upset Robin even more, the older woman acquiesced. "All right. I'll have it checked out." She grasped both of the smaller hands and held them tightly within her own. "Now, I want you to do something for me. Promise me that you'll talk with Dr Richmond about everything that's happened. She's on the outside of this, and she can see things from a different perspective." Jess paused, then continued. "It's not good to keep things inside, sweetheart. If you ever want to talk, I'm here. But, if you'd rather talk with Dr. Richmond, that's okay too. Just don't keep it inside. Will you promise me that?"

The blonde head nodded. "I promise." Robin nestled her body up against the larger one and snuggled close, taking in the familiar scent. "Have I told you lately that I love you."

That brought a crooked smile. "I think maybe you might have mentioned it a time or two."

"Oh." The younger woman hid a smirk. "Well, in that case, I wouldn't want to overdo it or anything. Perhaps, I just shouldn't mention it anymore."

Two long fingers hooked underneath Robin's chin, lifting it up a bit. "That would be absolutely unacceptable."

"Is that so?"

"Yep." Jess grinned. "House rule number seven, Robin, specifically states that each party living in the dwelling otherwise known as The Ranch shall use the "L" word in connection with the other party at least once per day."

"I see." Robin pretended to give the rule careful consideration. "So, then that would mean that there's still one party living in this dwelling who hasn't complied with house rule number seven yet."

Jess was thoroughly charmed. "Really now."

"Yes. At least that's the way I see it." Petite fingers drummed expectantly on the sofa cushion. "Did you have something you wanted to say to me?"

A deep chuckle. "You're not supposed to ask for it."

"I don't think there's anything in house rule number seven about asking or not asking, Jess."

"Um...." Dark eyebrows knit together. "Okay. This is the amended house rule number seven. Each party living in the dwelling otherwise known as The Ranch shall use the "L" word in connection with the other party at least once per day at times when the other party does not ask."

Robin cast her gaze at the floor in a slight pout. "Okay." A green eye then peered upward. "Um...I'm not really asking or anything, Jess, so if you do have something you want to say, you can say it."

At this point, it was simply impossible for Jess to resist. *She's so damn adorable.* Long arms wrapped around the smaller woman and positioned her down along the length of the plush sofa, the larger body coming to rest gently upon her. A low alto voice whispered seductively into a petite ear. "So as to strictly comply with house rule number seven, Robin, let me make this absolutely and perfectly clear. I love you, and I most definitely intend to prove it to you."

Robin threaded her fingers through the dark hair as sea-green eyes fixed onto cool blue. "Then I'd say you'd better get busy." She brought lips up to meet the ones above her own, effectively sealing her statement with a searing kiss.

Oh my. Jess momentarily had to clear her mind. Intense blue eyes bore solidly into green. "You drive me absolutely crazy." Without further hesitation, long, wandering fingers began to unbutton Robin's blouse, button by button, lingering at each one just long enough to graze the soft skin beneath it. "You know, it occurs to me that house rule number seven doesn't have a limit on the number of times either party can use the "L" word." Jess ran her fingers up and down the length of Robin's bare stomach and chest. "So..." Soft lips followed the fingers' pathway. "Let me say it to you again." Those same fingers expertly unhooked the younger woman's bra and removed both it and the blouse all at once. "I love you."

Smaller fingers simultaneously made their own progress on Jess's clothing, managing to remove most of it before the younger woman felt the metal zipper on her pants slowly lowering and those same long, wandering fingers exploring, then massaging a very sensitive area. Robin's breathing became labored as the pressure increased, her own lips and questing fingers likewise teasing and massaging several sensitive areas on the body hovering above her own in what quickly became a sensual dance.

Between gasps and her own labored breathing, Jess repeated her mantra, again and again. "I love you. I love you."

The dance enveloped them both in its seductive embrace, its rhythm setting pace to an imaginary symphony, all other time and space ceasing to exist. In perfect, almost synchronized choreography, the intensity steadily built, then increased even further, until both bodies finally arched and cried out in unison, their passionate song reaching its high crescendo, before tumbling back down into earth's stratosphere once again.

Jess collapsed on top of Robin, burying her face against the younger woman's shoulder and breathing heavily. Unable to will her muscles to move, she instead focused her attention on their rapidly beating hearts keeping time together in a musical sonata all of their own. Finally, she lifted her dark head and gazed adoringly into slightly unfocused sea-green eyes. "How do you do that?"

A small hand stroked the older woman's cheek, as one golden eyebrow arched ever so slowly. "Um...are you sure I need to explain this?"

A crooked smile followed. "Not that. What I meant was, how do you almost render me unconscious?"

A slight blush, then a chuckle. "I'm pretty sure it's not all me." Robin lifted slightly and placed a tender kiss on Jess's lips. "You have the exact same effect on me, you know."

"Well, then I guess it must be magic." The older woman leaned in and once again captured Robin's lips in several long, slow, and sweet kisses. She pulled back and cocked her head to one side in apparent contemplation. "Yep, it's official. It's most definitely magic."

Magic. Robin savored the moment, enjoying the pleasant weight of the larger body resting upon her own. And indeed, it was truly magical. *I don't understand how anyone could object to this.* "So..." She drawled out the word, tracing her finger back and forth along the older woman's jaw. "Have I told you lately that I love you?"

"Um..." Jess suppressed a smile. "I think you might have mentioned it a time or two." She leaned in and kissed along the base of Robin's neck, nibbling lightly as she saw fit. "I also think that's what started this in the first place."

It was incredible, the skin to skin contact. "Does that mean you're complaining?" Twinkling green eyes prodded.

"Absolutely..." The distracting nibbling continued. "Positively..." The nibbling continued further. "Not." The nibbling continued even further still.

The younger woman kept her presence of mind just long enough to whisper into a conveniently placed ear. "Then come to bed with me, Jess." Before Robin could utter another word, she was essentially whisked to her feet and led down the long hallway into the master bedroom.

Considering all of the evidence, one might say it was indeed magic.

****

The week progressed slowly, adding further anxiety to an already frustrating situation. There was, however, one bright spot to focus on, even if only temporarily. Valentine's Day. It had arrived without much mention or fanfare, and in truth, in light of everything else going on, it was nearly overlooked. Nevertheless, Robin should have known that even though Jess was understandably distracted, she wouldn't let the event pass by without the day's formal acknowledgement.

As the very long day came to its close, Robin pulled her sporty metallic blue BMW into The Ranch's two-car garage and shut off the engine. She hesitated just long enough to lift from the passenger seat the single long-stem red rose which she'd found waiting for her on top of her desk at work earlier that morning. A simple card had been placed with it containing a small phrase that meant more to her than the words themselves appeared to convey. She removed the card from its plain white envelope and read the words to herself again for what must have been the tenth time that day.

Be mine.

J

Robin smiled just as she'd done the nine previous times she'd read the card, then stepped out of the car and entered the house, long-stem rose and briefcase in hand. Before she had a chance to venture too far inside, she was immediately greeted by her taller companion in a manner which consisted primarily of whisking the briefcase from her hand and drawing her smaller body into a strong and heartfelt embrace. Both women stood there for a very long time, wrapped together in each other's arms, simply enjoying their deep emotional connection.

After a few lingering moments, Jess softly whispered her more formal greeting into Robin's ear. "Happy Valentine's Day, sweetheart."

With the red rose still clasped tightly in her hand, Robin took a half step backward and looked into the cerulean eyes in front of her. "Happy Valentine's Day, Jess. Thank you for my rose." She drew the flower closer to herself and breathed in its sweet fragrance.

"You're welcome." Jess gave her a dazzling smile. "I received a very lovely bouquet delivery today. Thank you."

There just seemed to be something about the older woman tonight that absolutely captivated Robin. Jess was positively glowing, and in the wake of it, Robin felt almost shy. "You're welcome."

"Come this way with me." Jess led them both into the formal dining room where she displayed a beautifully set table accented by several long red tapered candles placed in the center. The colorful bouquet Jess had received earlier that day rested prominently on the far end of the table, while at the closer end, two place settings of formal imported china complemented by genuine crystal glasses were expertly situated beneath a white lace heirloom tablecloth. "Dinner will be ready in a few minutes if you'd like to change into something a bit more...comfortable."

Green eyes gazed at the table, nearly mesmerized by the low incandescent lighting and the soft glow of the small flames dancing atop each of the slender red tapered candles. "It's beautiful." Robin commented, very much in awe.

Jess gently took the rose from Robin's fingers and laid it across the center of the table, completing the setting. "There." She smiled. "Now it's perfect."

And that, it was. Perfect. In a mystical, magical way, at that one singular moment in time, it was if the world outside with all its heartaches and troubles simply ceased to exist. As Robin absorbed one vision, she turned slightly, only to observe another. Her eyes all at once caught the near halo effect surrounding the taller woman as cast by the glowing and flickering candlelight. It was quite magnetic, and much too powerful to resist. She quickly closed the gap between the two of them, and took hold of Jess's hands. "The answer's yes."

"Yes?"

Petite fingers reached up and rested against the older woman's cheek. "What you put on your card. My answer's yes."

"Oh." *Be mine.* Jess leaned in and placed a very tender kiss on Robin's lips, then swallowed a bit harder than she had intended. "Um...it occurs to me that you should go ahead and get changed now, or we'll never make it to dinner." She flashed Robin another dazzling smile.

The blonde head nodded. "I think that's a very good idea."

While Robin set about changing into more comfortable attire, Jess put the finishing touches on dinner. A soon as the younger woman returned to the dining room, her companion pulled a bottle of chilled Chardonnay from the nearby ice bucket. "Care for some wine?"

"Yes, thanks." It all seemed rather formal in nature, but in a very good and very romantic way. "Dinner smells really great. What'd you make?"

"Chicken Cacciatore." Jess handed a glass of wine to Robin. "It's ready. Let's go ahead and eat."

"Okay." Curious green eyes peered into a nearby serving dish. "Um...Jess? You said you made Chicken Cacciatore?"

"Yes." The dark head nodded confidently.

"So then, that's what's in there?"

"Yep." Jess assured.

Right. Robin suppressed a smile. "But that's not all that's in there, is it?"

"Um...." Innocent blue eyes blinked several times. "I don't know what you're talking about."

A frank look. "I think you do."

There was absolutely no way out now. Jess had to come clean. "Okay, well maybe I did improvise the recipe just a little bit."

"You improvised a little bit?"

"Yes. I thought that those of us who preferred chicken could have the chicken, and then those of us who preferred...the other thing, could have the other thing."

She's so hopeless. Robin couldn't suppress her smile any longer. It now turned into a full grin. "That's quite convenient and very resourceful of you."

"Yes. The recipe's very flexible. It works out perfectly this way."

The blonde head nodded agreeably. "I can see that."

"So..." Jess looked at Robin in all seriousness. "Would you prefer the chicken or...the other thing?"

It was absolutely delightful, Robin decided, and thoroughly enchanting, that they could so easily combine their familiar banter with such an incredibly romantic setting. In fact, it served only to heighten the intensity of it all the more, given the low lighting and the flickering of the candle flames. And curiously, something in the back of Robin's mind told her that Jess had indeed planned it this way all along. *She's the most irresistible person I've ever known.* Sea-green eyes, now hiding absolutely nothing, captured, then held, crystal blue in a smoldering gaze. "I think I'll have the chicken with a little bit of the...other thing on the side."

Oh my. Jess swallowed with difficulty, her gaze never wavering. "Okay. And I think I'll have the other thing with a little bit of the chicken on the side." At this point, they could have been talking about absolutely anything and the intensity would still have been just as strong.

"Good." The gaze held further.

"Good."

Dinner, although thoroughly enjoyable, was finished rather quickly that evening.

****

"Jess?" Robin fumbled around in the darkness, finally finding her nightshirt and slipping the crisp cotton fabric over her head.

"What?" The older woman once again donned her Calvin Klein boxers and sleep shirt and lay comfortably on the waterbed.

"I don't know if I've ever told you this specifically, but you are very romantic."

Perfect white teeth almost glowed in the darkness. "Is that so?"

"Yes." The petite body curled up next to the larger one. "First there was the rose this morning, then dinner, and now...."

Jess silenced her with a kiss. "Now?"

"Um..." The younger woman momentarily forgot her train of thought, as a larger hand wandered underneath her nightshirt, finally coming to rest on her bare stomach. "I think perhaps we got dressed too quickly."

I am in so much trouble. Jess arched an eyebrow unseen. "Perhaps we did." She gave Robin several long, slow kisses.

"So..." Another drawled out sentence. "Why didn't you tell me?"

Quizzical silver-blue eyes stared at gray-green in the dark. "Why didn't I tell you what?"

"About what you wrote inside the ring."

"Oh, that." Jess seemed somewhat embarrassed. "I wasn't sure you'd remember."

A petite finger traced a dark eyebrow. "October 12. How could I forget?" Robin leaned in and placed a very gentle kiss on the older woman's lips. "The day we met."

"Yes."

"See what I mean? You're very romantic."

That brought a crooked grin in the dark. "Well, I aim to please." A large hand grasped a smaller one. "So...why didn't you tell me?"

"Um...why didn't I tell you what?" Actually, Robin had a pretty good idea of what Jess was going to say next.

Azure eyes held a hidden twinkle. *Two can play.* "Why didn't you tell me what you inscribed on the ring?"

"Oh, that." *She caught me.* "Well, to be honest, I wasn't sure that it made sense."

"Of course it did." Jess recalled the inscription quite clearly. *'Yours.'* "I think it's pretty self-explanatory."

Robin snuggled further against Jess and rested her head on the broad shoulder. "It's the other half."

The other half? Try as she might, Jess couldn't seem to connect the full meaning of that statement.

At the prolonged silence, the younger woman realized that she was originally right. Jess hadn't indeed made the connection. "It doesn't make sense, does it?" Robin buried her face into the fabric of the Calvin sleep shirt, now not wanting to look into questioning silver-blue eyes. She waited another moment, but as the silence continued on, she finally clarified the inscription's intent. "The bracelet's the first half. The ring's the other half."

Silver-blue eyes blinked, then closed fully as Jess recalled the inscription on the white and blue sapphire bracelet. *Forever.* The realization of the meaning of the two words taken together hit the older woman with an unexpectedly powerful force. *Forever yours.* Long arms tightened around the petite body. "Yes, sweetheart, it makes perfect sense." She kissed the top of the blonde head. "Absolute perfect sense."

Robin brushed her fingers idly back and forth against Jess's forearm, feeling the tiny fine hairs covering the soft skin. "So, is it okay?"

"Better than okay." Perfect white teeth showed themselves once again. "You know, kiddo, you're very romantic, yourself."

For some reason, that made Robin beam. She shifted and inched herself higher to look directly into silver-blue eyes, her own gray-green eyes now twinkling. "Well, I do my best, you know."

"And I must say, you do it very well." The older woman pulled Robin closer, capturing her lips in what turned into several long and slow kisses. After many moments, she pulled away again and breathed deeply in contentment. "I have a good idea."

"Jess..." Robin whispered playfully into a nearby ear. "We already did that."

A deep chuckle. "That's wasn't what I was thinking."

"No? Then, spill it." The blonde head rested on the pillow next to Jess.

"Okay. I was thinking that maybe we could take a trip to Tampa this weekend and tell my mom about us...and our rings."

"You haven't told her?" Robin was quite surprised.

"Well, no. I thought we could do it together, if you want to." Jess gave a wry grin. "I learned my lesson last time about telling my mom something important about us without including you."

The smaller woman thought about that. "I don't mean for you to keep things from your family if you'd rather tell them. You don't need my permission for that."

A long finger hooked under Robin's chin. "When it concerns the both of us, and it's important, I think we should do it together." The finger then traced along the petite jaw line. "So, what do you think?"

"I think it sounds like a great idea." Pale eyebrows knit together in further thought. "What about your brother? Do you want to tell him, too?"

"I've been thinking about that." The older woman sighed, not sure how much she should go into it. She always figured that telling her mother was a given, and that in telling her brother, he would most likely understand, but in reality, Jess wasn't at all sure of what her brother's wife would think about this type of revelation. "Peter doesn't know about us. I think he'd be okay with it, but...."

Robin hitched up on one elbow, her gray-green eyes studying Jess's profile in the dark. "But, what?"

"His wife, Peggy...." Completely within character, Jess shifted her gaze to the digital clock on the nightstand. "I just don't know how she'd react. She's deeply religious, and I'm not sure whether she'd have a problem with it. I don't want to create a family rift."

I guess it was too much to hope that her whole family would understand. "I don't want to come between you and your family, Jess."

Silver-blue eyes turned slowly toward Robin. "Sweetheart, you're my family, too. Eventually, they'll have to know about us." There was a slight pause as Jess pondered all the options. "Maybe we should do this. We could talk to my mom about it this weekend and see what she thinks. She's around Peter and Peggy more often than I am. I think she'd know how to handle this."

"Okay." Robin agreed. "Are you worried, though?"

There was no reason not to be honest. "A little. But I know I can count on my mom to help us."

All things considered, if they were going to talk with Jess's mother about this, they might as well get everything else out in the open, including the situation with the firm. In truth, Robin was very anxious about this issue. After all, it was her own father who had put Jess's career at risk. The blonde woman abruptly stopped herself from casting further blame. *No, that's not entirely true. I knew all along what I was doing.* Although she was uncomfortable about it, Robin nevertheless decided to ask. "Do you think we should tell your mom about what's going on with the firm?"

"Yes." There was no hesitation in Jess's voice.

The younger woman laid back down, now very quiet. Too quiet.

What's the matter? "Hey." A slender finger tapped lightly on Robin's wrist. "Is something on your mind?"

Robin swallowed, then finally put voice to her fear. "What if your mom blames me for everything that's happened?" *What if she thinks it's my fault that you might lose your partnership?*

Shit. How many times do we have to go through this? "Listen to me, sweetheart. My mom won't blame you, so don't even worry about that. Nothing that happens to me is your fault. Your dad did what he did for his own reasons, nothing more, and you had absolutely nothing to do with that." Jess shifted to her side to face Robin, briefly combing her fingers through the blonde bangs, then patiently continued on with her explanation. "We both knew the risks in continuing our relationship. We talked about them many times. I made the ultimate choice to be with you because I couldn't imagine my life without you. So, whatever happens with the firm, my mom will understand why I chose you over everything else."

"Do you really think she'll understand?"

"I know she will."

The blonde head nodded slightly in acknowledgment. "I didn't tell you earlier, but Harry called me today and told me I'd be meeting with the Management Committee next Monday."

"Yeah, he called me, too, and said that I'd need to meet with them Monday, as well. He said the delay this week was in trying to reach your father. Apparently, they wanted something in writing from him as to his intentions. I suppose that makes sense. If the State Bar complaint is off the table, then the Management Committee can deal with this matter internally and very quietly."

Robin sighed audibly. "How long do you think it'll take before they make a decision?"

They've probably already made up their minds. Jess considered the question for a moment longer. "I'd say they'll decide sometime next week. There's no reason to drag this thing out any longer than necessary. The sooner it's resolved, the better." It was becoming quite apparent now that Robin was very tense about this whole matter, and it showed. "C'mere."

The petite body instinctively snuggled against Jess, then shivered slightly.

"Everything's going to be fine, sweetheart. No one can touch us. You got that?" The older woman felt Robin nod against her chest. "I forgot to mention it before, but Barbara Roberts called me today."

Now Robin was intrigued. "What'd she want?"

"She wants to meet me for lunch tomorrow."

"Really? Any particular reason?"

Long fingers combed leisurely through Robin's short blonde hair. "She didn't say, but my guess is that she knows what's going on at the firm and wants to talk with me about it. I didn't get the impression it was anything negative, though."

At that moment, Jess felt Robin unsuccessfully stifle a yawn, and then watched silently as a petite hand very discretely edged its way underneath the Calvin Klein sleep shirt and came to rest flatly on Jess's stomach. It was a role reversal that was becoming increasingly commonplace as the days continued on. That, alone, was worth contemplating further. It seemed more and more as if they each needed to protect, and also be protected by, the other, in a give and take of strength which they both drew from somewhere down deep within themselves. The warmth of the petite hand resting against her skin brought a soft smile to the taller woman's lips. Then again, it was so much more than warmth. It was a type of energy, a current, passing from one to the other, and then back again in a continuous circuit.

And the unbroken connection it provided felt very good.

****

The small Italian restaurant was bustling at noonday with the usual lunch crowd, which made parking directly outside rather difficult. After finally locating a newly vacated parking spot, Jess entered the restaurant and immediately spotted Barbara Roberts already seated at a nearby table. Amidst the typical clinking of beverage glasses and dishes, the junior partner made her way past the hostess and joined her luncheon companion.

"Sorry to keep you waiting." Jess took a seat at the table. "I always forget how bad the traffic is this time of day."

Barbara smiled graciously. "Don't you worry a bit. I've only just arrived, myself." She picked up her menu and perused the day's specials. "Let's order lunch first, and then we can chat a bit."

Without too much difficulty, they made their selections and put in their lunch orders with a very efficient waiter. Once their beverages were brought out to them, both women relaxed and settled back comfortably into their chairs. There was a certain air of expectation, and although Jess had an idea of what the topic of their lunch conversation would be, she waited for Barbara to broach the subject first. She didn't have to wait long.

Barbara leaned forward slightly. "I wanted to mention to you that Harry told me about the situation at the firm with you and Robin. I certainly don't want to pry, and if you'd rather that we not discuss it, I'll understand completely, and we can talk about something else."

Well, let's find out if she's for us or against us on this. The junior partner took a sip of her iced tea, then smiled. "It's okay, Barbara. I don't mind discussing it."

"I must tell you that from the times I've seen you and Robin together, I sensed that you two were more than simple coworkers."

Blue eyes met the older woman's gaze. "Does that bother you?"

It was unexpected, but Barbara smiled widely. "Heavens, no. Robin is a very lovely young woman. Let me tell you something. I know how easy it is to get so caught up in your work that you forget to take care of yourself. You might not know this, but I've often worried about you, Jess, working so hard but not seeming to enjoy the good things in life. There's no substitute for sharing your life with someone whom you care about, whoever that person may be. A job is a job and will come and go, but a person does not define him or herself solely by the job he or she holds." The older woman looked directly at Jess. "Many, many years ago, I told my husband that exact same thing. He wanted us to start the new law firm, and I told him that if the firm didn't ultimately succeed, for whatever reason, he and I still had a full life ahead of us together."

The junior partner considered everything that had just been said. *She seems supportive.* "So, what you're saying is that whether or not the firm asks me to sever my partnership, the law firm itself isn't the most important or enduring thing in my life."

She's a very bright one! "That's absolutely right. You just remember that. Now, since I have quite a bit at stake, myself, in the firm's continued well-being, I will tell you that it is both my husband's and my opinion that you are one of the law firm's stars. Harry has constantly praised you and your work throughout the years, and I'm sure you know how hard he fought last year to make you a full partner. Of course, you absolutely deserved it."

Jess gave a frank smile. "Well, Barbara, maybe that's true, but I've put the firm at substantial risk with my relationship with Robin. Harry may now regret having gone to bat for me." She sighed, then look down at her hands. "I should have considered all of the ramifications. I just never suspected that Robin's father would have interfered the way he did. I understand now that he's agreed not to file a complaint with the State Bar, and while that's certainly positive, there's still the problem that I knowingly continued a personal relationship with someone whose performance I evaluate."

"Yes, but this situation isn't unsolvable, Jess. There's been no real harm to the firm, and I'm sure you and Robin will be even more careful now. I do know one thing for certain. The well-being of the firm would greatly suffer without having the benefit your continued skills in their employ." Barbara smiled reassuringly. "And that's precisely the reason I've indicated my intent to speak with the Management Committee on Monday regarding this matter."

In a gesture that surely would have been comical were it not for the seriousness of the subject matter, Jess's mouth fell wide open, although she'd have been hard pressed at that moment to find a way to speak. Instead, she grasped her iced tea glass and took a long sip of the cool beverage. Finally, having cleared her mind, she set the glass down and looked back across the table. "You really don't have to do that, Barbara."

The wife of the litigation department chairman casually smoothed the linen napkin resting upon her lap, her eyes twinkling ever so slightly. "Well, now that's a matter of opinion. I would seriously object to a very talented attorney such as yourself being let go from the very firm that I, myself, worked so hard to get up and running in the first place."

The waiter approached with their entrees, resulting in a break in the conversation. If truth be known, Jess was really quite stunned. She had always sensed that Barbara most likely would be supportive, especially considering all the times Barbara seemed so eager to socialize together, and with Robin present, as well. What the junior partner never would have imagined in a million years was that Barbara would, in fact, actually be willing to defend her before the Management Committee, itself. The waiter placed their meals on the table, and then left the two women alone once again.

Jess cleared her throat softly. "I don't know what to say."

The older woman gave Jess another reassuring smile. "You don't need to say a thing. I want to see you have a happy life together with someone whom you care very much for, and I also want to ensure that our firm has the best and brightest legal minds available for its benefit. That means that it's in the firm's best interests to work through this thing with you, and I'm going to make sure the Management Committee understands that." With her point having been successfully conveyed, Barbara picked up her fork. "Now, enough of all that. Let's eat and talk about much more enjoyable matters, like that wonderful sale they're having this weekend at Burdines Department Store."

The junior partner flashed a wide grin. *Harry was right. There's absolutely no doubt who's the boss, here.* "All right. Thank you, Barbara." As if on cue, Jess's mind flashed back to Robin's profound and very knowledgeable explanation of the real purpose of shopping. A dark eyebrow arched. *To have fun.* Jess leaned in a bit, putting her fingers to the side of her mouth conspiratorially. "I understand from a very reliable source that shopping is so much more fun when you find something which you weren't looking for, which you certainly hadn't intended to buy, which you most definitely don't need, but which nevertheless is on sale to a point where you simply just can't resist."

Barbara's eyes twinkled mischievously. "I see your source has clearly trained you well."

Oh God! I am so transparent.

****

The early Saturday morning sun cast its rays through the partially closed Venetian blinds, spilling across the crisp linen sheets of the queen-sized waterbed. A petite form slumbered contently beneath the covers, blissfully unaware of the day's beginning. Something unusual, though, filtered through to her mostly unconscious mind. It was not necessarily a tangible sensation, or anything remotely concrete, but the sense was present nonetheless. The petite body stirred slightly and inched over toward the edge of the bed, comfortably slipping further underneath the warm covers. The strange and unusual sensation, however, persisted. Now becoming somewhat more alert, the small form crinkled her nose a bit, then hesitantly opened her sleepy green eyes. Quite suddenly, she was startled, nearly jumping straight up in surprise upon seeing the clear azure eyes staring directly back at her from alongside the waterbed.

"Jess." Robin blew out a breath. "What are you doing?"

No answer, only further staring.

"I'm trying to sleep, here. What's going on?"

The azure eyes narrowed slightly. "You know very well, Robin, what's going on."

Unimpressed, the younger woman drew the covers back around herself. "I have absolutely no idea what you're talking about. Not to mention the fact that it's practically the middle of the night right now." She closed her eyes. "I'm going back to sleep."

The staring continued. "Number one, Robin, it's most definitely not the middle of the night, and number two, don't play innocent with me." Jess put on her best menacing voice. "I want you to give them back."

A green eye popped open. "Give what back?"

"You know very well what. I put them right over there in the corner, and now they're gone."

The green eye closed once again. "If you lost something, Jess, when I get up I'll help you look for it, but right now, I'm going back to sleep."

That was a totally insufficient response. "I don't think so, Robin. You tell me where they are first, and then you can go back to sleep."

That prompted the blonde head to bury itself underneath a second pillow.

"I'm not leaving, Robin, until you give them back."

A muffled voice filtered from beneath said pillow. "I presume you're talking about those obnoxious bright yellow Tweety Bird slippers which you insist on wearing just to get back at me."

"For your information, Robin, I wear them, number one, because I like them, and number two, because they're very comfortable. It has nothing whatsoever to do with your unbelievably over-sized rabbit slippers."

"They're bunny slippers, not rabbit slippers, and they are not over-sized." The tousled blonde head pulled itself out from underneath the pillow and resituated itself back in its original position, eyes still closed. "So now you do admit that you wear them on purpose just to get back at me."

"I admit nothing." Jess rested her chin defiantly on the edge of the waveless waterbed. "It occurs to me that you're cleverly diverting the issue away from the whereabouts of the items you clearly took. I'm giving you one last chance, Robin. Give them back. And let me warn you that if you refuse to tell me where they are, I will be forced to take drastic measures."

Drastic measures? The same green eye popped open once again. "What type of drastic measures?"

"Well, I seem to recall that I didn't get to complete my lovely musical rendition of last weekend, and you know which one talking about. In fact, I have very many other musical renditions just waiting to be heard. A particular theme song from 'Gilligan's Island' immediately comes to mind."

She wouldn't. The younger woman continued to contemplate the implied threat.

"Come on, Robin. Spill it. Mr. Bluebird's starting to warm up, here. And the Professor and Mary Ann aren't far behind."

She's not getting a word out of me. "Blackmail doesn't suit you, Jess." With that, Robin rolled over, intent on resuming her blissful slumber.

That's it! "Fine, Robin. If that's the way you want it. But don't say I didn't warn you." The older woman leaned in very close to a conveniently placed petite ear and began her musical tribute to television's finest island adventure series. The tune was unerringly on-key, and in perfect pitch. "Just sit right back and you'll hear a tale, a tale of a fateful trip, that started from this tropic port, aboard this tiny ship." Jess paused briefly, and when no reaction was forthcoming, she continued on with her cheerful melody. "The mate was a mighty sailin' man, the skipper brave and sure. Five passengers set sail that day for a three hour tour, a three hour tour. The weather...."

Good grief! "Okay, okay." Robin rolled over on her back and rubbed her face briskly. "They're in the closet, Jess. I just moved them there last night because their obnoxious yellowness was distracting me while I was trying to read." Still foggy green eyes narrowed. "Happy now?"

A wide, satisfied smile. "Very."

"Now, will you please, please be quiet so I can go back to sleep?"

"Certainly." Jess replied in her most innocent tone of voice, then happily retrieved the slippers in question from the closet and put them on. "I'll go ahead and start breakfast in a little while, if you think you'll be up by then."

Robin chose not to acknowledge that little remark, and instead watched discretely beneath half-closed eyes as Jess padded toward the doorway. "You are very dead, you know."

"Ooooh." The taller woman flipped a look back over her shoulder. "I think I'm afraid."

"You should be."

What came next was a mischievous chuckle, as Jess promptly headed out of the bedroom happily completing the remainder of the aforementioned musical rendition solely for Robin's benefit. The strains of the lovely melody echoed down the hallway. "The weather started getting rough, the tiny ship was tossed. If not for the courage of the fearless crew, the Minnow would be lost, the Minnow would be lost...."

Robin drew the covers around herself once more and attempted mightily to go back to sleep. Instead, however, she found it unexpectedly difficult to do so, tossing and turning several times before finally giving up on the futile effort altogether. The cause of her troubles, it seemed, was the unfortunate fact that a certain television theme song kept running itself unceasingly around and around in her sleepy mind, absolutely refusing to relinquish its newly acquired domain. With an audible groan, she sat up straight against the headboard and contemplated her very grievous situation.

She's going to pay! I'm definitely deducting massive points for this.

****

Shortly before noon on Sunday, the silver Mercedes entered the modern subdivision and pulled into the driveway of the two-story Tampa townhouse. Jess and Robin exited the car and made their way to the front door, stopping briefly to notice the now sunny and pleasantly warm late winter day taking hold. Jess knocked firmly on the front door, then retrieved her spare house key and let herself and Robin inside. Green eyes took in the familiar dwelling, as Robin recalled with a sense of warmth and inner peace her last visit to Jess's mother's house back on New Year's Day. What stayed with the younger woman, even now, was the fact that Jess's mother seemed so at ease and comfortable in the presence of both her and Jess together. There was no angst, no disapproving glances, no disappointment, and no awkwardness. Just sincere and genuine delight. And yes, as Robin remembered their visit that day, it was indeed absolutely and positively delightful.

Just then, Elaine Harrison made her way down the staircase. "Jessie, is that you?"

"Hi, Mom." Jess greeted her mother with an enthusiastic hug, then couldn't help but beam. "You remember Robin."

"Of course I do." Elaine stepped forward and gave the younger attorney a warm hug, as well. "Robin, it's so nice to see you again. I'm glad Jessie finally brought you back here for a little visit."

"It's so nice to be back." Robin grinned from ear to ear, quietly suppressing a small chuckle. She then cast Jess a sly sideways glance. "I've been telling...Jessie for the longest time that we really should come back and see you again."

Blue eyes narrowed slightly in Robin's direction. *Jessie?* "I'd be very careful if I were you, Robin."

The petite frame leaned in closer to Elaine. "Don't worry about her. She gets kind of cranky sometimes."

Elaine chuckled, then winked. "I'm so glad you've figured her out, Robin. Jessie can be quite temperamental at times."

"Mom...." Jess's expression combined embarrassment with exasperation. "Do you remember that little matter we discussed the last time Robin and I were here?"

"What little matter was that, dear?" Elaine watched as her daughter rolled her eyes and leaned closer to whisper to her.

Robin, of course, watched all of this, thoroughly amused. In fact, she couldn't help the giggle that escaped. "Yes, Jessie, please tell us, what little matter, exactly, was that?"

Suddenly, a large hand landed squarely at the back of Robin's neck in playful menace. "You are so dead."

"Oh, just ignore her, Robin. Like I said, Jessie...." Elaine caught herself, then enunciated her daughter's name very clearly. "Jess...can be quite temperamental at times."

While this exchange was going on around her, Jess cast both her mother and Robin an extremely bored look. "Are you two finished?"

"Yes." Elaine winked at Robin conspiratorially. "Let's all go on into the living room and relax. I'll bring in some lemonade for us."

Once the three women were comfortably situated in the living room with their tall glasses of lemonade, it seemed that now was the right time for Robin and Jess to share their secret with Jess's mother. Both of the two attorneys were seated together on the velour sofa, while Elaine relaxed in the adjacent swivel chair. Jess spoke first, trying to preface the announcement with a bit of logic. "Mom, Robin and I wanted to talk with you about something. You know that we've been...together for several months now, and Robin's now living at the house with me...." As Jess began her rather lengthy explanation, the ring on her finger conspicuously gave her away.

"Jess...." Her mother gasped in true delight. "Look at that beautiful diamond ring you're wearing."

"Um...." Jess froze, then glanced down at her finger. Well, so much for the long-winded approach to commitment revelation. The cat, as they say, was definitely out of the bag. "Yeah. That's really what we wanted to talk with you about." She took Robin's hand in her own and smiled broadly. *Here goes.* "Robin and I exchanged rings last weekend. We've decided that we want to spend the rest of our lives together."

Robin instinctively smiled, then spoke quickly. "It's true. We want to be together."

There was a genuine warmth in Elaine's next words as she looked from her daughter to Robin and then back again. "I am very happy for you both. It's important to have someone in your life to love and to be loved by. I see clearly that you make each other very happy." She reached for Jess's hand and examined the diamond cluster ring. "I must say, this is absolutely gorgeous."

By now, Jess was nearly too caught up with emotion to speak. She managed, however, to say one thing, which although quite obvious, held significant meaning, nevertheless. "Robin gave it to me." Simply stated, but accurate just the same.

"And it's lovely." Elaine next focused her gentle gaze on Robin. "Now Robin, I hope my daughter had the good sense to give you a ring at least as half as nice as the one you gave her."

The younger attorney smiled shyly, then extended her left hand to Jess's mother. "Yes. Jess gave me the most beautiful ring I could ever imagine." And in Robin's eyes, that particular statement was the absolute truth.

Jess's mother examined the diamond solitaire. "I do believe you're right, Robin. This is a truly exquisite ring. My daughter did, indeed, do very well." She looked at the younger woman fondly. "And not just in her choice of rings."

Robin was genuinely touched. She internally delighted in Jess's mother's approval, not just of the rings themselves, but also of what they represented. *Why couldn't my own parents have been at least a little happy for me?* "Thank you, Mrs. Harrison."

"Please, Robin, call me Elaine. You're a member of the family now."

Green eyes sparkled in happiness. "Okay, Elaine."

"Mom, there's something we wanted to ask you." Jess stared at the floor for a brief second, then voiced her concern. "This obviously isn't something we can keep from Peter and Peggy. I'm not sure how they'd feel about the fact that Robin and I are together. We certainly don't want to cause any family issues if either one of them might have a problem with it." She looked at her mother. "What do you think we should do?"

Elaine didn't hesitate. "I think your brother would be just as delighted as I am. As for Peggy, well, that's a bit harder to judge. I think it might be best to give your brother a quick phone call right now and ask him to stop over for a little chat. You could tell him your news and also get his opinion on how Peggy might react."

Jess considered her mother's recommendation. "Okay. That sounds like a good idea. I'll go call him now."

As the older attorney left the room, Elaine focused back on Robin. "Now, while Peter and Jess are visiting later, why don't you and I go for a leisurely walk around the neighborhood. It is an absolutely gorgeous afternoon outside."

"I'd like that, Elaine."

Jess quickly strode back into the room. "He's coming right over." She addressed her next comment to Robin. "Um...would you mind if I spoke with him alone at first? He doesn't know anything about us." Blue eyes searched green, hoping for understanding.

As if reading the older attorney's mind, Robin stood up and gently placed her hand on Jess's forearm. "No, I don't mind at all. Go ahead." A wide grin then followed. "Besides, your mom and I are going to take a nice walk outside together."

Suspicious blue eyes shifted toward Elaine's seated form then back to Robin. "You are?"

"Yes." Green eyes twinkled playfully. "And just so you know, I plan on taking this opportunity to pry quite a bit of useful information out of her about you."

"Oh, you do, do you?" Both dark eyebrows lifted.

"Yes." Robin was quite pleased with herself. "Especially since you're most definitely not off the hook for that little television show rendition you so eagerly sang to your heart's content yesterday morning." A petite finger wagged purposefully in Jess's direction. "Preventing me from going back to sleep, I might add."

A now patented bored look. "That was your own fault, Robin. If you had just told me what I wanted to know in the first place, none of what followed would ever have been necessary."

She can't win this one. A satisfied smirk. "Let's just say that I can't wait to hear all about your terrible two's."

The older attorney quickly stepped over to her mother and spoke in a very low tone. "Promise me, Mom, you won't tell her anything embarrassing about me."

"Jessie, dear." Elaine chuckled, then stood up and patted the side of her daughter's cheek. "I do believe you're way out of your league here."

Damn. It's a full-blown conspiracy!

****

"Let's stop over here and take a little rest." Elaine led Robin to a park bench situated around one of the subdivision's several small ponds.

Robin followed and sat down on the bench next to the older woman. "This really is a very nice neighborhood, and very modern looking."

"I've lived here about five years now, and one thing I certainly have to say is that the homeowner's association keeps the grounds up very nicely." Elaine attempted to engage Robin in a little conversation about herself. "So, tell me, how are things going with you? My daughter mentioned a while back that you'd had some difficulties during the past year. If you'd rather not talk about it, I would certainly understand, but do I hope you're doing better now."

Perhaps I could talk a little bit about it. "I...um...don't know whether Jess told you about this, but last summer, I was about to be engaged when my boyfriend was involved in a car accident." Robin took a shaky breath. "He didn't make it. I've been having a hard time coming to terms with all that's happened since then." She looked directly at Elaine. "But Jess has helped me through a lot of it."

"At least you have someone you can turn to." The older woman grasped Robin's hand and gave it a gentle squeeze. "My daughter absolutely adores you, you know."

That brought a warm smile. "And I absolutely adore her." Golden eyebrows knit together slightly as an additional, more complicated, thought came to mind. "It's been hard lately because my parents haven't accepted our relationship. They don't understand." The younger woman stared blankly at the small pond in front of them, desperately wanting to unburden her heavy heart. "My father's caused some trouble for us at the firm, and for Jess in particular, because she was functioning as my immediate supervisor. She'll probably tell you more about this later, but the firm...um...could take some action against her." Green eyes now became slightly watery. "Sometimes, I feel as if it's my fault that all this is happening. That she could end up losing things that she's worked so hard for."

Elaine listened, but didn't pry. She let Robin tell her as much or as little as she felt comfortable in doing. Jess's mother also sensed that Robin needed to talk about some things, perhaps even the very things that she couldn't share with her own mother.

"I wish my family understood how I feel about Jess, or at least be happy for me that I have someone in my life who I love and who loves me. But..." Robin trailed off for a moment, then resumed. "They've interfered in my life so much, mainly because of what they want, not because of what I want. I'm just not sure whether I'll see them again, or whether they'll want to see me, especially if they don't approve of how I've chosen to live my life."

It's so sad to see her so troubled. Elaine finally spoke. "I'm very sorry for the things you've been going through. Whether or not your parents ultimately come to accept the life you've chosen to live, I want you to know that you're also a member of our family now, and anytime you want to talk about something, or rant and rave about something, or complain about my daughter's hardheadedness, you just come and talk with me." The older woman winked and gave Robin a reassuring smile. "And one thing's absolutely for sure, if my daughter is in need of some serious shaping up, you may enlist my help in that department, no questions asked."

Robin giggled in spite of herself. "I'll keep that in mind."

"Good." Elaine grinned. "Now, I believe you were interested in Jessie's terrible two's."

Green eyes grew wide. "Do you have some dirt I can use on her?"

"Well, let me think. There was one time when I believe she was almost three-years-old, and we were living in our previous house. We had a gardener who came over every week to take care of the landscaping and occasionally do some other odd jobs around the house for us. One day, our backyard fence was in desperate need of a new coat of paint. Ellis, our gardener, had just finished opening a fresh can of brick red paint as Jessie toddled by. He looked at her and told her to be very careful not to step in the paint. Well, about two minutes later, Ellis heard what he said was a very suspicious sound."

Robin brought her hand to her mouth and chuckled. "Oh no."

"Yes, you guessed it. Ellis turned around, and there was Jessie, trying very hard to look perfectly innocent, standing with one foot completely submerged inside the newly opened paint can. It was quite a sight."

"Oh my." The younger woman was beside herself with laughter, wiping tears from her eyes. *This could be very useful.* "That's unbelievable."

"Yes. One thing we can safely say is that we never have a dull moment when my daughter's around."

"I'll say." Robin finally regained her composure and used the opportunity to gather a bit of further information. "Tell me, Elaine, how did Jess develop her very strange addiction to shrimp?"

"Oh, that." Elaine waived her hand casually in front of her. "She's not nearly as addicted as she pretends to be."

Pretends? "Um...I don't think she's pretending. In fact, it seems a little bit obsessive to me."

"Oh, don't get me wrong, Robin. She has a definite fondness for shrimp, but she can't resist playing it up just a little bit for an audience."

Robin contemplated that theory for a moment. "No, I think I'd have to disagree with you on that. If you'd seen the things I've seen lately, you might think differently about it. For instance, do you know that she actually tried hiding it from me one night? She came home with some Chinese take-out, and I started looking through all the bags for the shrimp with lobster sauce, which she always gets, but it wasn't there. Then, I left to go get the drinks, and when I came back, the shrimp with lobster sauce had somehow magically appeared on her plate. She actually thought that I wouldn't notice that she'd snuck it in." Blonde eyebrows knit together in continued thought. "Then, there was also the one morning when she made shrimp shaped pancakes for breakfast, claiming that they supposedly taste so much better than the plain old boring round ones."

"Hmmm." Elaine chuckled a bit. "I see what you mean. Well, perhaps it really has become more severe, and I just haven't noticed."

"And I won't even get into the time we went fishing and used live shrimp for bait. Let's just say that it's a very good thing I brought a picnic lunch that day."

"Now, that does sound serious." The older woman stood up from the park bench. "You'll definitely have to keep me apprised of this situation. Right now, let's walk on over past the clubhouse and pool, and then we'll go back and see what my children are up to."

"All right." Robin stretched and took a second to breath in deeply the spring-like fresh air, noticing with interest as pair of squirrels played hide and seek in a nearby tree. The young attorney joined Jess's mother on their continued walk and reflected on their recent conversation. And, of course, mulling further one very interesting paint

story in particular. Robin giggled lightly to herself.
Paybacks, Jess.

****

The tall dark-haired man settled himself comfortably on the living room sofa and waited as his sister brought in a couple of glasses of lemonade. There was a bit of an awkward silence as Jess searched her mind for the best possible way to broach the delicate subject prompting Peter's unscheduled visit. Unfortunately, she ended up procrastinating even further, engaging in trivial pleasantries, unsure of just how to begin the conversation.

Her brother set down his lemonade on the coffee table in front of him. "So tell me, what's this burning issue that you needed to talk over with me?"

This is so much harder than I thought. "Well, you know that Robin works at my law firm, and she has moved into the house with me." Jess looked at Peter and received confirmation of her statement. "Over the course of the several months that Robin and I have known each other, we've become very close. That was one reason we decided to live together." She looked at him again to gauge whether he was processing the information. However, his face remained expressionless as he reached again for his glass of lemonade. "Another reason we wanted to live together was that we...um...realized that...." *I'm not doing this well.* "The bottom line, Peter, is that I love Robin, and Robin loves me."

At this, her brother's dark eyebrows lifted. "Okay."

"Robin and I love each other very much, and we've decided that we want to spend the rest of our lives together." Jess wet her lips nervously. "Do you understand what I'm saying?"

Peter took a sip of lemonade, considering what he'd just heard, then cleared his throat. "You and Robin...love each other?"

"Yes." Jess likewise reached for her glass of lemonade, suddenly finding herself more than a little thirsty.

"Are you saying is that you and Robin are...together?"

"That's a good way to put it, yes."

"I see." Her brother continued to contemplate what he'd been told, his expression now somewhat shocked, then leaned further back against the sofa cushions. "Wow. I'd never have expected that." He fiddled somewhat nervously with the rim of his glass. "Does Mom know?"

Jess nodded. "Yes. Robin and I told her today about our plans."

"Your plans?"

"We...exchanged rings last weekend." Her gaze tracked from her glass of lemonade to the ring she wore, then as if on reflex, she extended her left hand to her brother to verify the statement.

Peter took a closer look at the ring. "It's very nice."

There was a definite stiffness to her brother's demeanor, and Jess was starting to become worried. "Does this bother you?"

Her brother took a moment to gather his thoughts. "To tell you the truth, I'm not sure what I think. From what I've seen of Robin, she certainly seems like a very nice person. And, if you love her, and you're happy together, then I guess that really is the most important thing."

Don't fall over yourself, Peter. "Listen, if this makes you uncomfortable...."

"No." Setting his glass down again, he edged closer to his sister. "It just took me a moment to put it all into perspective. The most important thing is that you're happy and that this is what you want." He captured Jess's eyes with his own, showing that he was completely sincere. "I won't say I'm not surprised, but if you're happy, then I'm happy for you." He smiled. "Robin really does seem like a very nice person."

Jess's own tense posture softened. Coming from a man, and one's own brother even, Peter's statement was in reality a ringing endorsement, and she knew it. "Thanks." She swallowed and brought up the other touchy subject that had been on her mind. "Peter, about Peggy, do you think she'll have a problem with this?"

Her brother's brows knit together in concentration. "You know that Peg's quite religious and is involved in many church activities, but I don't think she's judgmental. She already knows you quite well, and she met Robin on New Year's Day. It may take her a little bit of time to get used to the idea, and she may feel awkward about it at first, but I think eventually she'll be okay with it."

"Robin and I don't want to cause any family problems. If Peg isn't comfortable with this, Robin and I can work around it and maybe visit mom at times when Peg won't be around."

"Let me talk with her." Peter stood up. "I'll fill her in, and then I'll let you know if there's a problem. Would it be all right with you if I did that?"

That's reasonable. "Yeah. Thanks."

Just then, the front door opened and Elaine and Robin stepped inside. It didn't escape Jess's notice that both of them were laughing a little bit too conspiratorially for her comfort.

"Hi, Peter." Elaine entered the living room and gave her son a hug. "How are Peggy and the boys?"

"Good, Mom." He looked at Robin, a genuine warmth in his eyes. "It's very nice to see you again, Robin. My sister's told me about the very good news. We're very happy to have you a part of the family." He stepped over and spoke softly to Robin, albeit purposefully loud enough for all to hear. "Make sure you keep my sister in line. If you need any help, you know who to call." He winked and motioned with his thumb toward himself.

That brought a grin and a giggle from Robin. "I may just take you up on that."

Now, it wasn't normally in Jess's nature to be prone to conspiracy theories, but as she watched this interaction with avid interest, and then considered her mother's not so subtle betrayal of her earlier, Jess was quickly coming to the distinct conclusion that a vast conspiracy against her was indeed underfoot. *They're all in cahoots, I just know it!* She was brought out of her overly suspicious musings when her mother announced that dinner would be ready in an hour.

Elaine looked across at her son. "Can you stay for an early dinner, Peter?"

"No, sorry, Mom. Peg's got dinner planned already. I really need to get on home." The tall man said his goodbyes to all present, then left the household.

Jess glanced over at Robin, all too aware of the younger woman's exceptionally giddy mood. "Can I speak with you a minute?" She grasped the petite hand and led them both over to the sliding glass doors, while her mother stepped into the kitchen to continue with the dinner preparations. "All right, Robin. Spill it. What'd she tell you about me?"

She's so paranoid. And definitely cranky. "I have absolutely no idea what you're talking about." Robin grinned innocently. "Your mother and I had a delightful walk around the neighborhood."

Still suspicious blue eyes studied Robin further. *I'm not buying it.* "Fine. But when we get home, I want to know word for word exactly what you two talked about."

"What makes you think I'd tell you that?"

Jess stepped very close to Robin, as her low alto voice whispered seductively into a petite ear. "Because I can be very persuasive."

Robin swallowed hard. *Ooooh. I think I'm in trouble now.*

Chapter 8

The boardroom began to fill with all five members of the Management Committee, nearly everyone first pouring a cupful of freshly brewed coffee before filing in and taking a seat around the oblong cherry wood conference table. It was grim start to a Monday morning, as anyone would admit, a cool misty rain dampening the spirits of each and every member present during the Monday early morning hours. Most would have much preferred to be in any other place but where they currently found themselves, in a conference room about to ponder and then decide the most politically expedient way to handle what was, at best, a delicate situation. Gordon McDaniel took his seat at the head of the far end of the table, and after reviewing his notes on a legal pad in front of him, addressed the members of the Management Committee.

"Let's begin." The managing partner's expression was serious. "Before we speak this morning first with Robin Wilson, I've been informed that Barbara Roberts has requested that she be allowed to briefly say a few words to the Committee." He glanced over toward the head of the litigation department seated to his right, and upon seeing the nod from Harry Roberts, continued. "Unless there are any objections, Harry will ask Barbara to join us first for a few moments."

The room remained quiet, and hearing no objection to the request, Harry stepped out into the lobby and quickly returned and guided his wife toward an open seat in the center of the conference table. Barbara settled into the cool leather chair and looked down the length of the table to where Gordon McDaniel sat, smiling warmly at her old friend.

"Barbara, it's good to see you." The managing partner opened the dialogue.

"Thank you, Gordon, and thank you for allowing me just a few moments to speak to your Committee this morning." The wife of the litigation department chairman smiled again graciously, then paused and glanced around the conference table just long enough to extend a gentle greeting to each member present. Aside from her husband and Gordon McDaniel, those seated at the table were partners Tim West, Matt Singleton, and Patricia Jenkins. Although Barbara wasn't familiar with Tim West, the newest member of the Management Committee, she knew and frequently socialized with both Matt Singleton and his wife. She recognized Patricia Jenkins, a very aggressive corporate law attorney, who had been with the firm for nearly fifteen years. In fact, Patricia was the first female attorney employed by the firm who would eventually hang around the good ol' boys long enough to obtain partnership status.

Gordon continued on. "I've mentioned to the Committee that you've requested an opportunity to address the entire Committee as a whole, so if you're ready now, we can begin."

"Very well." The wife of the chairman of the litigation department folded her hands together in front of her and proceeded to address the members. "As you may know, I don't commonly involve myself in the daily running of this firm anymore. I left all of those administrative chores years ago to my husband and Gordon and their very capable staff. I don't mean to intrude on your judgment on the matter before you today, however, I want to offer to you my thoughts, and then you may proceed as you see fit."

"Well..." Tim West leaned forward and interjected. "I don't believe we've met, Mrs. Roberts, but I'm certainly willing to listen to whatever you have to say. I'm sure you realize, though, that the Committee members here today have a unique perspective on this matter in that we work inside the firm's environment day in and day out. We not only need to consider the inter-workings of the law firm in general, but also the risks any matters brought before us may have on each of our partners."

"Yes, of course you're right, Mr. West." Sensing a bit of opposition, Barbara decided to move quickly to the point. "May I be frank with you all?"

Tim West sat back. "Please do."

"Some of you may not know this, but Gordon, his wife, Lynn, Harry, and myself began this law firm so many years ago. As you can imagine, it took a lot of hard work to get the firm established and then to acquire and maintain a client base. In those early days, we weren't sure we'd make it, but ultimately, with perseverance and a little luck, we did." Barbara's gaze settled on Tim West. "One thing we strived for was to see that this law firm recruited the best possible legal minds available, and then to do everything possible to hold on to them once they were here."

Gordon looked up. "I know where you're headed Barbara, and I agree with you to a point. The problem in this situation is that the Committee just simply can't turn a blind eye to the fact that a partner of this law firm deliberately ignored the policies established by this Committee, and instead, acted in her own self-interests, putting all partners at risk in the process. While I agree that Jessica Harrison has a stellar record as a litigator, and up until this point has been a tremendous addition to this firm, what would it say to all our other attorneys if the Committee were to simply overlook her indiscretion?"

"Gordon, I'm not suggesting that the Committee ignore the matter. What I'm saying is that if Jessica were to leave this firm, you and I both know that some other law firm would snatch her up before her feet even hit the pavement, and this firm would be none the better for it. Perhaps the Committee, in this instance, could see a way to work out this matter with her, and Robin, if need be."

It was Patricia Jenkins' turn to speak up. "And if the Committee did see a way to work through this, what would prevent another attorney from doing whatever he or she wanted to do, regardless of the best interests of the law firm and its partners?"

At first blush, Patricia's question seemed damning, but Barbara noted the subtle gleam in Patricia's eye as she glanced toward Tim West. *Perhaps she's playing devil's advocate.* "Well, I'm quite certain that this Committee could structure an agreement which would adequately protect the firm from harm as it pertains to this particular situation, and which would also send a sufficient message to all other partners and attorneys of this law firm as to an acceptable code of conduct."

It did not go unnoticed by any member of the Management Committee that throughout this entire exchange, Harry Roberts remained silent, sitting in the chair next to his wife, his posture clearly supportive. He was permitting his wife to have the floor entirely to herself, and everyone knew it. Office politics cut both ways, and when the wife of a founding partner, who also assisted in the founding of the firm herself, deemed a matter of such importance that she felt the need to express her opinion, politically speaking, it was in everyone's best interests to listen and take the matter seriously...that is, unless you happened to be one particular new and quite brash member of the Management Committee, itself.

"I'm sure..." Tim West spoke out again, an overly polite quality coloring his voice. "This Committee will make an appropriate determination as to the proper course of action to take in this matter involving all concerned." *Giving Barbara Roberts respect was one thing. Giving her ultimate say in such matters via pressure tactics was quite another. After all, she has no real vote here.*

Barbara smiled deceptively. *He's a lost cause. Perhaps a little additional persuasion is necessary. Something for all of them to chew on.* "Very well. Let me just leave the Committee with one last thought, then. Which of these would be the greater harm? A stigma associated with this law firm for intolerance of alternate lifestyles which, no matter how vehemently that intent is denied, will nonetheless be perceived to be true within the legal community, or a subtler arrangement whereby sufficient action is taken to protect the firm in this matter, and at the same time, dissuade any like conduct from happening again by any other partner of this firm?"

Matt Singleton finally voiced a thought. "Yes, I think it's a point worth considering."

Harry sat forward in his chair and focused his attention on the managing partner. "What do you think, Gordon?"

What a mess! The sad fact of the matter was that if the firm chose to make an example of Jessica Harrison in this instance, the real reason for the disciplinary action would be obscured by the sensational aspects of her chosen lifestyle. But still...partners are not free to play the system in a game of Russian roulette, betting that a delicate enough situation will in the end serve to protect them from potential professional harm, allowing them free reign to act in whatever manner they so chose. Gordon sighed. Either way, the ultimate message would be lost. "All right, Barbara. We'll consider it. It's the best I can say at this point. Let's speak with both Robin and Jessica, and then see where we stand. The way I see it, a lot rides on each party's intent."

Suddenly, Matt felt a headache coming on. He had just finished preparing Jessica's will and was privy to certain privileged information. Still, it was not enough to warrant excusing himself from the Committee. As a matter of fact, as he thought about the situation even further, having prepared her will actually gave him greater insight into each party's intent. But either way, he would be remiss in not disclosing the matter to the Committee at this point. He felt compelled to speak. "I want the Committee to know that I have conducted a few personal probate matters for Jessica Harrison. I trust that my work for her will have no bearing on the subject matter currently before us."

"No." Gordon waived his hand casually. "I don't think that other matters conducted for Jessica or Robin on a personal level are material to the matter before the Committee today." He glanced over at Matt. "Unless you know of some reason why such probate matters might impair your ability to serve on this Committee."

"No." Matt shook his head. "I just wanted to advise the Committee of the issue before we proceed."

"All right." Gordon looked down the conference table to the wife of the litigation department chairman, who had been patiently, albeit curiously, observing the Committee's previous exchange. "Thank you for coming in today and speaking to us, Barbara. We appreciate your concerns and insights with regard to this difficult matter."

"It was nice to meet with you all." Barbara stood up and waited as her husband joined her and guided her out into the firm's lobby. Once safely outside the door, with an audible sigh, she turned to face him. "Oh dear. I think this may be a bit more difficult than I had anticipated."

Harry looked at her thoughtfully. "Well, you gave it your best shot, dear. Unfortunately, Jess brought a lot of this upon herself, and now, it'll be up to her to see her way clear of it. I'm betting, though, that she's up to the task." He led his wife to the elevators. "And although I don't condone what she's done or how she chose to handle it, I'd really hate to lose her."

His wife stepped onto the arriving elevator car and gave him a serious look. "If I were Jess, after seeing that bunch in there today, I think I might just leave this firm and start my own practice, taking Robin along with me. Gordon's Committee might be very wise to think about that." With that thought, the elevator doors closed.

Inside the conference room, Tim West closed his eyes and shook his head in frustration. It was absolutely outrageous. Management decisions were to be made by Management Committee members. Period. Secretaries don't have a say. Mailroom clerks don't have a say. Word processing personnel don't have a say. Associates don't have a say. And most definitely, partners' wives don't have a say. Not in the least. No matter who those partners' wives happen to be. *Perhaps Gordon and I need to have a little chat about certain things before we continue.*

****

Robin sat at the oval conference table, drumming her fingers apprehensively on its solid cherry wood top. Gordon McDaniel had stepped out of the room to take a quick phone call, which now had apparently turned into a lengthy phone call. After several more moments, the conference room door swung open and the managing partner joined the assembled Management Committee members and their star witness at the table.

"Robin, please excuse my delay." Gordon looked down the table at the young associate. "We won't take up too much of your time here today. We just have a few things we need to discuss with you, and then we can let you get back to work."

Let's get this over with. "That's perfectly all right." Robin smiled politely, careful not to show her anxiety. "I'll answer your questions as honestly as I can."

It wasn't entirely unexpected, but an uncomfortable silence settled over the room as the Chairman of the Management Committee appeared to be struggling for an appropriate way to begin the inquiry proceedings. He cleared his throat uneasily, then began. "I want you to know that we aren't here to pry into your personal life. On behalf of the firm, we need to make sure that there is no potential risk to the law firm as a whole as a result of your personal relationship with one of our partners, Jessica Harrison. As I'm sure you're aware, your father could have created an enormous amount of trouble for us if he had chosen to do so. As is stands now, we've received a signed letter from him indicating that he agrees not to file a complaint with the State Bar Association implicating this firm in any claims of improper conduct resulting from your relationship with Jessica Harrison."

Implicating this firm? What about implicating Jess? "Would the agreement he signed extend to all partners of the firm?"

Both Harry Roberts and Gordon McDaniel nodded at the same time. Harry was the first to answer Robin's question. "Yes. That was one of the things we wanted to make sure that your father agreed to. We didn't want him coming back later on and try to implicate any partner of this firm in this matter. As you realize, implicating one partner implicates, by extension, all other partners."

"Yes, I do understand that." *So, he let Jess off the hook, too. At least that's something.*

"Now..." Gordon interjected. "Please remember that we're not asking anything of a personal nature, and everything you say here will be kept strictly confidential. What the Committee would like to know, first of all, is at any time since you starting working with this law firm, have you ever felt pressured or otherwise compelled to maintain a personal relationship outside of work with Jessica Harrison out of fear for your continued employment?"

Green eyes went wide, then became determined. "Absolutely not. If you're asking whether I ever believed that my job was tied to my personal relationship with Jessica Harrison, I can tell you that I never, ever once believed that it was." Robin glanced around the table, noting that all present were looking uncomfortably down at their hands, save for Tim West. His gaze held hers for a slight moment, then Robin looked away.

The managing partner quickly asked the next question. "Were you aware of the firm's policy regarding personal relationships between those with supervisory responsibilities over employees whom they supervise?"

"I became aware of the policy a couple of months after I started working here."

Tim West spoke up. "How was it brought to your attention?"

The young associate grimaced internally. *He knows how.* "Jessica Harrison mentioned it to me."

"And yet, despite this, you and Jessica decided to continue your personal relationship, thereby leaving the firm open to accusations, the nature which your father recently threatened. Is that correct?" His point made, albeit a bit harshly, Tim West sat back comfortably in his chair.

He's out for blood. "Let me say something." Robin glanced from Tim West to the other end of the table where Harry and Gordon sat. "Because I never felt that my job was in any way tied to my relationship with Jessica Harrison, the allegations made by my father never even occurred to me or to her. It was never an issue with us. I never believed that such a claim was at all supportable, mainly because I absolutely deny it." Her voice had gained a hard edge as she fought hard to keep her resentment at both her father and the Management Committee in check. "My father had absolutely no basis to make such a claim, and no right to threaten to do so."

The head of the litigation department sensed tensions rising, and softened his voice in an effort to calm things down. "All right, Robin, that's all we were asking. We just wanted your honest interpretation of how you felt about being placed in the situation you were in. Our main interest is that you didn't feel that your job was tied to certain requirements which may or may not have been imposed on you."

His words were said with such sincerity that Robin just couldn't take offense. She gave him a reassuring smile. "I understand why you're asking, and let me state unequivocally that I never felt pressured in any way. I chose to maintain a relationship outside of work with

Jessica Harrison of my own free will. The allegations my father put forward never crossed my mind, and therefore they were not an issue with me. I want you to know that I've made it clear to him that what he did was unacceptable, and furthermore, I absolutely and positively deny any such allegations."

"Okay." Gordon was now obligated to pose another query. "We also want to know whether you were either pressured or felt obligated to keep the whole matter quiet, either for fear of your job or for any other reason.

What are they really afraid of? "Let me make this perfectly clear, so you have no doubts. I absolutely was not pressured, in any way either to continue my relationship with Jessica Harrison or to keep it quiet, nor did I feel any such obligation to do so."

As certain people are prone to do, the newest member of the Management Committee was just itching to play the hero and turn up something of substance. "Robin, you, and Jessica in particular, chose to remain silent about your relationship even though you were both fully aware of the firm's policy. If you weren't keeping silent because you personally felt pressured to do so, then what reason did you have for agreeing to keep it quiet?" Now, either Tim West was trying way too hard to make his point, or he really was stupid after all.

"Because..." Robin looked pointedly at him. "The nature of my relationship wasn't something that I personally was ready to disclose." She paused to let that sink in. "I'm sure you understand what I mean."

If the other members of the Management Committee weren't so busy looking at their hands, they might have seen the bright red blush that crept up Tim West's face. If truth be known, he was hoping for some deep dark calculated admission, not merely the obvious and sympathy producing answer he got. "Yes." He cleared his throat. "I do understand what you mean."

Why not just put it all on the table? "An important consideration was that Jessica and I wanted to continue working together." She looked back up the cherry wood conference table toward Harry and Gordon, directing her further response mainly to them. "We seem to work so well together that it's really amazing. I've gained invaluable practical experience and have learned an enormous amount about litigation practice just in the short time I've spent working with her. She's guided me through many first-year associate pitfalls, and during our trial together last December, I gained a great deal of courtroom working experience. I felt it was beneficial to me and my career to work with her, and so I wanted to continue doing that."

Tim West's head jerked up. This was interesting and certainly could be used as fodder to fuel further interrogation. "You both put your own self-interests ahead of this firm's interests? Is that what you're saying?"

"Take it easy, Tim." Patricia cut him off and now spoke to Robin for the first time. "I can understand how you'd want to gain as much practical knowledge as possible, especially when you're first starting out in this business. It's just an awkward situation because of the ultimate appearance this takes on, especially if it had been brought before the State Bar."

Robin's green eyes closed, and she lowered her head slightly, speaking softly. "I know that now. But it still doesn't change the facts. I never felt pressured, and I wanted to keep the matter quiet because I was the one who was not nearly ready to reveal it. And yes, I also wanted to gain as much practical knowledge from Jessica as I possibly could."

"Robin?" Matt Singleton had been reluctant up until now to ask any questions, considering his recent role in Jess's probate matter, but he thought it best to clarify absolute intent on this matter. "Is it correct that your intention was to keep this matter quiet purely for personal reasons, not as a careless disregard for this firm's well-being?"

Thank you, Matt. "Yes. And I also state unequivocally that it is my understanding from what I know that this was Jessica's intent, as well."

Apparently, everyone was satisfied by her answers, or pretended to be, as the room once again became deathly silent. Either that, or everyone was just too embarrassed to ask anything else. Finally, mercifully, Gordon spoke again. "All right. Thank you, Robin. I think that's all we need."

The associate nodded and stood to leave. "You're welcome." She turned to Harry and gave him a quick smile, then straightened her shoulders and silently left the conference room.

The boardroom remained eerily quiet after Robin's departure. Harry rubbed the bridge of his nose above the rim of his glasses and shook his head. Leaving aside the fact that he didn't quite understand Robin and Jess's relationship on a personal level, he nevertheless found it rather disquieting to air it all out in a business setting. There was just something unsettling about the precedent. And unsavory. *Perhaps a policy revision is in order.*

Perhaps so.

****

Tedious wasn't quite how one would describe it, but it was close enough. Jess sat at the oblong cherry conference table, fielding question after question posed to her by various members of the Management Committee. Most questions, not surprisingly, were accusatory in nature. Through it all, though, she was able to ascertain that what they were really after was intent. They harped on it time and time again. What was her intent, first, by maintaining a relationship with Robin, and second, by then concealing it, a concealment which ultimately put the firm at risk? *But why focus on intent alone and not on the facts of what actually happened?* It was puzzling, to say the least. The Committee members made no pretense of any politeness or tactfulness in their questioning. After all, the survival of the firm, as they saw it, had come perilously close to being jeopardized by her actions. In all honesty, it was not really surprising when Jess thought about it. After all, how was the Committee supposed to react to the fact that one of their own partners had put everything at risk? Jess closed her eyes and took in a long, deep breath before fielding the next barrage of questions. *As if my life isn't complicated enough....*

Tim West glared at the junior partner. "I think this Committee still needs an acceptable reason as to why you took such measures to hide your relationship with Robin Wilson, however you wish to categorize that relationship. Would you mind explaining it again for us, because I don't think we totally understand your intent?"

Shaking her head wearily, Jess reiterated her previous answer. "Robin and I work well together. I wanted to continue that, and I knew that by disclosing our relationship, she'd have to be reassigned. As you're no doubt aware, most people don't work well with me, nor I with them." She paused to let that truism sink in. "Without Robin to help me, associate assistance is limited, at best. The last thing I wanted was to be stuck with Mark Stevens again. It's no secret that Mark and I don't get along, as I'm sure you know." She grimaced in an unconscious gesture, recalling a near-malpractice catastrophe which had occurred with Mark Stevens just before Robin had been assigned to work full-time with her. "And the other reason Robin and I both decided not to disclose the nature of things between us is simply because we, ourselves, weren't ready to publicly reveal it. It's a...very sensitive thing, as I'm sure you're all aware."

"So, what you're saying is that your intent was to put yourself and your workload above the best interests of this law firm." Tim West folded his hands in front of him, confident he'd seen the true motivations behind her actions.

Bastard. Blue eyes leveled a devastating glare at him. "My intent, Tim, was to do the best job I could and to have the best possible assistance in doing so. In addition, I also wanted to be sensitive to both mine and Robin's comfort levels with regard to the public knowledge of this thing." Her gaze hardened further, and she cocked her head slightly. "Does that make my intent clear to you?"

"All right." Gordon stepped in, sensing an unpleasant altercation. "I think we're now clear on what your intent was, Jessica." He flipped through his legal pad. "The other problem we have is that, as Robin's supervisor, you were required to prepare her performance evaluations. It stands to reason that given your personal relationship, your ability to be objective might be compromised. How would it be possible for you separate yourself from your personal relationship with Robin far enough so that you could prepare those evaluations objectively? As you're no doubt aware, that is precisely why we created the policy in the first place. Favoritism is a motivation killer for everyone else in the workplace. Surely you know that."

That was my original thought when all this started. "Listen, Gordon, I was well aware of the favoritism perception, and I took extreme caution to avoid any appearance of preferential treatment. I oftentimes counseled Robin on many ways to improve her skills as a litigator in an endeavor to do just that. But the truth of the matter is, she's a very good attorney, and her instincts are top-notch." The junior partner shook her head in wonder at her protégé. "Besides, Robin and I work together almost like clockwork. She can anticipate what I need and what is required, without me even asking. She demonstrated that to me time and time again. I was more than pleased with her overall performance at our trial last December." Jess looked at her hands sadly. "I had every hope of continuing that working relationship."

A smirk passed across Tim West's face. *You should have thought about that before you broke the rules.*

Harry cleared his throat. "What Jess says is true, Gordon, and you know it." *Perhaps client satisfaction will carry some weight.* "You remember how Phil Jones of RSJ Industries told both of us how pleased he was with Jess and Robin's work on the trial. He's promised this firm all of his future work in the Southeast from now on because of it." He sighed. "I'm interested in keeping him happy right now so we don't jeopardize the deal. I've already fielded several calls from some of our other clients who are uneasy with someone other than Jess handling their work."

"Yes, Harry." Gordon sighed. "While that may be true, we can't have the perception of favoritism infecting this workplace, and we certainly can't have one of our own partners deciding on her own what's best for everyone concerned. There are other considerations here, aside from clients and workload requirements, as you know."

The head of the litigation department shook his head. It was becoming clear that Gordon may be a lost cause in this matter. Harry spoke his mind. "Yes, there are other considerations, and I'll tell you one thing, keeping a lid on this whole thing might be the best this firm can hope for at this point."

Tim practically shot up from his chair. "You don't really believe that after what she's done."

"Let's settle down." Gordon tried to regain some semblance of decorum in the already a tense atmosphere. He looked over at Jess who was watching the interplay with interest. "Is there anything else you'd like to say about the favoritism issue?"

Jess's better instincts told her to be quiet. She glanced at Matt Singleton sitting across from her suspiciously silent. *Damn, Matt.* She'd disclosed to him everything about her finances and probate wishes, clearly indicating her intent as far as the sincerity in her relationship with Robin, yet he had chosen to remain quiet throughout the meeting. *Is it too much to ask, Matt, that you could say something positive, here?* Resigned that fate had to take its course, she let the matter rest. "No, Gordon, I think I've conveyed my intent on that matter clearly."

"All right." Gordon continued. "The last issue is the sexual harassment claim...."

The junior partner, with lightning quickness, stopped him immediately. She held one finger up in the air, and spoke succinctly. "There is no sexual harassment claim."

Finally, Patricia Jenkins voiced her concern and clarified the managing partner's point. "What Gordon is referring to is the potential sexual harassment claim threatened by Mr. Wilson."

"Which has since been dropped." Jess interjected.

Patricia nodded. "Yes, and which has since been dropped."

Why the hell even bring this up? It's a non-issue. The junior partner took a steadying breath in an attempt to rein in her growing anger, then pointed her finger once again up in the air in a gesture of determination. "Number one, Robin's father had absolutely no standing whatsoever to bring or even to threaten such a claim. Number two, Robin expressly denies it. And number three...." Here, she paused to make her point explicit, steeling her gaze individually on each member of the Management Committee one by one, before she continued, her voice deep with barely controlled emotion. "Number three, I never,

ever, even once, in any remote way, intimated such a thing in my relationship with Robin. Never. Nor would I ever do so, and I don't like the implication that I would." Jess shook her head in annoyance, then attempted to calm herself. She studied at the blank faces looking back at her and sighed inwardly. It was now becoming abundantly clear that certain people were determined to hang one issue or another on her in order to justify any potential disciplinary action the Committee ultimately might take. And she didn't like it.

"That may be true." Patricia retorted. "But the point here is that a serious claim of a very unpleasant nature could have been made, and the mere allegation alone could have damaged this law firm in more ways than one. I'm sure you realize that." Her eyes then softened a bit. "Listen, I'm not insensitive to your situation. Really, I'm not. But what I'd like to know is whether you realized the potential peril you were putting yourself and this law firm in by maintaining such a clandestine relationship with a person whom you supervised. And further, whether you understood that as Robin's immediate supervisor, any such allegations of a sexual harassment nature could reasonably have been perceived to be true."

The smug look on Tim West's face didn't escape Jess. That was expected. What she couldn't figure out was Patricia Jenkins' angle. Was the older partner providing her with a way out, or was she just getting ready to put the last nail in the coffin? Blue eyes closed slowly, then opened in resignation. *Whatever happens, happens.* "Let me say this. As to whether I realized the potential peril I may have been placing myself and this firm in by my keeping my relationship with Robin quiet and that in my supervisory capacity it could have been perceived as sexual harassment, my answer is that I did not realize that particular scenario until Robin's father made his threat. To be honest, since the claim was never even remotely true, it just never crossed my mind to consider it. Perhaps it should have, but it didn't. So, if you're asking whether I deliberately chose to subject this firm to the risk of being tarnished with a sexual harassment claim, my answer is that I did not."

Patricia seemed satisfied at the answer, and sat back in her chair. She jotted something onto her legal pad, but otherwise remained quiet.

For his part, sensing that the issue was in danger of falling by the wayside, Tim West quickly jumped back into the questioning, unable to just sit back and let the junior partner off the hook so easily. "But you were Robin's supervisor, were you not? What about Patricia's question about whether you knew that such a claim, if it was made, could have been perceived to be true, regardless of whether in reality it actually was so? You should have known that."

This guy's getting the hell on my nerves. "Listen, as to whether since I was Robin's immediate supervisor I understood that such a claim could possibly be perceived to be true, let me say this again." Jess held up her finger once more, this time pointedly in Tim's direction. "Since in reality the claim was never even remotely valid, that potential did not cross my mind. Had I realized that such a claim could reasonably have been made, I would have taken steps to avoid it immediately. I absolutely and unequivocally would have done so, and I don't particularly like your implication that I'd do otherwise. Furthermore...." She leveled another devastating glare directly at him. "As to the issue of whether I should have known how it could potentially have been perceived....well, hindsight is always twenty-twenty, isn't it, Tim?" *You better hope I don't catch you screwing up, buddy, or your ass is mine.*

"You didn't answer the question." Tim snapped.

Things were fast becoming out of control as almost everyone now felt compelled to throw in their two-cents worth at once. Both Harry and Gordon, nearly in unison, shouted across the fray in an effort to calm everyone down and regain some semblance of decorum. It took a few moments, but the assembled parties finally quieted. Jess focused her eyes on her hands, realizing now that whatever decision the Management Committee ultimately made, her relationship with her partners was seriously damaged.

We need to end this quickly before it all but destroys us. "All right." Gordon shook his head somberly, then glanced up at the junior partner. "I think that's all we'll need for today. If the Committee has anything further, we'll let you know. As soon as a decision's been made, either Harry or I will inform you."

Jess nodded but surveyed the managing partner's demeanor. *Something else is eating him.* "I have one question for the Committee." She met and then held Gordon's gaze. "My understanding is that Robin will receive no disciplinary action resulting from this matter or as a direct result of the Committee's decision on this matter. Is that still the case?"

"Yes." Gordon nodded. "The Committee has agreed that Robin is not the responsible party. Further, Robin still has standing to file a claim, if she so chooses."

Oh. I see it now. Jess held back a smile as she realized the actual game being played. *It definitely explained their obsession with intent.* She almost laughed at the reverse implication, whether or not the Committee members realized that they'd just given it away. The

Committee was taking no action again Robin, in part because the Committee was afraid that the young associate, herself, might file a claim against the firm. They'd obtained a waiver from her father, that was true, but they'd obtained no such waiver from her. Any disciplinary action against her would likely be seen as retaliatory in nature. *Well, whatever leverage works here, works for me. Just as long as Robin's protected. And Tom Wilson, ol' buddy, I can do blackmail with the best of them.* "Fine." Jess stood up to leave. "Then, I'd say that it would be wise of the Committee to include in its final written decision that Robin is cleared of any and all wrong-doing."

Gordon raised an eyebrow. He wasn't sure whether or not the junior partner's statement was a thinly veiled threat. His mouth opened slightly as he mulled that thought over. It was just quite possible that a less than favorable decision against Jessica could result in Robin's filing a sexual harassment claim against the firm. Of course, Robin's taking such an action would also necessarily implicate the junior partner, which was highly unlikely to happen. Still, if things eventually turned sour between Jessica and Robin, all bets were off. He sighed wearily. "All right. We'll consider putting something to that effect in our decision." Having given that concession, he sat there stoically and watched as the junior partner exited the conference room, her shoulders unexpectedly confident.

Good grief. Can this day get any worse?

****

Robin sat at the dining room table, pouring intently over the household finances and going over the bank statements from her and Jess's joint checking account. She'd been studying their domestic financial situation for a significant part of the evening, and what she saw was not good, at least not from her perspective. In fact, it was downright aggravating. And disturbing. For the past two months, ever since Robin had moved into The Ranch, she had been depositing money into their joint checking account every week to help cover the everyday household expenses which she and Jess incurred. Now, in reviewing the bank statements, Robin found that every single dime she'd put into that account was still in there, left entirely untouched and wholly unspent. The bills, however, were all paid up, with not even a single one left owing. Green eyes closed in frustration. This could only mean one thing, and one thing only. Jess had been depositing twice the amount of money into the checking account as Robin had been, far more than enough to cover the entirety of their household expenses.

Ordinarily, Robin would have calmly and rationally inquired of Jess about her discovery, just in case there was some logical explanation for what she'd found. But these were not ordinary times. Many trying events had recently occurred which would have put even the most calm and rational of persons on edge. As such, Robin fell victim to her compounded and unresolved anguish and anger. The list of culprits seemed endless. There was the intrusion into their personal lives by the firm's Management Committee. That was true and trying enough, but taken together with the betrayal by her father, which was very fresh in her mind, his revelations about his influence on David, and the apparent lack of confidence which her parents ultimately viewed her capabilities, Robin took her additional discovery about the household expenses as yet another personal insult. Rightly or wrongly, she fumed about the revelation, and that fuming became more intense as the minutes ticked by. Jess, it seemed, did not value her ability to contribute to the running of the household, so much so that the older woman took it upon herself to pay all of the household expenses regardless of Robin's good faith contributions. *Why won't anyone take me seriously?*

Robin stewed about this for several more moments until Jess returned into the living room. The junior partner had just spent an inordinate amount of time sending e-mail messages attempting to calm down several of her clients, most of which were unhappy and nervous about her extended leave of absence from their cases. It didn't seem to sit well with any of them that other very capable partners of the law firm were handling their cases during her unscheduled hiatus. They wanted Jess back on the job, plain and simple, and they were becoming increasingly restless with each passing day. Now, as it turned out, restless clients correlated well with one very restless junior partner, and the result wasn't pretty. Not in the least bit. And since Jess was not used to being idle for so long, she was going absolutely and positively stir-crazy. And that was putting it kindly. Restless and stir-crazy was a volatile combination, and as such, not surprisingly, led to one on-edge and very cranky attorney. This time, the word 'cranky' was most definitely not a term of endearment.

The past several days had been filled with anxiety and anticipation awaiting the Management Committee's decision, which now at mid-week, was still not forthcoming. It was a fact that only served to add more tension and stress to an already tense and stressful period of time. Adversity can make one stronger, as both Jess and Robin so recently experienced, and although that was generally a truism, it was also a truism that adversity can test even the strongest of relationships, sometimes stretching them to nearly the breaking point. That being the case, what followed next was only natural and bound to happen, and in reality probably should have happened sooner. Jess and Robin finally reached the precipice of that breaking point, the household finances only proving to be the catalyst toward that ultimate path.

Robin eyed the taller woman entering the living room. "Jess, could you please come over here for a minute?" Although it was phrased in the form of a question, and very politely, too, the younger woman's tone of voice and demeanor served notice that it was, in reality, a distinct command.

Coming out of her e-mail preoccupation, Jess approached the dining room table, surveying the assorted piles of cancelled checks, bank statements, and paid bills as she did so. If she had an inkling as to what Robin was up to, she didn't let on. "What's up?"

"I've been going over our joint checking account, and I see that there's quite a bit of money remaining in there even though all our bills are paid up. Do you know why that is?"

"Well, I'm assuming that it's because we've got some extra money in the account right now."

I'm in no mood for games. "Jess, let me explain this. For the past two months, I've deposited money in this account every week to take care of our household expenses. We agreed to that. Now, I want you to look at this." The younger woman held up the check register for the older woman to see. "Do you see how much money we have left-over in the account after all our bills have been paid for the past two months?"

Blue eyes squinted to read the amount reflected on the last line. "Yes." It was a purposefully succinct answer.

"And that amount, coincidentally, is just a little bit more than everything I've ever deposited into the account." Green eyes hardened. "Jess, how could you do that?"

Both dark eyebrows rose. "How could I do what, Robin?" The taller woman really didn't understand what Robin was so upset about.

"Don't pretend you don't know. We agreed that we would both deposit money into the joint account for household expenses. I've done my part, but you've obviously taken it upon yourself to deposit more than enough money to cover all of our bills yourself. That was not what we intended, and you know it." Robin glanced at the check register once more. "Again, Jess, tell me, how could you do that?"

"Listen, Robin..." The older woman's tone of voice became very careful and deliberate. "We have plenty of money in the account. All the bills are paid in full. There is absolutely no problem. If you're asking why there's a surplus in the account, I thought we'd keep a reserve in there just in case we needed to do some maintenance on the house this spring and summer. That's all."

"That's all?" It was a rhetorical question. "Well, you could've at least discussed it with me. But no, you just took it upon yourself to make that decision, instead."

"I really don't see the problem, here." The dark head shook in exasperation, analyzing the matter. "It's only prudent to keep a reserve fund so we have money to fix the air conditioner or buy a new refrigerator or fix the roof or do whatever else we might need to do to keep this place going. This is really a very minor issue, Robin...." A large hand gestured in front of the stacks of papers on the table. "And besides, I really don't see what you're so upset about. The agreement was that you deposit money in the account, I deposit money in the account, and we pay the bills from the account. End of story. There was never any restriction on how much money either party could deposit, was there, because if there was, I certainly don't recall it?"

The younger woman stood up abruptly from the table. *That's it!* "Don't you do that. Don't you play word games with me. You know full well what the agreement was. The agreement was that we would equally share in paying the household expenses. Equally, Jess. It was not that one of us would pay the bills and one of us would keep a reserve fund. That wasn't how it was supposed to work, and you know it."

I don't need this. "Number one, Robin, I don't need your permission to pay the bills, and number two, I've been taking care of things around here just fine for many years now, and I certainly don't need you telling me how to run my house."

The blonde head snapped up. "Your house? What happened to our house? Every time I turned around, you kept on telling me that this is my house, too. Now, all of a sudden, it's your house?"

Jess took a long, deep breath to try to gather some perspective and calm herself. All things considered, she wasn't totally unsympathetic to Robin's point of view on the matter. She let go a sigh, then offered up her explanation. "I only meant that I know what it takes to keep up the house. I've been doing it for many years. It's wise to keep a reserve fund for maintenance and repairs. Things happen, and we have to be prepared. That's all I was trying to do."

Green eyes gauged Jess's demeanor. *She just doesn't get it.* Robin sighed sadly and sat back down at the table, shaking her head slowly in bewilderment. It was one thing for Jess to want to be prepared, and it was quite another to make such decisions without discussing it together. Just as Jess turned to head back into the living room, something down deep inside of Robin, something she didn't recognize, lashed out, and she said something she never thought she'd ever say. "You don't have any faith in me. You're just like my father. And David."

Upon hearing that statement, Jess stopped dead in her tracks. She didn't move for a very long time as she considered the damning accusation. The older woman knew full well that she was many things, and she certainly could be difficult at times to get along with. She also believed that she had been doing extremely well in trying to be empathetic with Robin's difficulty in dealing with David's death, so much so that she had put down her own admittedly irrational jealousy time and time again upon merely hearing the man's name. But now, being compared to the manipulative and controlling man that Robin's father was, and then having David thrown back in her face like that....well, it nearly caused the older woman to lash out, herself. She absolutely didn't deserve that indictment from Robin, and she took it very personally. Blue eyes blinked several times very slowly, then, rather than say something she knew she'd later regret, Jess made a fateful decision. *I need some air.* Without a backward glance, she strode over to the kitchen, grabbed her keys from the counter top, and headed straight for the garage door.

From that moment on, everything seemed to happen in slow motion. Robin caught the older woman's movement out of the corner of her eye. She saw Jess stiffen her shoulders, take a step toward the kitchen counter, pull a set of keys roughly into her hand, and then rapidly proceed toward the door leading to the garage. *And to the car.* And suddenly, it was as if Robin's whole world was collapsing right in front of her eyes in a surreal instant replay that was both eerie and uncanny in its familiarity. In an action she'd later not remember, the younger woman, in fit of panic, bolted from the dining room table, raced across the length of the room, and headed straight for the garage, trying desperately to block the older woman's exitway. As she did so, her voice rang out in a guttural, agonizing cry that defied all possible description, a mixture of stark fear and terror that echoed off the room's surrounding walls in an urgent and considerable appeal which seemed to go on forever. "Noooooo!" She rushed to the door and braced her arms wide on either side of the metal frame, looking straight on into shocked azure eyes, before crying out in the same agonizing fashion once more. "Noooooo! You promised me!"

213

Jess stared at Robin in utter confusion, trying to read into the depths of the frightened sea-green eyes locked intently upon her own. *What the...?* The older woman's gaze slowly tracked from Robin to the keys resting loosely in the palm of her own hand, and then, with a sickening clarity that caused her to reel unsteadily backward, she nearly collapsed as the realization ultimately hit home, and hit home hard. *Oh, dear God. What am I doing?* She watched almost mesmerized as the keys, wholly of their own accord and in slow motion themselves, helplessly fell onto the tiled floor, clanking with a deafening intensity that shattered the ensuing vacuum of all discernable sound. For very long moment, they both stood there, locked trance-like in each other's gaze, each unable to move amid the absolute silence that followed.

Finally, Jess, in an action totally within her better character, rushed forward and gathered the younger woman in an all-encompassing embrace, her hold tightening as she felt the smaller body simply fall into her own. She heard the heavy sniffling increase and then clung to the trembling petite form even tighter, trying with all her might to come up with something, anything, to make up for her horrible misjudgment. Her tongue, however, inexplicably remained silent, and all she could do was cleave in utter and complete remorse to the one who held her heart. Finally, with her own tears streaming unchecked down her face, she offered up the only words she possibly could. "I'm so sorry. I'm so, so sorry, sweetheart. Please forgive me." Long fingers combed through golden strands of hair as Jess whispered her desperate plea over and over again. "Please forgive me. Please. I'm so sorry."

Robin buried her face into the older woman's chest, trying to calm her all too real fears and leaning even further into the safe haven standing before her. Finally, tear-filled sea-green eyes gazed quietly up into remorseful blue as a petite hand reached forward and cupped the older woman's cheek. It was another moment before Robin found her voice well enough to speak, and when she did so, she whispered her heart's greatest fear. "I'd be lost without you, Jess. I couldn't bear it."

How could I have done this? "I know, sweetheart. I know. And I'm so very sorry." Jess kissed the top of the blonde head, briefly taking comfort in the younger woman's spring rain scent, then rested her forehead gently against Robin's. "Let's go ahead and sit in living room, okay? We need to talk about this."

Robin nodded and followed Jess over to the plush sofa, sitting down so that they were face to face with each other. She came to realize that she had her own apologizing to do, and that the accusations she'd leveled against Jess were entirely out of line. Perhaps it was all the tension and stress of what they'd been going through, but there was still no excuse to lash out at the one person who was her entire life. "Jess...." A petite hand grasped a larger one. "I'm very sorry for what I said. I didn't mean it." She looked down, trying to gather her thoughts. "You're nothing like my father or David. It was way out of line for me to say that, and it's not true. You're the sweetest and gentlest person I know, and I know you love me with all your heart." The younger woman brought the hand she held to her lips and placed several soft kisses on the knuckles. "For a moment, I thought you wanted to control my life just like my father and David did, but I was wrong. You have always protected me, and I know that whatever you do, that's what's foremost in your heart."

It took a long moment of reflection, but Jess finally spoke. "I'll admit that when you compared me to your father, I was very angry. I certainly don't mean to control you. I'd never want to do that." It was a risk, but she decided to admit the real cause of her behavior just moments ago. "But when you mentioned David....I just completely lost it. It made me crazy."

It's harder for her than I thought. The younger woman knew that David was a sore subject, but she had to know exactly what Jess was thinking, otherwise they'd never be able to deal with it. Robin ducked her head and caught Jess's gaze, her voice very soft and gentle. "Tell me why." Petite fingers rubbed the back of the larger hand in a soothing motion. "Why does it make you so crazy?"

Blue eyes broke the gaze and characteristically glanced away. "Because he has a part of your heart that I'll never have."

Robin understood now, as she recognized the jealously for what it was. She tightened her grip on Jess's hand. "No, honey. You have my whole heart. Just you. No one else." Green eyes closed briefly, then reopened. "I will admit to you that he's inside my mind sometimes, and it sometimes distracts me, but you're inside my heart all the time. Every moment of every day. It's only you. Please believe that." She paused, as if setting her mind to something, then made a fervent vow. "I'm going to learn how to deal with David's memory, and put it in the proper place. I promise you that."

A long silence followed. "It's just that sometimes I can't help feeling jealous of him." Jess suddenly felt very ashamed at the admission. "I know it's not rational, but it seems as if he's always there, always between us, like a ghost that just won't go away."

She's hurting so much over this. Petite fingers continued to gently rub the back of the larger hand. "You are such a brave person. You've been so understanding with me, even though I know it's been really hard for you." Robin knew she had to ask the next question, although in truth, she wasn't sure she really wanted to know the answer. "Jess, is he really there between us?"

And now, here was the ultimate dilemma. To be honest or to be kind. Jess, unwilling to hedge the truth at this point, chose to be honest, however much it might hurt. "Yes, Robin, sometimes he is."

The smaller woman took a deep breath, nodding her head reflexively. "All right." She swallowed. "Then, I'll work on that. I can't deny that he was a part of my life, or that some things about him and our time together still affect me, but I'll work on that with Dr. Richmond."

This doesn't seem right. "No, Robin. It's my problem, not yours. I've got to accept that he is...was an important part of your past, and I have to deal with it. And I promise you...." Jess's gaze locked onto Robin's with an intense determination. "I promise you, no matter what, I will never, ever try to leave like that again. Never."

"I know." But even as Robin said it, in her heart, she really did not know. Her heart still clung to the fear, and it wasn't giving it up easily. But at the moment, she had more repairing to do. "I also want you to know that I know you weren't trying to control me. You were only doing what you thought was best." A small hand reached out and tenderly stroked the older woman's cheek. "I'd just really appreciate it if you and I could make these decisions together." Her voice was very soft and gentle, and this time, held no reproach. "Okay?"

The dark head nodded. "Okay. I promise, from now on, we'll do that." Jess leaned in and gave Robin a sweet kiss. "I'm very sorry for the way I acted tonight."

"And I'm very sorry, Jess, for the way I acted tonight."

God, Jess, you really screwed up. "I'm pretty tired, now. How about we call it a night?"

"Yeah." The smaller woman rose from the sofa. "I think that's a very good idea."

Adversity, in whatever degree it comes along, can make one stronger. That fact had already been demonstrated with the attempt by Thomas Wilson to tear Jess and Robin's relationship apart. And now? Well, perhaps allowing the really unpleasant things to come fully out into the open was a start to maintaining an even stronger, unbreakable bond. If a relationship could withstand the tests and trials of real life wholly intact, then nothing of an earthly origin could ever destroy it. And by the same token, if a relationship could withstand the tests and trials of the heart wholly intact, then nothing of the spirit could ever destroy it, either. The events of the evening, although tragic in a way, were entirely necessary and most likely inevitable in coming. For if wounds are left to fester, the tests and trials of real life can ultimately threaten to overcome the strength of the heart.

And had that happened tonight, that would have been the real tragedy.

****

As it turned out, it was much too early to sleep, even though both Jess and Robin made heroic attempts to do so. They each laid separately in the waterbed, resting on opposite sides, neither speaking nor sleeping. Both were mulling over the events of the evening in their minds. And both were feeling intense remorse. Finally, as the prolonged silence and distance became entirely too uncomfortable to withstand another moment longer, Jess turned her head toward the smaller woman and sighed. "Robin?"

"Yeah?" Came the much too quiet reply.

"Are we okay?"

Silence was the only response.

Damn. Well, maybe things will look differently in the morning. Just as Jess had given up expecting an answer, Robin silently inched over and snuggled up next to the larger body, wrapping her arm securely around the taller woman's waist. That action, so familiar and yet so simple, hit Jess hard, releasing a flood of emotions in its wake, most of which she simply couldn't process. Shuddering slightly, she took a deep breath before whispering what was truly in her heart. "I love you, sweetheart, so much. Please always know that. No matter what ever happens, or my inconsiderate behavior, you're the most important thing in my life."

A small hand slid underneath the Calvin sleep shirt and rubbed circles in a soothing motion on the soft skin of Jess's stomach. "And I love you, Jess. More than I can say. I don't know why I said those insensitive things to you. I feel so ashamed about that." Robin lifted herself up on one arm and brushed her lips tenderly against a soft cheek. "I never want to fight with you again. Never."

"Me, either, sweetheart. It hurts my heart."

"And mine, too." Robin's heart hurt in more ways than one. There was something she really needed to know, and she knew she had to ask. "Jess?" Her voice became raspy. "Would you really have left tonight?"

Damn. How to answer that. Silver-blue eyes closed briefly. *Honesty hurts, but lies hurt worse.* "I really don't know what I would have done. Yes, I would have gotten into my car, but I'd like to think that after that, I'd have realized what I was doing, and then have come

217

back inside. But to be honest...." Sliver-blue eyes focused somberly on gray-green in the dark. "I just don't know." *I broke my promise.*

The blonde head nodded slowly. It hurt to hear the admission. "Jess, but you said it won't happen again, right?" There was a definite note of uncertainty in the question. "Right?"

Long arms reached out and engulfed the smaller woman in a tight embrace, and in doing so, Jess almost lost her composure. With a fervent, almost fierce vow, she whispered her answer. "Yes, I said it and I meant it. It will never, ever happen again. I promise you that, Robin, with everything I am, and I pledge to you that I will never give you cause to worry about this again."

"Thank you." A simple response, yet filled with much more meaning than the words themselves conveyed.

"So we're okay, then, right?"

Relieved, Robin rested her head on a broad shoulder, and the movements of her hand resting on the older woman's stomach now became playful in nature. "Yes, Jess, we're okay." The hand became even more playful. "But, I think we have one more very serious matter to discuss."

It was hard, but Jess bravely maintained her self-control under the tickling assault to her stomach. "And just what serious matter is that?"

It has to do with house rule number eight."

"Um..." Dark eyebrows furrowed. "There is no house rule number eight."

A giggle. "There is now."

"Is that so?" The older woman grabbed the increasingly playful hand. "And just what is house rule number eight, if I might ask?"

"House rule number eight specifically states that in the morning when one party is asleep, the other party, no matter how tempted, shall not wake the first party up with renditions of certain songs."

"Um...I have absolutely no idea what you're talking about, Robin."

"I think you do." The hand resumed its playful adventures. "And it's not allowed."

Jess tried hard to reign in a chuckle. "You wouldn't, by any chance, be talking about my favorite two songs in the whole wide world, would you?"

"Well..." A playful finger poked the bare stomach. "If they're the ones you sang to me in the morning on several occasions, then yes, I would be talking about those." Robin could sense the exaggerated pout that followed. "And pouting about it won't work, Jess, so don't even try it."

"Fine." *She never said I couldn't think up other songs.* "You win, Robin. I agree to abide by house rule number eight."

That was way too easy. "You do?"

"Yes."

"Just like that?" *She's up to something.*

"Yep. Just like that. You have very persuasive powers, you know." An aggrieved sigh. "But I'm sure gonna miss ol' Gilligan and the Skipper." Another aggrieved sigh. "And the Millionaire and his wife." It was official. Three aggrieved sighs in a row. "And of course, the Movie Star." Make that four. "And we certainly can't forget the Professor and Mary Ann, can we now?" A large hand recaptured the playfully assaulting hand once more. "And I'm really, really going to miss good ol' Mr. Bluebird and that marvelous zip...."

"Don't say it." Robin reclaimed her hand and went about her previous task.

"Well, as I recall, house rule number eight says nothing about lyrics, Robin, or mentioning said lyrics at nighttime."

She's impossible. "It says songs, Jess, which includes lyrics. Just so we're clear, I've now amended house rule number eight so it clearly makes reference to any time of the day or night, waking up or going to sleep."

One last aggrieved sigh for evening before Jess closed her eyes, ostensibly to sleep. "Okay, fine, Robin. Just remember Scooby Doo."

Scooby Doo? "You are very weird." The playful petite hand stilled and gray-green eyes closed, well on their way toward sleep. After a brief moment and a sudden thought, one gray-green eye quickly popped open. *She wouldn't dare.* The other eye likewise popped open, as a certain cartoon theme song came rushing very clearly to mind.

Yes, she would.

****

The pale dawn sunlight cascaded across the tiled floor through the living room's sliding glass doors, signaling the start of a brand new day. As if prompted by daybreak alone, the motorized pool sweeper outside began its daily ritual, flicking its tail wildly at times and occasionally spraying bursts of water up into the crisp morning air. Robin settled herself into the easy chair next to the sofa after retrieving both a cup of gourmet coffee and the morning newspaper. In an unusual occurrence, Jess had not yet gotten up, apparently preferring to spend her morning sleeping in just a little bit later rather than worrying about not being at the office. The younger woman had just gotten comfortable when Jess's wide awake form strode purposely into the living room, something of great importance obviously weighing on her mind.

"Good morning." Robin sipped her coffee.

No response.

Hmmm. A little grumpy this morning? "Didn't you sleep well?"

"I slept fine, Robin." Blue eyes studied the smaller figure sitting casually in the chair, then proceeded over toward her. "What are these?" Jess presented Robin with the items in her hand.

Sea-green eyes glanced from Jess to the items in question, then back to Jess. "I would think that would be quite obvious. Don't you?"

Dark eyebrows narrowed slightly. "Funny. I know what they are, Robin. What I want to know is where they came from and what happened to the other ones."

A shocked expression. "Are you accusing me of something?"

"Let's just say, to use a phrase you, yourself, said to me very recently...if the shoe fits."

Robin stifled a giggle. "Well, they do seem to be more your style."

That comment brought a pair of raised eyebrows. "More my style? What was wrong with the other ones?"

"Aside from the fact that they were obnoxious and hurt my eyes, they never really did suit you."

"I thought they were lovely."

The smaller woman played along. "Yes, Jess, they were indeed very lovely. Just not quite...you."

"And these are?" Large hands lifted the items to Robin's green eyes for inspection once again.

"Yes. I think they suit you perfectly."

"Perfectly?" Jess mouthed the word. "Um...I'll have you know, Robin, that I am nothing like this."

"And you were everything like the yellow Tweety Bird ones?"

"Yes." The older woman proclaimed proudly. "All bright and sunshiny."

Now, Robin simply couldn't hold in the chuckle any longer. "I don't think so, Jess."

Blue eyes fixed righteously on green. "I won't dignify that remark. And besides, since when did slippers become a running commentary on personality types, anyway?"

She's so much fun. "Since you decided to poke fun at my bunny slippers, that's when." Robin nonchalantly resumed her paper reading.

"I happen to think I have a very sunny disposition."

A giggle escaped from behind the newspaper. "Right. Sunny. I don't think I'd bet the farm on that."

With that retort, Jess took a seat on the plush sofa and contemplated the items still in her hand. Finally, she bent down and put both of said items onto her feet. *They fit well.* "All right, Robin, have it your way. But I'll have you know that I am absolutely nothing at all like these. Nothing. I most definitely am not in any way remotely like the Tasmanian Devil. Not even a little bit. I just want to be perfectly clear about that."

Another giggle, this time muffled. "If you say so, Jess."

"I do." The tall form got up from the sofa and knelt down next to the easy chair, grasping the newspaper and setting it down on the smaller woman's lap. "Because if I was anything like that, Robin..." She leaned in for a good morning kiss that had a tad bit more to it than just a simple good morning. "You'd most definitely know it."

Uh oh. The younger woman swallowed. "I think I might have given you ideas."

A playful, yet satisfied grin. "Oh, you can definitely count that."

The easy teasing and playfulness didn't escape either one of them. Humor has healing properties, and they both knew it well. Jess, herself, realized that Robin's slippers swapping scheme was really an overture, a way of letting the older woman know that everything was really okay between them. In fact, one could say that any prolonged lack of their usual teasing and joking banter could have clearly been seen as a warning sign, one of very deep concern. The fact that Robin sought so quickly to reaffirm their relationship with humor was in reality a testament to the solid foundation upon which their relationship was actually based. It was a brand new day.

Just then, a ray of bright morning sunlight streamed in, reflecting off of Robin's diamond ring in such brilliant and dazzling flash of light that it caused both women to momentarily stare at it. Jess took the smaller hand into her own and gave the ring on the petite finger a gentle kiss. She then stood up and padded toward the kitchen, raising an eyebrow and casting a parting glance over her shoulder as she did so. "Tasmanian Devil, huh?"

A very wide grin. "Yep. Tasmanian Devil."

Chapter 9

Robin approached the closed office door, then hesitated briefly. *The managing partner's office.* It seemed so imposing, even forbidding, much the same as the principal's office had seemed during her younger school days. *I've never been called to the principal's office before in my life.* Nevertheless, here she found herself being summoned. But summoned why? She fervently wished that she were anywhere, anyplace, other than where she actually was. *All right.* She sighed. *Let's get this over with.* Now resigned to her fate, the young associate steeled her nerves and knocked lightly on the heavy wooden door. Upon hearing the muffled voice from the other side admitting her in, she slowly turned the knob and entered the office. Inside, she found both Gordon McDaniel and Harry Roberts seated formally at a small table adjacent to Gordon's large heirloom desk.

"Robin, please have a seat." The managing partner motioned her over to join them.

I wonder what this is about. The young associate surveyed the situation as she stepped inside the office and quickly confirmed her suspicions. Something definitely seemed up. The question was, just what was it?

As Robin took a seat at the table, Gordon continued. "Harry and I have a matter we'd like to discuss with you, Robin." He smiled somewhat deceptively, then produced a neatly typed document which he set in front of her. "As you know, the Management Committee has been deliberating this week regarding the status of Jessica Harrison's continued partnership with the firm." He paused very briefly, then proceeded. "However, in the course of those deliberations, the Committee has determined that a minor issue needs to be resolved before the Committee can render its final decision."

The young attorney glanced at the paper in front of her. *This is a release.* The pieces were now starting to fall into place. "Okay. What issue is it, exactly?"

Harry spoke up. "Robin, as you know, the firm has received a waiver letter from your father as to any potential allegations which he could possibly have made against Jess. What the Committee recognized in its review of the matter was that although it had a release from your father, it had no such release from you." Sensing the young associate's increasing discomfort, the head of the litigation department eased his posture and spoke in a more fatherly tone. "Robin, we like you here at the firm, and we greatly value your contributions. We certainly don't wish to make you in any way uncomfortable. However, the simple fact is that the firm as a whole must be protected against any potential liability with regard to...." He hesitated uneasily. "With regard to the relationship between you and Jess."

"I see." Robin nodded. But in truth, she really did not see, and was, in fact, steaming inside. All this time, through all the negotiations with her father and all of the Management Committee's theatrics at the hearings, putting she and Jess through intense stress and awkwardness in discussing aspects of their personal relationship which, to be generous, were nobody's business, it suddenly now all came down to whether or not the Committee had a release. And the real irony was that they sought a release not just from her father who'd made the original threats, baseless as they were, but also from Robin who'd made no threats nor had she even hinted at such. She sighed internally. *Why do people always think the worst of me?* And further, why hold hearings in the first place if all you need is another release? It made no sense. Then, it hit her. In fact, it was becoming all too clear. The Management Committee wanted to strong-arm Robin into signing a release, setting the firm free and clear, and then the Committee would do whatever it wanted to do to Jess, anyway. *Well, not if I have anything to say about it.* Robin made no comment, but rather just continued to listen.

"Robin..." Gordon cleared his throat. "The Management Committee hopes to wrap this matter up quickly and issue its decision before the weekend approaches, which as you know, would be tomorrow."

Pressure tactics. It was textbook coercion, through and through, and the young attorney didn't like it one little bit. She glanced one more time at the document in front of her. "Then, I assume you'd want the signed release prior to that time?"

The managing partner's slightly balding head nodded affirmatively. "We'd need it very soon, yes. Today would be best."

The screws tighten. Then, something occurred to Robin. Perhaps, there was more going on, here. She now took particular notice of Harry's uncharacteristically uneasy posture, despite his attempts to relax it, and Gordon's over-eagerness to obtain her signature on the release. Could it be that the pressure was actually on them and not on her after all? She thought about that. Liability insurance, perhaps? Malpractice insurance? Ethical concerns? *Not that I'd agree that there was anything of an ethical nature to be concerned with regarding my relationship with Jess, anyway.* But still, why else bring this whole release thing up at this late date unless it was being forced upon them? And if that really were the case, perhaps Robin could play it to her advantage. She smiled casually, giving nothing of her insight away. "Let me understand. Basically, if you have a release from both myself and my father, then the firm would be free of any potential liability."

"Yes, that's right." Harry answered.

"I see." *They're afraid of something. Perhaps, that I might really file a claim against them, or perhaps liability or malpractice insurance coverage issues.* "And if the firm is free of any potential liability, then all of the firm's partners would be free of any potential liability, as well."

"Yes." Harry answered again, now knowing that Robin had indeed connected the dots. *She's very perceptive. A true attorney.* He was proud in spite of himself and let a small smile slip. To be sure, his first allegiance was to protect the firm, but Robin's intuition had given her, and Jess too, a potential win in this situation.

"So, if all partners of the firm would be free of any potential liability, then the firm would no longer be placed in any type of potential jeopardy arising from this situation." The young associate caught Harry's eye, reading from his expression that she, indeed, was on the right track.

"Yes." The head of the litigation department held her gaze and nodded affirmatively. "If that were the case, there would be no risk of jeopardy to the firm."

That's all I need to know. Harry was subtly telling her that all she had to do was sign the release and Jess would retain her partnership. It was that simple. It was that clear. It was that reasonable. And yet, it was blackmail just the same. Robin felt the stirrings of anger return. *I will not be blackmailed.* She didn't know, of course, that Jess had the exact same thought when Robin's father had threatened to reveal their relationship to the firm and file a complaint with the State Bar

Association. *Blackmail.* Green eyes shifted once more to the document in front of her. Then again, the young associate reconsidered, she had to give Harry credit for maneuvering a way out for Jess, as she was now sure that he had done just that, coming up with this whole release issue and maybe even throwing in liability and malpractice insurance concerns as a way to enable the Committee to resolve the matter in Jess's favor. *Maybe.*

The managing partner interrupted her musings. "Will you need some additional time to review the document?"

Again, green eyes tracked deliberately, first from the document, then to Harry, then to Gordon. *Maybe Harry engineered this. Maybe. But I want more.* Having determined that Gordon and probably most of the Management Committee were apparently worried that without a release, she might someday file a claim against the firm, Robin made a key decision. She'd press for one additional thing in return for her so highly sought-after signature on the piece paper sitting in front of her. After all, she had a card to play now. "Yes, if it's all right with you, I'd like to review it this evening and then return it to you first thing in the morning."

"Of course." Gordon was agreeable, sensing victory. He sat back in his chair and exhaled slowly, now visibly more at ease. "That will be fine."

Before anyone else could voice another word, Robin broached one more topic, in effect playing her card. She fingered the corner of the release, then spoke in a disarmingly deferential tone of voice. "I have a question, if I may ask it?"

"Certainly. What is it, Robin?" Harry asked easily.

Here goes. "As I mentioned before to the Management Committee, I believe that working with Jess has been very helpful to me professionally. Should the Committee decide to retain Jess's partnership, is it possible that something could be arranged where I may have the opportunity to work with her again?"

The managing partner was quick to shake his head, dismissing the idea. "I'm sorry, Robin, but that would make her your direct supervisor, and as before, we simply couldn't risk the problems that such a situation would certainly create."

He's obviously not understanding me. Undeterred, the young associate tried to make her point once again. "What I'm saying is that I think that I have learned a great deal from Jess about the practice of law these past several months." She looked pointedly at Gordon. "I believe that if I were to resume working with her, both myself and the firm would definitely benefit greatly from that." Her expression remained inquiring, but her intent was clear as she deliberately glanced down at the piece of paper in front of her for maximum effect. *Yep. I can blackmail, too, Gordon.*

The room was eerily quiet as the full impact of Robin's statement dawned on the two older attorneys. The young associate didn't realize it at the time, but she had indeed learned a lot from Jess, and not just in the practice of law. Robin, herself, may not have realized it, but the head of the litigation department, mentor to Jess and surrogate father combined, sure did. Jess's protégé had, in fact, turned the tables, and quite effectively, to say the least. And not only that, it bore noting that Robin had gained a great skill in the whole process. She had gone from being secretly angry and on the defensive in the beginning of their meeting, to being totally in control and on the offensive in the end. She didn't allow her anger and self-righteousness to cloud her perception of the situation, and she was bright enough to accomplish what she knew she wanted to do. In short, she played the game masterfully. Not bad for a day's work.

"All right, Robin." Gordon spoke slowly, realizing he'd just been beat at his own game. "I understand what you're asking. Let me confer with Harry, and I'll see whether something can be arranged." In truth, the managing partner didn't at all like being backed into a corner. Who would? But the again, it was his own fault. He'd apparently underestimated the young associate, and now the burden rested upon him to obtain that signed release from her one way or the other. The Management Committee was counting on it. *His* Management Committee was counting on it. Gordon sighed to himself, resigned to the situation as it stood now. He looked at Robin. "Okay. I'd like you and Jessica to come in first thing tomorrow morning so we can all put a welcome end to this saga."

I did it. I won. Robin quickly released the breath she was holding, then stood up, grasping the document from the table in front of her as she did so. "Yes, sir. We'll be here." And with that piece of business satisfactorily concluded, she turned to leave.

Harry and Gordon watched in silence as Robin exited the managing partner's office. Both men, interestingly, had the exact same thought.

Damn. She's gonna be one hell of an attorney.

****

Jess stared at her newly acquired Tasmanian Devil slippers and pondered the previous evening's events. *The argument.* It was true, she and Robin had made up. The slippers were tangible evidence of that. But still, something preyed on her mind this bright and sunny morning. Something all too familiar and all too common. Ever-present guilt. It was always there, always just beneath the surface, and never far from making itself known. At the very least, it was never far from making itself known to an audience of one. So Jess being Jess, it was only natural that her internal voices had ratcheted up quite a lively exchange on the matter. And, in typical fashion, Jess being Jess, it was only natural that she reluctantly and flippantly engaged the internal fray.

It's about time you showed up.

The alternate internal voice was quick to retort. *'Listen buddy, I've had a few other things on my mind lately, or don't you keep up with the news bulletins.'*

My, my. We are grumpy this morning, aren't we?

No comment.

Regardless, we've got quite a lot of work to do.

'Yeah?' The alternate internal voice grumbled. *'Such as?'*

Quit playing dumb. If everything was fine, I wouldn't be here.

The alternate internal voice didn't miss a beat. *'Speaking of dumb, I have a particularly fitting suggestion for you, but I think I'll save it for now.'*

That would be wise. So, what happens to be on your mind today?

'You tell me. You seem to have all the answers.'

All right, if that's the way you want it. It appears that you committed not one, but two, major faux pas last night, did you not?

'Maybe.' The alternate internal voice equivocated. *'But, if I did, Robin forgave me for that. See my new slippers?'*

They're lovely.

'Thank you.'

But that's not the issue, is it?

'I don't know what you're talking about.' It was a typical response, although not terribly honest.

This is growing tiresome, but if you must have everything spelled out for you, then fine. The issue in both of those cases is trust.

'Trust?' The alternate internal voice assumed an indignant tone. *'What the hell are you talking about?'*

Robin has to be able to trust what you say to her.

'Of course, she can trust me.' The alternate internal voice insisted. *'She can completely trust me.'*

Oh really? Did you or did you not promise Robin that you'd never leave upset if you and she ever argued?

After careful consideration, the alternate internal voice responded with total confidence. *'Yes, and I absolutely have kept my promise.'*

Oh please.

'Oh please, what?'

Don't even try it. The only reason you didn't drive off last night was because Robin stopped you. Admit it.

'I will not admit it.' The alternate internal voice once again turned indignant. *'For your information, pal, I wouldn't have left last night even if she hadn't stopped me.'*

If you really believe that, then you're delusional. You had one foot out the door. Gone. Practically halfway down the street. Admit it.

'No. There is nothing to admit.' The alternate internal voice adamantly refused to even consider the obvious. *'I absolutely, positively, and most certainly would not have left. End of story.'*

Denial doesn't suit you. Have you considered drug therapy?

'Listen, Dr. Freud, I know what I would and would not have done, and I'm telling you, I wouldn't have left the scene.'

The scene of the crime?

'Yes...I mean, no...I mean, there was no crime.'

Just who are you trying to convince? You know full well how important the whole issue of leaving when angry is for Robin, and yet for some reason, you refuse to deal with what happened.

The alternate internal voice, now in full righteous indignation mode, lashed out. *'Yeah, well she shouldn't have thrown all that David B.S. at me in the first place. I am nothing like David.'*

I see. So, we're back to David again, are we? No real surprise. Listen, Robin needs to be able to trust you. You'd better understand that before all of this gets out of hand. And by the way, you seem to have more of a fixation on David than she does.

'What the hell is that supposed to mean! The alternate internal voice was now annoyed beyond belief. *'I'd be happy never to hear the man's name again, but every damn time I turn around, there he is.'*

If you keep putting him in the forefront, he'll stay there. You'd be wise to keep him safely tucked in the background where he belongs.

'Right. Easy for you to say. You don't have a ghost following you around.'

Clever, but no cigar.

The alternate internal voice was confused. *'What in the world are you talking about?'*

David isn't the issue here, and you know it. He's just a clever diversion on your part to avoid dealing with the real issue.

'And what, pray tell, is the so-called real issue?' The alternate internal voice snipped.

Trust.

'Are we back to that again? I told you, Robin can trust me. I promised her that I wouldn't leave, and I didn't. I kept my promise.'

You didn't act on your own volition. Robin stopped you from leaving.

'I kept my promise.' The alternate internal voice repeated.

That river in Egypt is getting longer and longer by the minute. You'd do well not to sail it.

Unfortunately, it was like talking to a brick wall, as evidenced by the alternate internal voice's next statement. *'I have nothing more to say about this. My answer is my answer.'*

You need to face the facts before it's too late. Nothing can replace lost trust. Nothing. You need to think about that. Don't pretend that the issue isn't there, because it is, and don't blame your own behavior on everyone and everything else but yourself. You'll only regret it.

A dismissive sigh. *'If I had wanted a sermon, pal, I would have gone to church. My answer stands.'*

Fine. Then it appears you'll need a bigger boat. Next issue: Trust.

'Trust? Wait a minute. We just talked about that.'

You're very perceptive today. Grumpy, but perceptive. The previous issue was about Robin's trust in you. The issue now is about your trust in Robin. See the difference?

The alternate internal voice just couldn't help making light of the matter. *'What I see is that you're a cup and saucer short of a full place setting. That's what I see.'*

Funny, but not constructive.

'Um...two tacos short of a combo platter?'

Attempts at diversion by humor won't work.

The alternate internal voice, unfazed, kept going. *'One can short of a six-pack?'*

Fine. Are you finished now?

'Nope, just getting started. A few clowns short of a circus? A joker shy of a full deck? A couple of peas short of a pod? One brick short of a full load? A few pickles shy of a whole jar?' The alternate internal voice paused mid-thought. *Is any of this working for you?'*

No. Now, let's continue before yet another millennium starts, shall we?

'Party pooper.'

Whatever you say. Do you trust Robin to be a full partner with you in maintaining the household? Answer yes or no.

'*Yes or no.*'

Cute. Make all the jokes you want, but your avoidance of the issues will come back to haunt you.

'*Geez, can't anyone have a little fun around here?*' The alternate internal voice now sighed, apparently unable to totally escape the self-psychoanalysis. '*All right, fine. Have it your way. The answer is yes. I absolutely trust Robin to be a full partner with me in maintaining the household.*'

But you still consider the house to be your house, don't you?

The alternate internal voice grew slightly impatient. '*I presume you have a point, here?*'

Figure it out.

'*What? You want me to figure it out? You know that I hate riddles. This is your game, buddy, not mine.*'

Well, it's a simple question. Do you still consider the house to be your house?

The alternate internal voice thought about that for a moment. '*If you're referring to the fact that I pay the mortgage, then yes, it's my house. I own it.*'

And that's something that will always be hanging over you and Robin, no matter how hard you try to cover it over.

The alternate internal voice feigned ignorance, although in reality the implication was painfully obvious. '*What do you mean?*'

Despite what you've just said, in actuality, you don't consider Robin to be a full partner with you in maintaining the household if you're, in fact, the one who owns the house.

'*Technical ownership of the house is a small issue and doesn't matter. Robin knows that the house is her house, too.*' The alternate internal voice did not sound convincing in the least.

Does she? She specifically heard you say that you know how to run your own house.

'*That was a poor choice of words on my part. I apologized for that.*'

And that makes it okay?

'*Yes.*' Guilt, however, was setting in. '*Robin understood that I didn't mean it the way it sounded.*'

It may be hard for you to acknowledge, but you hold that very issue over Robin's head every single day. You believe that you alone should make the final decisions concerning the running of the household.

231

'No I don't. We have a joint account to pay the household expenses.' The alternate internal voice argued.

Minus the mortgage payment.

'Of course, minus the mortgage payment.' The alternate internal voice reasoned. *'It's my responsibility and my mortgage payment.'*

And your house.

No response as the weight of the matter settled in.

Do you see now where this is headed?

'No. You're way off base.' The alternate internal voice, once again in denial mode, grew annoyed. *'That is not the way it is.'*

Really? You don't even trust her enough to pay for part of the household expenses.

'Wait just a minute.' The alternate internal voice was now grasping at straws. *'I absolutely trust Robin. She deposits her share of money into the account, and I trust her to do that.'*

And then you, yourself, decide not to spend it.

'That's not fair. I explained about that to her. I just thought we'd keep a little bit of a reserve for household repairs. That's all.' It really did sound like a reasonable argument, provided that someone bought it.

There you go again.

'There I go again, what?'

It all comes down to what you and you alone think because, after all, it is your house.

'Damn right it's my house.' The alternate internal voice snapped.

Aha. Your first totally honest admission today. Selfish, but honest.

'I resent that. I am not selfish.' The alternate internal voice tried once again to sound indignant, but failed miserably.

Whatever you say. But it's clear that you need to deal with these trust issues before they come back at you in ways you haven't even imagined. They're already coming between you and Robin.

The alternate internal voice sobered. *'It makes my heart ache when things come between us like this.'*

Then you need to resolve the trust issues once and for all.

'I suppose you have the perfect solution for all of this?' Well, it couldn't hurt to ask.

That's where you come in. You're a bright, albeit currently suspended at the moment, attorney. You can figure it out.

'Could you at least give me a little hint?'

No.

'Please.'

No.

'Rats!' The alternate internal voice groused. *'You're no fun.'*

That's a matter of opinion. Remember, if you refuse to deal with these issues, you'll come to regret it.

'I think you're being overly-dramatic.' The alternate internal voice downplayed the matter. *'I still maintain that everything's fine now. I apologized, Robin forgave me, and I even have my brand new Tasmanian Devil slippers to prove it.'*

Fine. Have it your way. However, if drug therapy doesn't work, you may want to try a lobotomy.

'Then, I'd be crazy.'

No argument there.

****

It was getting late. The sky had turned dark, and the office building had mostly emptied by the time the young associate hopped in her recently acquired metallic blue BMW and headed for home. She'd given Jess a quick call to say that she was on her way, but she hadn't elaborated much about her "negotiation session" earlier in the day with Harry and Gordon. A more private discussion with Jess was in order. *Very private.* She smiled to herself as she made her way away from the downtown streets and toward The Ranch.

Things were going to work out perfectly. The deal was set, and now much of the stress of the past several weeks would finally be lifted. She and Jess were going to be working together again. That was the important thing. *Together.* Robin grinned at the thought and remembered a revelation that had become firmly ensconced as truth. *We're meant to be together.* And further still, as an added bonus to her hard-won deal, she'd even gotten the impression that both Harry and Gordon, ironically, had developed a certain new respect for her as a result of their meeting earlier that day. On that particular point, the young associate wasn't wrong.

Finally, the BMW approached the driveway to The Ranch and pulled up into the garage. Its driver quickly closed the large automatic garage door, grabbed her briefcase from the front seat of the car, and entered the house. Inside, she found the junior partner nestled in the easy chair opposite the plush sofa busily reviewing the latest law review articles, and apparently totally absorbed in some nuance of a particular case she was reading.

"Hi." Robin came up behind her.

A bit startled, Jess snapped her head up. "Oh, hi kiddo. I didn't realize it had gotten so late."

233

"Interesting reading there?" The smaller woman smiled knowingly and took a seat on the sofa.

Blue eyes twinkled. "Fascinating." Those same eyes now turned very playful. "For instance, did you know that a court has now ruled that residential house rules must be strictly adhered to?"

"Really?" Robin propped her chin on her fist. "Tell me more."

"Well it seems that failure to comply with any and all existing house rules can be a very serious offense."

"Oh my." The younger woman set down her briefcase on the coffee table and moved over to kneel in front of the easy chair and its alluring occupant. "Well, then I must be very sure not to violate any such existing house rules."

"You must, indeed." Jess gave Robin her best serious look. "Otherwise, according to the court case I've just been reading, the consequences could be rather...dire."

She's so funny. "Ooooh, dire consequences. Sounds very serious."

"Yes." The dark head nodded somberly. "Afraid so."

"Well, then to avoid any potential violation of said house rules, I'll be sure to comply to the utmost with each and every one of them." Robin leaned forward so that she was just mere inches away from Jess's face. She raised a petite hand and rested it against the older woman's cheek, then moved in even closer. Tantalizingly closer. "For instance, so as to be in full compliance with house rule number seven...." Petite fingers brushed back and forth against the dark cheek. "I will mention the 'L' word in connection with the other party occupying this residence."

"You will?" Jess almost croaked.

"Yes." Robin lingered, enjoying the effect she was having on her previously playful companion. She then placed a delicate kiss on the older woman's lips. "If you're ready for such full compliance, of course."

By now, with the tables having been so effectively turned for the second time that day, this time on Jess, the older woman couldn't bring herself to move even if she tried. "Um...." For some reason, she had trouble remembering whether an answer was due. "Um..." Robin's breath distracted her further. "Was there a question?"

That brought a grin. "No." The grin widened seductively. "How about if I just take it from here?"

"All right." It was all Jess could say, and even that took enormous concentration.

"Good." The kiss that followed was tender and slow and long and sweet, with a hint of other things to come. After a very long time, Robin pulled back, green eyes locking onto blue. "I love you, Jess."

Jess gave Robin a quick kiss in return, regaining her equilibrium. "And I love you, Sweetheart."

Just then, the front doorbell rang, breaking the moment. *Damn. Great timing.* "That must be our pizza." The taller woman stood up, helping Robin to her feet in the process.

"Pizza?"

"Yep. After you called from work saying you were leaving, I decided to order a pizza since it was getting a little late for us to cook anything." Blue eyes glanced at Robin. "Are you up for pizza?" A chuckle immediately followed. "Ooops. What am I thinking? When are you not up for food?"

That comment brought a playful swat. "You are so mean to me."

"Just stating the facts, kiddo. Why don't you go ahead and get changed from your work clothes, and I'll get the pizza and the table ready for dinner? Sound like a plan, Stan?"

"Yep. Be back in a jiff, Biff."

Biff? A dark eyebrow raised as Jess mouthed the word. *Hmmm.* "Don't hurry. Take your time." She watched Robin saunter down the long hallway, then retrieved the pizza from the delivery boy. And that's what he was, too, just a boy, barely able to drive and certainly not old enough to shave. *Geez, the next thing you know they'll be sending preschoolers delivering pizzas on their tricycles.* The taller woman spent the next several minutes busily tucked away in the kitchen, then she efficiently set out the plates and silverware on the table. Just as she was pouring sodas for both herself and Robin, she spied the smaller woman sporting more comfortable clothes entering the dining room. "Boy, that was fast." A quick wink.

"Yeah, well I'm starving."

"Is that so?" A suppressed smile. "How unusual."

"Watch it, Biff." Robin sat down.

"Biff? Whatever happened to Bucko?"

Petite hands opened the pizza box. "You're still Bucko, but now you're also Biff."

Jess appeared to contemplate that for a moment. "I see. Another term of endearment, I presume?"

A blonde eyebrow arched. "If you prefer to think of it that way."

"I do." Jess grinned happily

Green eyes now gazed at the pizza inside the delivery box. "Um..." A slight pause. Then a longer pause. "Jess?"

Innocent blue eyes focused on an imaginary spot on the placemat. "Yes?"

"What kind of pizza is this?"

"Um..." A long finger traced a non-existent line. "You know, regular pizza."

Regular pizza? "I see. And what toppings are on this regular pizza?"

Those same innocent blue eyes looked up. "Toppings?"

"Yes." The blonde head nodded. "You know, those little food items that you put on top of the pizza? What are they?"

The imaginary spot on the placemat now seemed very interesting. "Well, there's sausage, and ham, and mushrooms."

Sausage, and ham, and mushrooms. Sea-green eyes tracked from the pizza to Jess. "Is that all?"

Silence.

"Jess?" *She is so busted.* "Is that all?

It was amazing. That imaginary spot grew absolutely fascinating.

"Jess, let me tell you what I think. I think that maybe you might have added just a teensy weensy little something else to the toppings. Did you?"

Now, blue eyes focused on Robin, dark eyebrows lifting comically. "I don't know what you're talking about."

The younger woman was secretly amused. *She's so hopeless.* "I think you do."

More silence.

"Jess, honey." Robin's tone was sympathetic. "It's okay to tell me. Did you add something to the toppings?"

"Maybe."

Maybe? A frank look. "Maybe yes?"

Having now been caught, Jess had no choice but to come clean. "Oh, all right. Yes, I added something to the pizza after it arrived, but just to half of it."

Green eyes scrutinized the pizza. "I see."

A dismissive sigh. "You don't have to have any of that half, you know."

Robin lifted a piece of pizza and put it on her plate. "I know." She took a bite. "I'm not."

In response, Jess took a slice of pizza from the opposite side of the box and began eating. "Suit yourself." After a few moments, she smacked her lips together, thoroughly enjoying her meal. "Mmmm. This pizza is very good."

"It's delicious."

The older woman took another bite. "Yes, but the half of the pizza that I have is exceptionally good today" She smacked her lips together again lightly. "Want some?"

"No." Robin resumed eating.

Long fingers grasped another piece of pizza and held it out to Robin. "Are you sure?"

"Yes."

"Okay." Jess playfully taunted, waiving the pizza in front of Robin. "But you're missing out."

That's it! The younger woman, with infinite patience, set her second slice of pizza on her plate and slowly wiped her hands on her napkin. She then looked down the table at Jess. "Let me explain something to you, just so you know. Sausage, ham, and mushrooms are perfectly normal toppings for pizza. Shrimp, on the other hand, is not. Do you understand what I'm saying?"

Silent contemplation.

"Jess? Do you understand?" Robin asked again.

More silent contemplation.

With no response forthcoming, the blonde woman resumed eating. "You keep thinking about it, and I'm sure you'll eventually agree with me."

Contemplation over, Jess finally spoke. "I'll tell you what I agree with." A happy grin. "I agree that my pizza is very good tonight."

Good grief. A significant eyeroll. "Whatever you say, Jess."

The larger body then leaned in very close to Robin. "I think I should point out to you that shrimp makes me very happy." Jess gave the younger woman a knowing nod.

Very happy? The smaller woman, catching the nod, stopped eating altogether. "Um...how happy?"

A long slender finger reached up and slowly traced Robin's lips. "Extremely, extremely..." The finger continued its path over the slightly parted lips. "Happy."

Oh. An audible swallow, then blonde eyelashes fluttered lightly. "In that case, I think you should definitely have another slice of your shrimp pizza."

Hearing that comment, Jess sat back in her chair, immensely satisfied with her victory. "Well..." She grinned widely. "I don't mind if I do."

Ooooh. I can't believe she got me again!

237

Considerable Appeal

****

The early morning sun had long risen above the horizon, casting a glowing light through the large floor-to-ceiling glass windows in the litigation department chairman's office. Jess and Robin entered together, taking seats in front of the large wooden desk, as Harry perused the morning newspaper, his cup of hot coffee perched conspicuously in front of him. Sitting in complete silence, all three parties waited for the managing partner's arrival. In reality, it wasn't a particularly uncomfortable quiet for any of them. After all, the deal was already set. The outcome was known. There was no particular suspense, no need for further negotiation, no uncertainty, no jockeying for position. Nope. Just taking care of some unresolved and unfinished business. That's all.

Jess cast a glance around the office, settling her gaze on Harry's form framed by the near-glaring sunlight. As Robin had told the story, he had orchestrated a way out of this mess for all of them, and had convinced the Management Committee to accept a deal. It was a shrewd move on his part. *Leave it to Harry to figure out a way to keep both me and the firm out of hot water.* But at what cost? Well, certainly, the cost was a slightly damaged reputation for Jess. Perhaps she'd even suffer a loss of respect by certain of her colleagues, perhaps even by Harry, himself. *Perhaps.* Then, there was Robin's release. *Damn.* The junior partner really didn't like the idea of Robin signing such a thing. What do they call it in the business world? Oh, yes. A "love contract". *Shit. Ten to one they'll ask me to sign the damn thing, as well.* The worst thing about it was that the release reduced both her personal relationship and her business relationship with Robin to a common contractual matter, a kind of prenuptial agreement, just in case the relationship ended. Jess sighed internally. *Ended.* Could that really happen?

The junior partner had to give Robin credit, though. She'd used her wits and keen sensing of the situation to seal the deal in the most favorable light possible. Blue eyes glanced over at the young associate. *She did a good job.* Robin's sensing of how badly the Management Committee wanted the release was good instinct, a trait that would serve her well in the future. And using the Committee's weakness to her own advantage by promising to sign the release in exchange for assurance that Jess's partnership would be secure was shrewd in its own right. In truth, the junior partner was really quite proud of Robin. There would be no greater test of Robin's abilities than in handling a situation which so intimately involved herself and someone about whom she cared greatly.

Just then, the door opened and the managing partner stepped inside the office. "I see that everyone's here, so let's begin." He approached the large wooden desk where Harry sat and stood off to the side, leaning casually against a long bookcase filled with old statute books.

Harry quietly set his newspaper down and took a long sip of coffee, obviously preferring to let Gordon deliver the Committee's formal verdict.

Noting the silence, the managing partner continued. "Robin, do you have the signed document with you?"

Well, he didn't waste any time. "Yes, all signed and notarized." Robin placed the release on the desk. "I made one small change on page two, but other than that, I have no other concerns about signing it."

Gordon picked up the document and reviewed the change. "Yes, that's fine." He nodded his assent. Now, he could breathe a little bit easier. He had the signed release in hand. That was what he was really after. The firm was protected. Everything else was perfunctory. Pure mechanics. There was just one other little detail to take care of. His gaze fell on the junior partner. "Jessica, did you have an opportunity to review this document, as well?"

Here it comes. "Yes, I did."

"Good. The Management Committee requests your signature on page three." Gordon set the paper in front of the junior partner and handed her a stylish pen. "Right there." He pointed to the signature line and stared at her expectantly.

Jess took the pen, and without further comment, signed the document. *A "love contract." It figures.* She handed it back to him.

"Okay." Gordon directed his remarks to Jess. "Here is the Management Committee's final decision. You will be permitted to retain your partnership with the firm provided that you agree to the following terms. First, you must reimburse the firm for its legal fees associated with this matter. Second, you must forfeit your partnership distribution for one month, prospectively. Third, your suspension, which you have served for the past two weeks, is without compensation. And fourth, any other matter involving you, regardless of subject matter, which is serious enough to be brought before the Management Committee and for which you are found to be the responsible party, will result in the permanent, irrevocable severance of your partnership. Those are the terms."

Jess nodded. *I suppose it could be worse.* "Agreed."

"Good." He stepped around the desk. "You'll receive a copy of the written decision of the Committee, and you'll also receive an agreement setting forth the terms I've just outlined which you'll need to sign prior to your reinstatement on Monday morning." Upon seeing her nod in the affirmative, his business was concluded. The main thing was that he got his release. The firm was free and clear. "And, as to the working arrangement between you and Robin, I'll let Harry hash that out with the both of you. Now, if you all will excuse me, I've got a Historical Society board meeting to attend right now." He started to leave the office, but instead hesitated, giving Jess a curious look. He then glanced briefly over at Robin, then back again at Jess. *I don't understand it. Why would anyone put their career in jeopardy for such a relationship? It makes no sense.*

I know that look. The junior partner held his gaze. *Not one word, Gordon.* Her face was an expressionless mask. *Not one word.*

Robin, who had remained deferentially quiet during the interchange between Jess and Gordon, caught the look he gave, as well. *What was that all about?* It certainly was strange, and she made a mental note to ask the junior partner about it later.

As Gordon exited the office, both younger attorneys turned their attention to Harry, who hadn't said two words all morning. The head of the litigation department slowly and deliberately moved his empty coffee cup off to the side of his desk and folded his hands directly in front of him. "Well." He cleared his throat. "What am I going to do with you two?"

"Harry...." Jess began to explain, even though she didn't exactly know what she was explaining.

He quickly put his hand up. "Let me finish." His demeanor was stern, but his tone of voice held a hint of affection. "As Gordon indicated, it's now up to me to find a way for the two of you to work together."

Work together? Jess had assumed that Harry would be assigning Robin to work with Clay Taylor permanently. It was inevitable, and although it didn't make her happy, the junior partner knew it was the desired protocol in this type of situation. But what was Harry talking about now? The junior partner cast Robin a questioning look.

The young associate simply shrugged innocently. For whatever reason, Robin had chosen not to reveal to Jess the part of the deal that allowed both of them to continue working together. Robin, herself, didn't exactly know why she didn't tell Jess. Perhaps she wanted it to be a surprise. Or perhaps a bonus to the deal. Or maybe she just wanted

Jess to be proud of her. On that point, she needn't have worried.

The junior partner shook her head, not understanding Harry's statement. "You're saying that you have to find a way for Robin and me to work together?"

He nodded. "Yes. Pursuant to the Management Committee's agreement with Robin, you two are going to be permitted to work together, and like I said, I now have to find a way for you to do that without raising any type of favoritism concerns. Not an easy task."

At this point, Jess looked over at Robin, raising both dark eyebrows appraisingly in the process. *How did she manage that?* A smile formed on her face. "Is that so?"

The young associate just smiled back sweetly.

Harry continued. "So, here's the way it's going to be. You both will operate as a team. I will act as the team's supervisor and evaluate the team's overall performance, thereby eliminating any potential favoritism allegations. Each of you is dependent upon the other. If the team succeeds, then you both succeed." He glanced at Jess and Robin. "Can you both work within those parameters?"

Jess nodded enthusiastically, still not entirely believing how all this ended up. "Yes."

Robin, likewise, followed suit. "Yes, sir."

"Good." He then broke into a wide grin and shook his head in seeming amazement. "Son of a gun." He shook his head again. "You are the only two people I know who could've pulled this thing off." He leaned forward in his chair and barely winked. "Just don't do it again."

Jess grinned, very relieved. This had worked out better than she could have possibly hoped. "Don't worry, Harry. Robin and I will be perfect angels from now on." She arched a dark eyebrow in Robin's direction. "Isn't that right, Robin?"

"Absolutely." The young associate wholeheartedly agreed. "Perfect angels."

"All right, then. Now, I think some of us have work to do today." Harry turned his head and stared longingly at his empty coffee cup. "Robin, as you head on back to your office, could you please ask Betty to bring me in another cup of coffee? And Jess, will you stay for just a moment longer?"

"Sure." The junior partner gave Robin a wink as the younger woman stood up and left the office, then settled herself more comfortably into her chair. "Okay, Harry, what's up?" A knock at the door interrupted them, and Betty brought in a fresh cup of steaming hot coffee. Jess watched as Harry's secretary set the coffee mug down on the corner of the large wooden desk and then retreated back to her cubbyhole outside. "So, now what's up?"

Harry sipped his coffee, then got serious. "Listen, Jess, I'm counting on you. Don't do anything to mess this arrangement up."

"I won't." The junior partner studied her hands, contemplating her next words. "Robin told me how you put together this whole release deal in order to keep me around." Sincere blue eyes met his. "I want you to know that I appreciate your faith in me and your support, and I promise you that I won't let you down."

"Good." The managing partner leaned forward and rested his forearms on the desktop. "Jess, you're a damn fine lawyer and very good for this firm. I have always supported you, and I always will. But..." He looked at her pointedly. "I need for you to come to me with any problems you may have here, large or small, from this point forward. Are we clear?"

"Yes. You have my word." She smiled. Harry really was a good man. "Again, Harry, thanks for working out the deal."

"Well, I think you can thank Robin for most of that. I did what I could, but Robin recognized the dynamics involved in the Committee's thinking and then turned around and used their own concerns as leverage to get what she wanted. She's a very smart young woman."

The junior partner grinned broadly. "That much I had figured out."

Harry nodded. "She's going to be one hell of an attorney." He tapped two fingers idly on the edge of his desk. "I have to tell you, when she went for more than the original deal with her insistence that the both of you continue to work together, I about fell out of my chair." He shook his head, recalling the meeting the day before with Gordon and Robin. "I never saw that one coming, and I guarantee you that Gordon didn't, either."

"Really? I'm impressed." And Jess really was impressed. Very impressed. "I wish I could've seen that."

"She reminds me of you. You sure have taught her well." The litigation department chairman winked, then quickly sobered. "But I need for the both of you to behave, now. As much as I'm happy that things worked out for you this time, and I admire how you both pulled this whole thing off, the Management Committee will not tolerate anything further from either of you. Gordon may have been backed into a corner this time, but I guarantee you that he won't let it happen again."

"I understand."

"Good." Harry turned all business once again. "Now, I'll see you on Monday. All of your previous cases will be waiting for you when you arrive."

"I'll be there." The junior partner stood up. She glanced at Harry, then decided she might as well broach the subject that had been on her mind all morning. "Can you tell me the outcome of the Committee vote?" Actually, she was itching to know.

I'm surprised she waited this long to ask. "Yes." He paused briefly, then answered. "Four to one."

Figures. Three guesses who went against me. As the junior partner turned to leave, she cast a fond look back at her long-time friend and mentor. "Hey, Harry?" At his glance up, she gave him a wry smile. "Thanks." He casually waived her off, maintaining his businesslike demeanor, but not fooling her for one minute. *He's really a teddy bear.* Her tall form left the office and stepped into the long hallway, closing the door behind her.

Now, let me find Matt Singleton. There's something I need him to do for me. Today.

****

"So, how you doing, Biff?" Robin snuggled against her taller companion on the plush living room sofa. The soft orange glow of candlelight surrounded them, the flames gently flickering to cast dancing shadows on the nearby wall.

"Biff is just fine, thank you." The dark-haired woman suppressed a grin, then kissed the top of the blonde head beside her. "Have I told you how proud I am of you?"

"Only about a million times, but I never get tired of hearing it." A petite finger traced random patterns on the cotton fabric of Jess's t-shirt. "To tell you the truth, I wasn't sure that my plan would work, but I had to go for it. I just couldn't let them get away with trying to get something for nothing."

"Your instincts were dead-on right, and you handled yourself very well." The taller woman brushed the bangs from Robin's forehead. "I have it on good authority that both Gordon and Harry were very impressed...well, as impressed as they could possibly be under the circumstances."

The blonde head lifted up, surprised. "They were?"

"Absolutely. It's not every day that a relatively young associate gets the better of them. Harry, of course, did warn me that they won't fall for it again, but I think you gained a lot of respect from them."

"Really?" Robin's hand trailed down and slipped underneath the hem of Jess's t-shirt, stroking the silky smooth skin. "Well, I did learn from the best, you know."

"Um...." Jess was becoming a little distracted. Well, actually, more than a little distracted. "Perhaps you deserve a reward for your efforts."

A reward? "What a great idea." The younger woman leaned in and whispered into a very convenient ear. "Was there something in particular you had in mind?"

All Jess could think about at that particular moment was the warm, moist breath caressing the nape of her neck. There was no doubt in her mind that she was with the only person in the whole world who could evoke so many intense emotions from her all at the same time. And what she was feeling right now was very strong, indeed. "Well, there is one thing...." Her thought was cut off by a long, searing kiss that left her nearly breathless. "Um..." She was clearly a bit dazed. "Um..." Azure eyes somehow managed to focus. "Come with me. I have a reward to give you."

Sea-green eyes never left crystal blue as Jess led them both into the master bedroom. Robin's heart picked up its beat, her pulse racing, as the tall form knelt in front of her and long, slender fingers unbuttoned her blouse, tossing it aside. Soft lips placed gentle kisses on every inch of exposed flesh, while those same long fingers slowly and deliberately removed each and every article of clothing in their pathway, creating an explosion of sensation in their wake. It was amazing. And incredible. No matter how many times they'd done this very same thing before, it was always so unbelievably intense.

Finally, Jess led Robin over to the waterbed, guiding her down with infinite tenderness and kissing her sweet lips with such feeling that Robin didn't know where she ended and Jess began. Large hands roamed and caressed and massaged and stroked Robin's body freely, intent on their sensual task, until finally, the smaller body arched and surrendered itself in the all-encompassing and shuddering waves that followed. The reward rendered was very sweet, indeed.

As Robin's heart rate regained its normal rhythm, she held the taller body tightly to her own for several long moments, enjoying the unique closeness. Then, as the smaller woman shifted herself to rest on top of Jess, petite fingers intent on a task all their own, began a journey of love and adoration reserved only for the one person in the whole universe who held the essence of her soul. And like all the other times beforehand, the connection between them was very moving, very intense, and very beautiful as they each cradled the other's heart in love's tender embrace.

As they laid together in the darkness, the soft moonlight from outside cast an ethereal glow throughout the bedroom. Jess brushed her fingers back and forth against Robin's cheek in a feather-light touch. "Everything okay?" The younger woman had been silent for a very long time.

"Yes." Soft lips placed a delicate kiss on Jess's chin. "I was just thinking about how glad I am that this whole thing with the firm is over now."

An internal sigh. *It's not over. It's just beginning.* "Well, we're back to working together again, and that's a good thing."

Robin detected something in Jess's response. She propped herself up on one hand. "Are you worried about something?"

Good question, and just how, exactly, to answer it? After due consideration, the older woman decided to let Robin savor the day's victory. Besides, there might not be anything to worry about, anyway. "Well, I think we'll have to prove ourselves as a team, but you and I are going to do the best damn job that firm has ever seen." She grinned in the dark, partly to reassure herself, and partly to reassure Robin. "I guarantee it."

Gray-green eyes regarded Jess fondly. "We sure do make a good team, don't we?" That earned Robin a quick kiss, which in turn elicited a slight giggle from the younger woman. "I take that as a yes?"

"You betcha, kiddo."

After a few more minutes of contented silence, Robin spoke again. "I saw that look Gordon gave you today when we were in Harry's office. What was that all about?"

The older woman characteristically stiffened. *Damn.* She'd intended to avoid the issue completely, but despite her best efforts to direct the focus away from the unpleasantness, Robin kept circling around it. Jess swallowed, then tried to put as best light as possible on the situation. "I believe that there may be some people at the firm who might resent the way all of this has turned out." Well, at least, that was an innocuous enough way to phrase it.

Blonde eyebrows furrowed. *That's not it, or at least not all of it.* Everything in Robin's instincts was telling her that there was more going on. She focused intently on silver-blue eyes in the dark. "Tell me, Jess. You can tell me."

Jess grasped Robin's hand within her own and kissed the knuckles. "There are some people who may not..." She searched for an appropriate word. "Understand our relationship."

What is she really saying? Then, it dawned on Robin, and she understood completely. There could be a backlash against them. It really wasn't a surprise. She'd actually known it all along. The smaller woman tucked their still joined hands snuggly underneath her chin. "As one very smart person once told me, it's none of their business. No one could understand how I feel about you." They were Jess's exact words, said to her only months before. In truth, Robin's saying them was a testament to how far she had come in the past several months. It wasn't too long ago that she'd have been worried sick over what other people might be thinking.

The significance of Robin's statement didn't escape Jess. She recalled saying those words to the younger woman when they were first beginning their relationship. Now, Robin was saying them to her. *How things have changed.* "So, then you're okay about it?"

"Yes." Gray-green eyes twinkled. "I'm wonderful."

"Yes." Amused silver-blue eyes twinkled back. "You most certainly are."

****

A petite nose twitched, then twitched some more as a delightfully delicious aroma emanated from the kitchen. *Ooooh, coffee.* It was rather late in the morning, after all, and it appeared that the proprietor of the household had been up for quite some time, no doubt concocting some infamous creation for breakfast. A green eye opened drowsily and surveyed the surroundings, instantly confirming the assessment. Bright sunlight streamed into the room through slits in the Venetian blinds, and the older woman was nowhere to be seen.

Robin inhaled the tantalizing scents wafting in her direction, now detecting a hint of frying bacon in the mix. *She's doing this just to wake me up. She knows I can't resist the smell of coffee and bacon in the morning.* The younger woman sat up, languidly stretching her limbs to the fullest before climbing out of bed and diligently searching for her beloved bunny slippers. Thankfully, they were just where she'd left them the previous evening. For the time being, at least, her highly-prized footwear was all present and accounted for. She slipped the items onto her feet and padded down the long hallway toward the kitchen, intent on taking a sneak peek at just what her housemate was up to.

It was a familiar sight. The dark-haired woman stood next to the stove, occasionally turning the bacon, knowing full well that Robin would soon be up and about just from the delicious smells alone. In fact, it was a sure bet that at any moment, her sleepy companion would indeed be darting into the kitchen, attempting desperately to snatch a piece of bacon at exactly the precise split-second that Jess wasn't looking. It was an art that the younger woman had perfected in several months of living with Jess, and today was no exception. True to form, before the larger body could even turn around, petite fingers had deftly pilfered a crisp bacon strip sitting unsuspectingly on the stove warmer. Jess immediately noticed the missing object and grinned. *Somebody's finally up. My plan works every time.*

Robin sat innocently at the kitchen table munching on her hard-earned bacon. In truth, as she sat there, she marveled at the dark-haired woman. For all of Jess's tough exterior, she was just a cuddly bunny underneath. She was one who could pick people apart at inane committee meetings, and at the same time, she was as kind and considerate as any human being ever could be. *And absolutely, positively, and without a doubt predictable.* "Good morning." Robin managed to get out between munches.

Blue eyes sparkled. "Good morning, sleepyhead. If you didn't get up soon, I was going to have to scrap breakfast altogether and try for dinner."

Green eyes narrowed. "You are so mean to me."

A mortified look. "Moi?"

"Yes." Robin snatched another piece of bacon. "And I'm on to your little scheme, by the way."

"Scheme?" Dark eyebrows lifted comically, ostensibly to convey absolute innocence. "Why Robin, I have absolutely no idea what you're talking about."

Another munch, then a frank look. "I think you do. You deliberately made coffee and bacon at the same time knowing full well that smelling them always wakes me up."

A shocked gasp. "I did?"

A petite finger wagged playfully in Jess's direction. "Yes, you did."

"Well, what do you know..." Jess cocked her head in thoughtful concentration. "I always wondered why whenever I fixed bacon and coffee, you always showed up."

Robin threw a bunched up paper napkin at Jess. "You're impossible."

"Yep. That's why you love me, kiddo." A wide, happy grin. "So, tell me, would you like eggs or pancakes with your bacon today?"

"Eggs, please, over easy." A slight giggle. "After your little shrimp pizza topping thing the other night, I'm not inclined to take any chances with your pancakes this morning. Who knows what could happen? As if your shrimp-shaped pancakes that one other time weren't enough...I shudder to think what could happen next."

A very bored look.

"And really, who ever heard of putting shrimp on pizza, anyway? No one I know, that's for sure. I mean, ham and sausage and mushrooms, and even onions and green peppers and black olives, are perfectly normal toppings. But shrimp...." The blonde head shook in utter disbelief.

The very bored look continued.

"You know, you probably shouldn't order shrimp pizza out in public. Other people may not understand about your fetish the way I do."

Blue eyes blinked ever so slowly. "Are you finished?"

"Yes." Robin smiled sweetly.

"Good."

The smaller woman poured herself a cup of coffee, then noticed a folded piece of paper resting on the table in front of her. "Hey, what's this?" She picked it up.

"Um..." Jess looked away. "It's your copy."

My copy? The younger woman unfolded the paper, noting the title printed in neat calligraphy across the top of it. "It's a deed." She perused the document further, also noting the legal description. "To The Ranch."

Jess remained suspiciously silent.

"But, what...?" Green eyes widened. There, prominently displayed in black and white script, was Robin's name. She let go a quick gasp. "Jess...."

The taller woman approached the table and set a plate of bacon and eggs in front of Robin before sitting down next to her. "Listen, I've added you to the deed here. I had Matt take care of it yesterday." Azure eyes, unable to look at Robin, instead focused on the plate of food. "Is that okay?"

She wants to know if it's okay. In truth, Robin was speechless. She never expected this. It turns out that Jess wasn't so terribly predictable, after all. "It's...." Eyes the color of the sea moistened, then found brilliant crystal blue and held them in an intense gaze. "Yes." All other words at the moment escaped her.

"I wanted you to know beyond any doubt whatsoever that this is your house, too, your home, in every possible way. It will never be an issue." Jess was, of course, referring to their disagreement a few days before.

A petite hand grasped a larger one. "Thank you. It means a lot to me that you wanted to do that." The gesture of Jess adding her to the deed was more than merely symbolic, and Robin knew it. The older woman had worked so very hard to hold onto the house after James had cleaned out her financial accounts all those many years ago and devastated her life and her heart in the process. Now, here she was, sharing ownership of her most prided possession with Robin. "Are you sure about this?"

Jess's gaze never wavered. "Absolutely sure."

Robin squeezed the hand she was holding. "You are an amazing person."

That brought a smile. "So are you. We're each other's family now. This house, everything I have, is yours, just as much as it is mine. I want you to know that. What's mine is also yours."

The blonde head nodded. "And what's mine, whatever I have, is also yours, Jess. I want you to know that, too."

"Thanks." A pause, then Jess tapped a long finger against her chin pensively. "Hmmm. You know, Robin, it just occurred to me that if what's yours is mine...." She conspicuously peered underneath the table. "Does that mean that your bunny slippers are mine, too?"

Green eyes quickly narrowed. "You leave my bunny slippers out of this."

The older woman held up her hands in mock surrender. "Hey, I was just asking."

"I know what you were doing, and you can forget it, Biff."

Well, you can't blame a girl for trying. "Fine. Let's eat, then." Mischievous blue eyes suddenly twinkled. "Oh, and by the way, Robin..." A playful smirk. "It's your turn to pay the mortgage next month."

Now, that remark was entirely predictable.

Considerable Appeal

Chapter 10

He stepped off the elevator without a sound, surreptitiously checking the lobby area for signs of life as he did so. Continuing on without notice, he stealthily made his way down the long corridor, past the glass-paneled library doors and toward the small kitchen. It was a dangerous game and he knew it, but it was nonetheless necessary to his ends. Upon reaching his destination, he ever so cautiously poked his head inside the doorway. *Empty.* He relaxed somewhat. *So far, so good.* Aside from his throbbing headache, things were going better than he had expected. He'd gotten inside undetected. *Whew!*

Now, to get on with it and get what he came for, then get out. He surveyed his surroundings for a long moment, finally fixing his eyes on his prize. The sight beckoned him forward for a closer inspection, presenting a dilemma he hadn't contemplated. It was clear now that he'd have to make an important decision. Pensively, he wrestled with his options, his eyes darting back and forth several times as he considered the course of action he was about to take. His plan hadn't allowed for such complexities, but it was too late to back out now. He glanced toward the area just outside the doorway. *Still clear.* His decision was made. Now was the time to act.

He set his briefcase down and hesitated briefly, more out of nervousness than caution, finally gathering together his courage. Then, in a bold and most unexpected move, he swiftly bypassed the carafe marked "Hazelnut" and poured himself instead a cup of the Colombian. He took a long deliberate sniff of the aroma, and his headache seemed to recede immediately. *Good decision.* Satisfied with the success of his mission, he reached down and grabbed his briefcase, then hastily made

251

his way out the kitchen doorway. And that, he would later admit, was his prime mistake, as he nearly ran head-on into a very startled blonde haired green-eyed young associate.

"Whoa." Robin swerved, neatly avoiding having coffee splashed onto her new pale blue linen suit. "Gosh, Paul, slow down a bit."

The senior associate stood there guiltily. "I'm sorry. I didn't see you." He frowned as he realized that his plan to sneak into the office unnoticed was now officially ruined.

"It's okay." A blonde eyebrow arched as the younger associate took in Paul's slightly disheveled appearance. "Just getting in?" It was now nearly 10:30 in the morning, well into the typical workday.

Paul rubbed his forehead. His headache had returned in full force, likely a remnant of his late night binge the previous evening. "Well, I had some matters to attend to this morning."

I bet. Robin slipped past him and poured herself a cup of the hazelnut coffee without commenting further.

Hangovers were not an especially common occurrence with Paul, but upon hearing news of the Management Committee's decision filtering through the office grapevine, the realization that he had absolutely no chance whatsoever with Robin had hit him particularly hard during the preceding weekend. And it was fair to say that he was a little bit bitter about that, as well. He'd always thought that Robin would eventually come around to him. As an added incentive, he'd even offered to be there for her if things got too rough during that whole committee hearing mess. What else was a guy supposed to do? He grimaced visibly. *Nothing's fair.* He looked over at Robin, his curiosity getting the better of him. "Can I ask you something?"

The younger associate turned toward him as she stirred cream and sugar into her coffee, her internal radar sensing that something was definitely up with him. She responded carefully. "All right."

The now present ring on Robin's finger caught Paul's eye and brought his bitterness even closer to the surface. There was a hard look to his eyes. "What does she do for you? I mean, all she's brought you is sorrow and grief, investigations and hearings, gossip and disapproval. It can't be worth it to you to be so miserable." It sounded bitter and he knew it, but he didn't care. It was the truth.

Robin was absolutely incredulous. Here was a guy who wouldn't know true emotional connection if it bit him, and he was standing there piously judging her relationship with Jess. "I simply can't discuss this with you, Paul." She turned and made a brisk move to leave.

His face softened slightly. "Look." He gently stopped her progress. "I'm just trying to understand."

Robin responded with an undeniable truth, one that applied not only to Paul, but likely to many others, as well. "I don't know that you will ever be able to understand." She looked at him directly. "I will tell you one thing, though. It's what I choose."

Well, that made absolutely no sense. "You choose to be miserable?"

"Who says I'm miserable? I have everything I want."

"Do you?" He rubbed his forehead once again, his throbbing headache growing more and more prominent by the minute. He knew this was a lost cause, but something nevertheless made him persist. "What I see is someone who's been through months of misery, something that didn't have to happen. If Jessica cared for you as much as you think she does, she wouldn't have put you through all of that. You couldn't have wanted what happened to happen."

"That's enough." Robin quickly shut him down. "Like I said, I really can't discuss this with you. I'd appreciate it if you didn't bring it up again." She swiftly made her way toward the doorway, making one last comment on her way out. "I'd say the only misery going on here, Paul, seems to be with you."

Silently, the senior associate watched her leave. *Well, that was unfair.* He ventured out into the hallway just as several secretaries heading for their morning coffee break were approaching. Having no interest in their gossip for today, he found himself now lost in a totally unrelated train of thought. *Maybe Sandy will go out with me.*

Poor Paul.

But, was there perhaps the tiniest grain of truth in some of what he'd said?

****

What a morning! Jess rushed into the lobby and headed for her office much later than she'd originally anticipated, her early morning meeting with a client lasting almost until noon. *Damn.* She had so much work to catch up on from being gone that it would take nearly an eternity just to make even a small dent. It was now clear that she'd be having many late nights for the foreseeable future. She rounded the corner and proceeded down the long corridor toward her office, stopping briefly at her secretary's desk. "Hi Angie. Anything happen this morning?"

Angie looked up from her magazine, then closed it quickly. "A few messages, none urgent." She handed them to Jess.

"Okay." The junior partner took the messages and watched as her secretary hastily slid the magazine underneath some papers on her desk. *I think it's time we had a chat.* Angie had been her secretary since the early days, a lifetime ago it seemed, when Jess had first started out as a fresh new associate with the law firm. It was true that Angie was an excellent legal secretary as far as secretaries go, always on top of things and aware of all of the appropriate and often obscure legal procedures, but her idleness and frequent gossiping had really gotten out of hand lately. *I can't afford to be undermined.* However, now was not the time to have that chat. It would have to wait, Jess concluded, at least until sanity returned to her workload and things were more manageable. *And I definitely can't afford any staffing problems right now.* "Here's a tape. On it, I've dictated a summary of my meeting with Anderson Rayburn this morning. Please have it ready for me to review before the end of the day." With that, Jess strode into her office and set her briefcase down on her desk.

"I'd like to speak with you, if you have a moment." A voice abruptly sounded from the open doorway.

What the hell? Without looking up, Jess recognized the voice instantly, turning her harried mood now decidedly bad. *Tim West.* This guy was the absolute last person she wanted to see, and the expression on her face gave no doubt to that sentiment. "Actually, no, I don't have a moment. I have a lot of work to catch up on." She was brisk about it, wanting no part of whatever it was he felt compelled to say.

The member of the Management Committee, however, remained undeterred. "This won't take long." He took a few steps inside the office and closed the door behind him. "I just want to set a few things straight." It was an unfortunate choice of words.

"Look, if you want to rehash things, I'm not in the mood, nor do I have the time. I have a great deal of work ahead of me today." *Which I wouldn't have if you hadn't been such a damned jerk about things.* Jess conveniently ignored the fact that one could legitimately argue it was her own actions and poor decision-making which had, in actuality, led to her previous suspension.

He continued on despite her objection. "I'm sure it's no surprise to you that I disagreed with the Committee's decision. Nevertheless, the Committee made its decision and so be it. I will tell you one thing, though." He leaned forward slightly and placed his hands on top of the chair nearest the door. "You may have won the battle, but you haven't won the war. What you did and how you did it cannot be allowed to remain as some kind of precedent around here. Standards have to apply,

254

and no one is immune from them."

Jess almost rose to his bait. She stood there for a moment, considered her response, then spoke plainly and evenly. "As you said, the Committee made its decision and so be it. Now, I have to get back to my work." To press her point, she opened her briefcase and pulled out some paperwork.

"Fine." He straightened up. "But I'm not letting this go. I'm giving you fair warning on that. The situation you put this firm in is unworkable. We will all suffer because of it. As a partner with an interest in this firm's well-being, I will continue to fight it."

Well, it was clear this guy had made this issue his personal mission in life. Jess couldn't hold back her retort any longer. "Listen, the Committee made its decision. That's the end of it. You didn't prevail. Deal with it. And I would further caution you not to interfere with my practice of law."

"Or what? You'll go to Harry? You've been protected here by him all these years. What happens when he finally decides he's had enough of this place and retires? Who will cover for you then? He won't be here to make all kinds of excuses for you. He won't be here to supposedly supervise you as a way to bail you out of your messes. He won't be here to run interference for you with Gordon. And he certainly won't be here to promote your way up the ladder."

Ah. Now, I see what this is about. There were, Jess had to admit, those in the firm who intensely resented her quick rise to partnership status. And that was the real issue. *Perceived favoritism.* It was ironic. What had concerned her all along about her own working relationship with Robin had itself much deeper roots. *Was it true?* Jess wondered internally. Had favoritism played a role in her own status with the firm? *No.* Harry had supported her because she was a damn good attorney and he knew it. That was the way it was. Despite the internal warring within herself, Jess dismissed Tim West's implied point outright. "You're way off-base. If you have a problem with what Harry does or does not do, go talk to him about it. I've got work to do here."

The Management Committee member turned to leave. "This is not over. Mark my words on that." He exited the office and briskly shut the door behind him.

Jess glared at the empty space where he'd stood. *Idiot.* She shook her head and sank into her leather chair, collecting a few more papers from her briefcase as she did so. She wouldn't readily admit it to herself, but the whole conversation had hit a bit too close to home. Perhaps it was true that she'd overcompensated with Robin because of her own experiences with Harry. Had she done that, though? *No.* The situation with Robin was entirely different. *Entirely.* There were absolutely no parallels involved. *None whatsoever.* It was as different as night and day. *Completely.*

While Jess sat contemplating the finer points of the matter, there was a light knock at the door. *Damn it. I'm busy.* "Not now, please." She called toward the closed door, then reached for the button on the intercom to make it clear to Angie that she wasn't to be disturbed for the rest of the day. Before she could do so, however, the door cracked open a tiny bit. "I said, not...."

"Hi." Robin cautiously poked her head inside the office, then closed the door discreetly behind her. "Bad day?"

An exasperated sigh. "I'll live."

"If this isn't a good time, I can come back."

"No, stay." The junior partner motioned for Robin to have a seat. "I'm going to need your help."

"Actually, that's one of the reasons I stopped by. I'm here to offer you my services."

A brief pause, then a dark eyebrow edged up as blue eyes twinkled mischievously. "Is that so?"

Robin blushed slightly. "You're incorrigible." She settled into the chair closest to the large window. "You know what I meant."

Feeling a bit better, Jess smiled. "Yep." She handed the young associate a pen and notepad. "Here's what I need you to do. On the Bronson Construction case, review the contract. I know there's a 'paid when paid' clause in there which they're relying on, but I also know the law states that those clauses are largely unenforceable. Research the issue and get me some case law on point. Second, if our client, as the owner of the project, paid Bronson but Bronson didn't pay its subcontractors, where did all of that money go? It was only after Bronson defaulted on the contract that our client stopped payments. What happened to the millions of dollars already paid to them, especially since they didn't put it into the construction work?"

"Did the subcontractors lien the project?"

"You got it. We've got a lien fest going on, so snoop around a bit. What did Bronson do with the money our client paid them? If they used it to finance their work on other projects, it's illegal under the statute and there are criminal ramifications in addition to potential civil liability."

"I'm on it."

Long fingers idly tapped the desktop. "And go ahead and trace the claims of lien back to the Notice of Commencement and the Notices to

Owner served by the subcontractors. See if everything was done timely. If not, those claims are invalid. That might knock out a few of them." The idle tapping continued. "Also, check out the Payment and Performance Bond. There may be a bond claim there, as well."

"Right. Anything else?" The younger attorney looked up from her writing.

"No, that'll do it for now." A look of intense concentration persisted for a moment, then the junior partner shook her head. "You know, something's fishy about this case, but I just can't put my finger on it." *Follow the money.* "Maybe if you get in there and dig into it a bit, you'll find something."

"Maybe. I'll see what I can do." A pause. "You okay today?"

The older woman's expression visibly softened. "Yeah. I just had a surprise visit from Tim West. He got under my skin."

"Oh no. What did he want?"

"He's apparently not going quietly. He's made it his pet mission to cause me trouble and insinuated that when Harry decides to retire, I'm basically screwed."

"Harry won't let that happen." Robin took a step toward the cherry wood desk. "You're too valuable to him."

Too valuable. There were absolutely no parallels, Jess kept telling herself. None whatsoever. The situations were as different as night and day. "Yeah, maybe." She promptly changed the subject. "How's your morning been?"

Green eyes rolled upward. "Fine until I ran into Paul in the kitchen. He questioned me about my relationship with you. Can you believe that?"

"Really? What did you tell him?"

"The only thing I said was that it was what I wanted and I really didn't want to discuss it with him further."

"But...?" Jess sensed there was more.

"Well, it was just a bit unsettling, that's all. I know he's harmless, but his interest in my life really creeps me out."

Hmmmm. "You know, it is a bit odd. You'd think he'd have gotten the message long ago." *But had he gotten the message? Good question. Perhaps a little reinforcement wouldn't hurt.* "Maybe I should speak with him. He's a decent guy, a bit self-absorbed, but he doesn't strike me as malicious."

"Well, if it gets him to back off, I'm all for it."

"Okay, let me think about it. I have an appeal brief I need from him later today. I'll see how he is with me, and if there's a problem, I'll deal with it." The older woman wouldn't admit it out loud, but her hackles were up. Her instincts told her that a spurned man could spell trouble in the long-run.

"You're the boss." Robin stood up, her stomach choosing that precise moment to rumble. "I suppose you don't have time for lunch, do you?" It was for all intents and purposes a rhetorical question.

"Afraid not, kiddo. Bring me back something, though?" Hopeful blue eyes begged.

"Done." A wide smile now appeared. "Hey, Jess?"

"Yeah?

"I'm really glad to be back working with you."

"Tell me that again at nine o'clock tonight when we're both still here working like dogs." A blue eye winked.

Rats. "You sure know how to show a girl a good time." Robin winked back.

"Just one of my many skills." Jess deadpanned.

A tiny chuckle. "Okay, see you later. I'll bring you back some lunch."

As the young associate opened the door to leave, Todd, one of the mail room clerks, appeared carrying several boxes, with several more of the same neatly stacked up out in the hallway. He stepped just inside the doorway, and upon seeing Robin, he hesitated briefly, then tentatively spoke up. "Uh...Ms. Harrison? Mr. Roberts asked that I bring these to you."

Robin peeked beneath the lid of the top box and surveyed its contents, then glanced over at Jess still sitting at her desk. "Your files."

Goody. My day is complete. The junior partner took a deep breath, resigned to her fate for the remainder of the day, then motioned to Todd. "Thanks. Just put them over there against the bookcase."

Robin simply grinned and quietly left the office as Todd went about his business. Once he'd finally gone, Jess groaned audibly. *This is turning out to be a very long day.*

And it wasn't even noon yet.

****

"Ooooh. God, Jess, this feels so good."

"I'm glad you think so." The older woman diligently went about her task, making sure she performed all the right moves.

"I think this is the best idea you've had all day."

"Well, occasionally I do have a brilliant thought." Twinkling blue eyes looked up only to be greeted with a playful splash of foamy heated water. The soothing Jacuzzi jets had hit their mark, and Jess eagerly settled herself back into the large oval Roman tub. "Champagne?" Having now successfully completed her task of uncorking the bottle, she carefully poured the chilled bubbling wine into two glasses, handing one over to Robin.

"Thanks." Petite legs stretched out across the opposite end of the marble tub as the water jets continued to work their magic. "Even though it's late and I'm really tired, this was exactly what I needed. I can feel myself relaxing already."

"Just wait until after you've had a few glasses of champagne." Jess quipped.

"It's all your fault, you know."

A shocked expression. "Moi?"

"Yes. You kept me at the office working my you know what off tonight, Miss big-time partner."

Another shocked expression. "I seem to recall how one very lovely young associate came to me earlier today and generously offered me her services."

Robin stifled a giggle, then sipped her champagne, the tiny bubbles tickling the back of her throat. "That was before I knew what you had in mind for me." The soft light of the wild berry scented candles flickered gently nearby, casting a warm glow about the spacious bathroom.

It was an opening Jess couldn't resist. She inched over closer to Robin. "I definitely have plenty in mind for you."

Oh. The seductive voice resonated deep within the younger woman causing her to swallow reflexively. "I'll just bet you do."

A slightly raised eyebrow was her only reply. "Here, let me get you a little more champagne." Jess reached over and expertly refilled Robin's glass, then her own.

A tiny chuckle. "Trying to get me drunk, I see."

"I have no comment."

"Right." A long, contented sigh followed. "You know, Jess, this is undeniably one of the most decadent pleasures I can think of. Whoever invented the Jacuzzi deserves a medal."

"I can't argue with that. Whoever invented champagne deserves a medal, too." Long fingers grasped the slender stem of the fluted champagne glass and toasted an imaginary inventor.

"And these gourmet chocolate truffles." Robin popped one into her mouth. "That person gets two medals."

"Who needs anything else? A Jacuzzi, champagne, chocolate, and you." A warm smile conveyed still unspoken thoughts, ones they both instinctively knew well though neither had ever voiced, a sense of something indescribable between them. Mesmerized by the flickering shadows on the tile walls, they sat in companionable silence, sipping their champagne and relaxing in the luxuriously warm swirling water. "What a day, though. I think at this rate I'll finally be caught up by the end of the week."

"Did anything fall through the cracks in your absence?"

"Miraculously, no. I think Harry stayed on top of things, thankfully." Jess reached for a truffle. "I did meet with Paul today."

"Oh? And how did it go?"

"I told him I was going to need to rely on him in a limited way to help me with a few of my cases, and if he had a problem with that, then he should tell me now. Paul may have his faults, but he's not an idiot. He knows he's on track to make partner soon and it wouldn't be in his best interests to refuse work at this time. He is ambitious, after all, in spite of his personal feelings, so he assured me in no uncertain terms that he'd have no problem working on my cases."

A thought had occurred to Robin earlier that day, and she momentarily questioned whether or not to mention it. *Might as well get it out in the open.* "Listen, Jess. I'm working with you on your cases, which is great and what I want to do. If you do need Paul's assistance on some matters, that's fine, but I'm really going to find it uncomfortable to be around him on those cases if he hasn't accepted the situation between you and me."

Jess could have kicked herself. Now, how did that get past her? She'd been so mentally absorbed in her own working relationship issues that she hadn't even considered the possibility that Robin would have some misgivings. *Damn. Way to go, Jess.* "I intend on using Paul's assistance mainly on appeal and bankruptcy matters because he's one of the few experienced lawyers in the firm in those particular areas." She looked directly at Robin. "You and I will be working on everything else. I promise you, if it becomes necessary for you to work on a matter that Paul is handling, I will personally assess the situation before asking you to do so. I won't put you in any situation that makes you uncomfortable. Is that fair?"

The younger woman breathed a sigh of relief. "Yes. Thanks."

"Good." A gentle smile. "Okay, enough shop talk for one day." The sparkling wine was beginning to have some effect on both of them, along with the soothing warm water loosening up their tired muscles, so much so that Robin's eyes had closed just a bit. Jess's larger form drew closer to her smaller companion. "Now, don't fall asleep."

The low vibration of the older woman's voice caused the sea-green eyes to open slightly. "I'm not falling asleep. I'm just relaxing."

Relaxing. "I see." Jess made a few little idle splashing sounds in the water beside her, then attempted to capture several tiny swirling bubbles rising to the surface of the water, all of which, one could argue, indicated that she was perhaps not quite as relaxed as her Jacuzzi partner seemed to be. Actually, relaxed wasn't exactly the word she would have chosen at all right at that moment. "Want another truffle?" She reached over and grasped one of the chocolate morsels from its gold foiled resting place. "There's one more here with your name on it."

Now that sounded enticing. "I'd love another one." No sooner had the blonde woman said the words when long fingers brought the gourmet confection up to her mouth for sampling. Both verdant eyes were still half-lidded as she took a bite, noting that Jess then proceeded to finish off the remaining half of the treat. Instantly, and before she could entertain another thought, chocolate coated lips covered her own, and she melted literally into their delicious softness. As the warm lips gently pulled away, Robin sighed in utter contentment. "Now, that was the best truffle I've ever tasted."

A deep chuckle. "I aim to please."

"And you do very well, indeed." The younger woman let her eyelids fall closed once again, savoring the lingering sweetness of the candy, and at the same time, the intense sweetness of the moment, itself. Suddenly, she felt a gentle tug first upon one knee, then the other. "Um...Jess? Did you drop the soap?"

Warm, moist breath tickled a petite pink earlobe as the low voice resonated into it. "Soap? Who said anything, Robin, about soap?"

Green eyes popped open, gazing squarely into darkening blue. *Oh boy.* As the steam rose from the heated water and the mirrors lightly fogged, all further cohesive thought from that moment on was quickly forgotten.

****

Jess heard the familiar rattling of keys against the door as she stood in the kitchen contemplating dinner options from the sparse offerings the refrigerator held. Having arrived home herself only a few minutes earlier, she'd managed to change from her business suit into more comfortable clothes and was just beginning to hunt down something for herself and Robin to eat for dinner. Even though they'd both left the office at the same time, the younger woman had been slightly delayed on her way home, taking a short diversion to pick up the week's dry cleaning. A dark head poked around the refrigerator door to greet the harried commuter. "You're home."

"Whew!" Robin made her way into the large kitchen and set the dry cleaning down across the glass tabletop. "Traffic's horrible today. The interstate is all backed up which caused the expressway to back up which caused everybody else in this entire city to take the exact same road I was taking home." She stopped to grab a bottle of water from the opened refrigerator. "I vote for a move out to the country."

A sympathetic smile. "I'll keep that in mind, kiddo." *Who needs to cook tonight, anyway?* "Hey, how about we order a pizza for dinner?"

"You read my mind." The smaller woman made an astute observation as she closed the refrigerator door. "We have to go grocery shopping, don't we?"

"Only if we want to eat." Came the predictable retort.

That earned Jess a gentle slap on the forearm. "You're hopeless." Robin turned and gathered up the dry cleaning. "This weekend, Jess. You do remember how to go grocery shopping, don't you?"

"Well, what I remember, Robin, is that grocery shopping requires a certain amount of hands-on experience, at least that's what I've been told." One azure eye winked suggestively.

The younger woman played along. "Yes, and you've made considerable progress in that department, I must say. Of course..." She put on her best serious expression. "You could do with a little more tutoring."

Tutoring? "Is that so?" Jess took a step closer and whispered into an adorable pink ear. "Well, then I'll definitely look forward to that."

A quick intake of breath. *I can't believe she still does this to me.* "Okay, then."

A slender finger traced a path along the petite jaw line. "Okay, then." Very soft lips then proceeded to caress those of the younger woman to further punctuate the point. "Tutoring it is."

Breathe. "Um...right." The blonde woman shook her conscious mind back to reality. "Let me...um...get changed, and you can order the pizza. Deal?"

Hiding a satisfied grin, Jess reached for the phone. "Deal." *I've still got it.* She set about her task of dialing the number to the pizza parlor, successfully placing their order without too much difficulty and requesting their usual toppings of sausage, mushrooms, ham, and of course, extra cheese. As soon as she'd set down the receiver, she recalled something which had slipped her mind from earlier, before her playful conversation with Robin had, in all frankness, distracted her. She walked down the long hallway toward the converted bedroom and gently tapped on the partially opened door.

"Come in." Robin had already donned more casual clothing and was in the process of hanging up her own portion of the dry cleaning. "Did you get the pizza ordered okay, or do you need my expert advice?" She chuckled lightly and tossed Jess an impish glance. "I know we don't have any shrimp in the house to put on the pizza, so I guess you're out of luck tonight, honey."

The face that greeted her was now more serious. "I forgot to mention something to you." Blue eyes captured green, then held them steadily. "I checked the answering machine when I got home, and there was another message on it from your mother."

There was a brief and rather disquieting silence, then the smaller woman hurriedly retrieved the remainder of the dry cleaning still resting on the daybed and resumed her previous task. "You know, I think I'm starting to get really hungry. Let me know when the pizza...." Before she knew it, she was enfolded by long, caring, comforting arms. Still, she said nothing.

Jess held on for a very long moment, then slowly broke away, trying to read what was going on behind those guarded eyes. She led Robin over to the daybed, sitting them both down and grasping the petite hands within her own. "I know it's difficult for you, but this is the fifth time your mother has called since...." She was at a temporary loss for words, finally settling upon the obvious. "Since everything that happened with your father."

Now, less guarded eyes revealed unspoken anguish, as Robin remained very still, the raw emotions plainly visible.

Jess sighed internally. Okay, so she'd finally said it. It was true, she and Robin hadn't talked much about the incident since it happened. In fact, they'd mostly avoided it, but how could they avoid it forever? *The incident.* Jess's jaw tightened reflexively at the memory of that hurtful night when Thomas Wilson paid a visit to his daughter shortly before the Management Committee hearing and wounded her so completely. *The incident.* Everything about that night made Jess's blood boil. Even so, she reasoned to herself, she also knew that Robin's estrangement from her parents was exacting a very heavy toll on her. And in spite of everything, and as much as Jess hated that man for what he'd done and the complicity of Robin's mother in the accumulated pain, she hated even more seeing Robin hurt by it all.

By now, anger had replaced the anguish present just moments before, and the blonde woman struck a defiant tone. "It doesn't matter." It was a thinly veiled lie, and both of them knew it.

Jess proceeded cautiously. "Listen, sweetheart, maybe it would be a good idea just to call her back and see what she wants." *How could it hurt?*

Uncharacteristically, Robin responded harshly. "I couldn't care less, Jess, how many times she calls. I'm not going to talk to her."

"But...."

"No. I'm not speaking with her, and that's final. Let it go."

Jess flinched, taken by surprise at the extreme reaction. Granted, she didn't particularly care for the way Robin's mother had treated her own daughter, to put it mildly, but after all, Robin's mother was Robin's mother, and no matter what anyone says, there's a bond there. Maybe it couldn't be salvaged in this case, but it has to be worth one last try, doesn't it? *Besides, what if her mother wants to make amends?* "Listen to me, Robin." It was a firm, yet gentle request. "She's your mother. Wouldn't it be better to at least find out what wants?" It seemed like a logical argument. Of course, understandably, Jess's perspective was colored by the very supportive relationship she had with her own mother.

The younger woman shook her head in complete disbelief. "How can you defend her? She betrayed me...us. Have you forgotten?" Robin couldn't for the life of her understand Jess's apparent sympathy for the woman after what her mother had done, how her mother had conspired against her, how she had kept the truth from her while her father proceeded to Florida to blackmail Jess into leaving her, and most of all, how it had almost worked. "How can you take her side after everything we've gone through because of her...because of them? I don't understand."

"I'm not taking her side. I'm just saying that maybe she wants to try to mend fences with you. You won't know unless you talk with her."

"I...." The blonde head turned angrily away. Several seconds passed, then both petite shoulders slumped and the smaller body began to tremble slightly. The voice was now very small as anguish once again replaced the dissipating anger. "I just can't."

"Honey, please." Long fingers reached around and gently grasped the smaller woman's face, guiding it back to meet a very concerned gaze. The tears were present, clouding those green eyes, just as Jess knew they would be. "I know it hurts." A thumb wiped away a falling teardrop. "Talk to me, sweetheart. Tell me why you can't speak with her."

Why don't you know? The wounds were deep, compounding the

already pervasive wound left by David's death, something Robin knew that Jess, as much as she tried, would never fully understand. Glistening eyes pleaded for recognition of the truth. "Because they destroy everything I love."

Crystal blue eyes searched the saddened green eyes just inches away. *That isn't true.* "No, honey, they haven't destroyed everything. They haven't destroyed our love. See?" Jess showed Robin her ring. "We're forever."

If only it were that simple. The blonde head shook slowly in resignation, the ultimate reality all too apparent and all too inevitable. "Don't you see? When I let them in, they destroy what I love."

The older woman felt helpless. Didn't Robin know that nothing in heaven or on earth could ever destroy their love for each other? Jess repeated over again in her mind the words Robin had spoken. *When I let them in, they destroy what I love.* They were simple enough words, but taken together in the current instance, they just didn't make sense. Hadn't she and Robin won? They'd prevailed at the hearing. They'd beaten them all despite her parents' best efforts. *So, what could she mean?* Then, the answer came to Jess, and it felt as if the air had been literally knocked from her lungs. *David.* The predictable jealously rose. *Damn it. But he's gone and I'm here. I'm here.* "No, Robin." She said it again. "They haven't destroyed everything."

Misty green eyes glistened once again. "I won't lose you, Jess. I promise you, I won't let them take you from me. I won't let them in again." It made perfect sense to Robin. The trouble was, it wasn't an entirely rational sense.

What? Then, comprehension slowly dawned and concerned blue eyes now turned misty, themselves. Jess understood. In Robin's mind, having her parents in her life meant that the things she loved ultimately were destroyed. Long fingers brushed back a stray lock of blonde hair from the younger woman's forehead as Jess spoke in a very soothing tone of voice. "Now, you listen to me." She made deliberate eye contact. "You and I are forever. That's a fact. Nothing, including speaking with your parents, will ever change that."

It was having absolutely no effect. The fear had crept far too deep within for anyone to reach, at least at this time. "I can't call them, Jess. I can't let them in. I won't let them destroy you."

The dark head nodded sadly. "Just like David."

She understands. "Yes." Robin released a relieved breath. "Just like David."

Oh, honey. Strong arms gathered the smaller woman up into a loving embrace. It was clear that Robin needed some professional help with this. "Sweetheart, can I ask you something?"

A faint sniffle sounded. "Yes."

"I haven't wanted to pry too much into your sessions with Dr. Richmond because I know that they're very personal, but will you tell me how they're going?"

"Um..." The younger woman sat up a bit straighter. "I've been told that there are layers of issues which have to be resolved one at a time and that this process will take a while to accomplish."

Okay. "Have you discussed the incident with your father and the trouble we had at the firm because of the things he'd done?"

"Well, we've discussed his attempted blackmail and his overall manipulation of the situation because he didn't like it."

Okay. There was no reason to hold back now. Jess delicately continued. "Have you discussed his involvement in what happened with David and how you feel your parents destroy the things you love?"

Blonde eyelashes blinked several times, the response slow in coming. "No, not yet."

Okay. Two slender fingers reached over and gently raised the petite chin just a bit. "Will you do a little favor for me?"

"What kind of favor?"

"Will you tell Dr. Richmond what you told me today and see if she can help you?"

There was no immediate answer. Instead, Robin stood up and stepped over toward the window overlooking a far corner of the shimmering swimming pool. The late day sun was now setting, its light casting long, streaming deep orange paths through the open Venetian blinds creating contrasting patterns along the carpeted floor. It was very quiet in the room except for the din of the wakening crickets just outside the window and the faint hum of the air conditioning unit pumping cooled air throughout the house. Robin could feel the slight breeze of the chilled air brush across the back of her neck as she stood in front of the glass window pane, a heightened awareness present as the silence now grew in length. Would she talk with Dr. Richmond about it? Why was that question so difficult to answer? Could it be that lending voice to the fear made it seem all the more real? Her heart, she knew, wasn't ready to hear the answer just yet.

"Robin?"

The colors of the sunset really were beautiful, so many pinks and oranges and reds, deep gold and even a slight hint of purple. It was fascinating how the light reflected just perfectly off the rippling water in the pool and the swaying palm branches cast gently moving shadows across the lush green of the freshly mown lawn. It was amidst the tranquility of this peaceful sight that long arms silently found their way around the smaller woman's waist from behind and a familiar chin rested upon the blonde hair glowing softly in the quickly fading sunlight. That perfect peace, all at once, magically transcended the deeply troubled soul, as if the mere joining of two complementary beings could alter cosmic karma and form a more certain destiny.

The long, protective arms tightened their hold, and a soothing, low voice whispered the words that would now begin to heal. "Robin, the love we share is eternal, like the sands of the desert or the waves of the sea, indestructible even to the most mighty, ancient yet still not born."

I know those words. The perfect peace now settled where fear once presided. *Indestructible.* Robin turned to face the taller woman. "Yes."

"Yes?"

"Yes, I'll speak with Dr. Richmond about the things we talked about today."

A warm smile graced the older woman's lips. "Good." There was nothing more to say. Progress was progress, one small step at a time.

Robin returned the smile, her heart now feeling considerably lighter. "You know, I never knew you were prone to poetic prose." A blonde eyebrow lifted as she proceeded toward the open doorway. "Keep it up, and you could earn big bucks for your efforts."

"Is that so?" Jess really had no earthly idea where the words she'd spoken had come from. They were certainly not her style, and yet, they felt eerily familiar, as if she'd heard them told to her sometime before. "Maybe I missed my calling." She joked. *Then again, maybe not.* She followed Robin out into the hallway. "You ready for some pizza? It should be here any minute now."

"Great. I'm starving."

"Why am I not surprised?" An ebony eyebrow raised in mock query, the question purely rhetorical in nature.

"Are you sure you can manage without your beloved shrimp tonight?"

Well, there was absolutely no way Jess could pass this one up. She grinned, winked rather conspicuously, then offered an entirely typical retort. "Why?" A pause for effect. "Are you planning on going somewhere, Robin?"

Ooooh. Sea-green eyes focused squarely on their target, then narrowed considerably. "You are in so much trouble."

Uh-oh. Long legs took off like lightning down the hallway toward the kitchen, a very determined petite body trailing not far behind. The only question was, what would happen when the chaser finally caught the chasee?

That, of course, was anybody's guess.

****

The smaller form stirred, then gravitated toward its larger companion in sleep, casting a petite arm around the familiar waist and snuggling into the long, dark hair haphazardly draped across the nearby pillow. A silent breath was taken, and within a heartbeat, a contented smile appeared, slowly easing across the petite owner's face as another deeper breath confirmed the earlier impression. Even through the haziness of slumber, the perceived fragrance imparted a particular comfort, its distinctive blend of sweetness and woody hints conjuring up subconscious images reminiscent of forests and rugged wilderness.

The taller body seemed to acknowledge the contact and nestled back further into the warm presence behind it. As a small hand made its way underneath a Calvin Klein shirt to rest upon the smooth stomach hidden there, a silent sigh escaped from the recipient of the touch. The sense was overpowering in nature, even in subconscious dreamland, and the feeling of visceral completeness registered in a most profound way. It was oddly familiar, arms encircling tightly from behind, laughter echoing as two figures galloped easily through the wind toward places uncertain.

But these sensations were fleeting, and the mind's images faded as quickly as they had appeared. Instead, an azure eye half opened as consciousness slowly asserted its dominance. The dawn was just breaking, dim gray tendrils of the morning's first light peeking faintly around the edges of the Venetian blinds in the windows. Resisting the bid to shake off the dwindling vestiges of sleep, the drowsy blue eye closed once again in a valiant attempt to recapture the previous dream. The conscious mind, however, was not to be so easily ignored, and instead persisted in an insistent attempt to waken its dozing host with a cacophony of internal commotion.

Gooooood mooooorning, sleeeeeepy heaaaaaaad!

It was a nightmare straight from the movie, "Good Morning, Vietnam," the alternate internal voice groggily reasoned. *'Shhhh. I'm sleeping, here.'*

No you're not. You're awake and you know it.

An internal sigh. *'I was having a perfectly lovely dream which you managed to rudely interrupt, thank you very much.'*

Sorry to disturb your beauty rest, but there are some things we need to discuss.

'*Let me correct you.*' The alternate internal voice was anxious to end this little chat and recapture the previous dream...something about galloping on the wind.... '*There's nothing that you and I need to discuss. I'm fine, Robin's fine, you and I are fine, everybody's fine. No problems, zippo, nada, nothing. Got it?*'

You are difficult, aren't you? I see you've chosen to bury your head in the sand and ignore everything that has happened over the past few weeks.

'*What's that supposed to mean?*' The alternate internal voice responded angrily.

Just what it sounds like. Your cozy little snuggle this morning notwithstanding, you haven't dealt with the issues that lead to a healthy relationship with Robin.

'*Oh please! Are we back to that again? I thought that was all settled.*'

If it was, you wouldn't be talking to me, would you?

'*Well, that's just great.*' The alternate internal voice conceded the point. '*Here I am telling Robin to go talk to the therapist and I'm the one who needs the shrink.*'

I have absolutely no comment.

'*Cute. Listen, I have to get back to my dream, so let's get on with this. What's the problem, now?*'

First, congratulations are in order.

'*Thank you.*' A pause. '*What for?*'

You skillfully negotiated out of your predicament at the firm and managed to retain your job and your working relationship with Robin in the process. Bravo!

The alternate internal voice accepted the rare compliment. *Thanks, I....*'

And you magnificently managed all of your cases so that nothing fell through the cracks while you were, shall we say, away from the office.

Pleased, the alternate internal voice continued to receive the praise. '*Well, yes, I am very thorough.*'

And let's not forget your splendid handling of Robin's emotional trauma regarding her mother's recent phone calls. Your insight into that situation was absolutely brilliant. A tremendously stunning achievement.

Detecting the tiniest hint of sarcasm, the alternate internal voice became annoyed. '*You have a problem with what I did?*'

Can you see a pattern developing? The only reason you retained your job and your working relationship with Robin was because Harry and Robin both bailed you out. The only reason your cases didn't fall through the cracks while you were suspended was because Harry and the people he assigned to your cases in your absence kept on top of things for you. And the only reason Robin agreed to talk to the therapist about her situation with her parents was not because she was ready to do so, but because she wanted to please you. Is the pattern clear now?

A bored tone. *'Since you seem to have all the answers, why don't you enlighten me.'*

Fine. Listen carefully. It's everyone else who has to do things for you, bail you out, manage your cases, try to please you. Any credit you give yourself for those things actually belongs to others.

'But....'

But nothing. The sooner you recognize your own culpability in the things that have happened, the sooner you and Robin can get past them.

'That's just gibberish.' The alternate internal voice retorted. *'I've recognized everything that's happened and taken full responsibility for things that were of my doing.'*

If you say so.

'I say so.'

Denial never did serve you well.

'You forgot the house.' The alternate internal voice was quick to raised point. *'Don't I even get credit for the deed thing?'*

Okay, if it's credit you seek, then it's credit you get.

Totally oblivious to the sarcasm, the alternate internal voice smugly replied. *'Thanks.'*

But before you get all full of yourself, you must understand that you have some outstanding issues to deal with, a prime example being your continued jealousy over you-know-who.

A dismissive tone. *'I'm dealing with that. Besides, it's not my fault he keeps showing up every five minutes.'*

Oh, that pesky acknowledgement of responsibility thing again. Nothing's ever your fault.

'It's not.' The alternative internal voice insisted. *'I'm not the one who keeps him alive.'*

Aren't you? You feel threatened even when his name isn't mentioned.

'I do not. Besides, he's gone, I'm here. End of story.' It was not a

very convincing argument.

See? We haven't once mentioned his name and you've become defensive.

The alternate internal voice considered the statement. *'Well, what, in your all-knowing opinion, am I supposed to do, then?'*

Realize other people's perspectives and accept responsibility for your own actions, feelings, and jealousies, and then deal with the consequences that arise from them. Letting things fester only makes them worse.

'That's a bit preachy.'

Say what you will, but it's the truth. And at the risk of sounding even more preachy, there are still issues that Robin hasn't dealt with either, such as her acceptance of what happened to you know who, her coming to terms with her parents' behavior toward him and then more recently, toward you, and her feelings about blaming God for all or part of what happened and what she fears might happen again.

'Yes, I know all that. It's why she's been seeing the therapist.' An internal thought. *'Maybe it's just because she blames herself that she's so hard on her parents and God.'* Another internal thought. *'And maybe she's afraid of blaming herself again.'*

Bingo.

'Of course, she has every right to be hard on her parents.' The alternate internal voice countered. *'After all, they've been manipulative and unsupportive, not to mention completely unjustified in what they've done.'*

Depends upon whose perspective you're looking at.

Realization started to hit home. *'That perspective thing.'*

Exactly. Now, you're catching on.

'It still doesn't excuse their behavior in any way, shape, matter, or form.' The alternate internal voice wasn't quite ready to give in on the issue.

Maybe not, but despite everything, they're still Robin's parents, and she may very well need them in her life, whether she realizes it now or not.

Silent contemplation.

So, as you can see, there are issues that remain for both of you to deal with sooner or later. You don't have to like them, you just have to deal with them.

'Great.' An internal frown. *'You know, you really have a way of putting a damper on things. And I was having such a lovely dream, too....'*

Considerable Appeal

The truth hurts sometimes, but don't be too hard on yourself. You've made some progress.

'*You think so?*'

Of course. Just don't think the ballgame's over. It's barely halftime, and you've got to keep the other side from scoring.

'*Right. If they don't score, I win.*' The alternate internal voice astutely concluded.

Correct. If they don't score you win.

'*Got it. Now, if you don't mind, I have a dream to get back to. In my dream, I was....*' Internal pondering. '*I was....*' More internal pondering. '*Damn. I can't remember now.*'

From the next pillow, a soft voice rough with sleep broke the silence, jarring the disappointed dreamer into a fuller cognizance. "Did you say something, Jess?"

Must've been mumbling. Long fingers reached down and covered the warm hand resting upon an already warm stomach, the low voice whispering gently. "No, sweetheart. Go back to sleep. It's still early."

In response, the smaller body snuggled more tightly up against its larger companion as the dream of racing freely along desolate shorelines and wooded landscape merged with the rustic scents of sweet pine and oak to once again embrace the slumbering subconscious minds of two inseparable beings.

****

Some time later, the mid-morning sun beat slivered paths across the queen-sized waterbed, the golden rays filtering inside the room through the tiny slits in the Venetian blinds leaving thinly striped patterns glowing in their wake. It was an unusually lazy weekend morning, nearly ten o'clock in fact, as one sleeping figure, then the other, finally stirred to welcome the warm springtime day.

Jess spared a quick look at the clock on the nightstand. *Is it that late?* She let her eyes adjust to the shaded light in the room, then stretched out her long form, feeling the muscles beneath her skin tense and relax in sequence. Noting the slight movement beside her, she turned to face her smaller companion. "Hi."

"Mmmmpf." A blonde head snuggled deeper into the older woman's shoulder.

An affectionate grin. "How's my beloved shrimp this morning?"

One unamused green eye cracked open. "You must have a death wish. You remember what happened the last time you called me that, don't you?"

"Um..." The grin now widened. "Why don't you refresh my memory?"

"You ran for your life until I caught you, that's what happened." Point made, the green eye closed once again.

Oh, I'd say you definitely caught me. "Yes, you're very quick on your feet, Robin." *Her hair smells like springtime. And rain.*

"And do you remember what happened after I caught you?"

"Let me see..." A look of intense concentration. "I believe your exact words were that I was, quote, your slave for life."

"Yes. And don't you forget it."

A low chuckle. "Oh, I wouldn't dare."

"Good." Robin stifled a yawn, then squinted considerably as her sleepy eyes gradually adapted to the subdued daylight in the room. "You were talking in your sleep, you know."

Dark eyebrows shot up. "Was I? What did I say?"

"Couldn't really tell. Sounded almost like you were talking to someone."

Oh. Right. I was in the middle of a dream, and then I was interrupted by...never mind. A quick change of subject was in order. "So, what do you want to do today, kiddo?"

Robin, now fully awake, propped herself up on one elbow. "It's the weekend, Jess. Did you forget what we're supposed to do this weekend?"

Slightly mischievous blue eyes gazed into sea-green. "Well, if I remember correctly, it has something to do with grocery shopping." A beat. "And tutoring."

That brought the expected blush. "You have a very good memory."

"It does come in handy sometimes." Long fingertips brushed lightly against the sleep tousled wispy blonde bangs. "So...exactly what tutoring do I need for this grocery shopping?"

Pale eyelashes fluttered closed in response to the gentle touch. *That feels nice.* "Let's see...." A petite finger tapped softly on the bed. "I think we should start with the basics."

"The basics?"

"Yes." A serious expression. "There are some important things to remember, and this is where hands-on experience can be very beneficial."

The older woman was listening intently. "Is that so?"

"Yes. Now, first, if you're looking for produce, say tomatoes, and you want to tell if they're ripe, you should try squeezing them. The ripe ones are always more soft."

"Are they, now." Jess moved a little closer. "Tell me more."

"Well, next, if you want something from the bakery department, they usually have a person standing there with little samples of things like cakes and pies and muffins...."

"Muffins?"

"Yes." Robin continued her explanation. "So, if you're not sure whether you'd like what they're offering, you could simply try a sample."

"I see." The voice was low and seductive. "So, you're saying that if I was perhaps...interested, I could always sample the muffins."

"Of course." A pause. *Oh, she is so busted.* "However, Jess..." The smaller woman smiled very sweetly. "I'm sure that you'd find certain particular muffins far, far more appealing than others." A pointed look. "Wouldn't you?"

Uh-oh. "Um...yes, Robin, that's absolutely true."

"Good. I'm glad you agree." The petite body slowly crept on top of the larger form, its weight settling firmly to trap its prey. "So, then..." The voice was but a whisper. "Perhaps we should review, just to make sure you're perfectly clear on the finer points of grocery shopping."

"Uh..." Slightly unfocused blue eyes looked up into smoky green, the tables having been effectively turned. "Okay."

"Grocery shopping..." Small fingers slipped underneath the Calvin Klein shirt. "Requires a certain amount of hands-on experience."

Jess suddenly lost her concentration. "Um...right."

"And if you're looking for, say tomatoes..." Robin kissed a chiseled jaw, then let the fingers beneath the Calvin Klein shirt wander in circular motions, teasing the soft flesh as they made their journey upward. "You should squeeze them in order to make sure they're sufficiently ripe." The fingers proceeded to punctuate that particular point rather nicely.

"Um..." It was impossible to think.

"And if you're passing by the bakery department, and you're interested in sampling the muffins..." The younger woman kissed a path from one tender earlobe down to the base of a very enticing neck. "Remember that certain particular muffins...preferably of the more familiar variety...are much, much more appealing than others." She slid the length of the long body and lifted the hem of the Calvin Klein shirt to fully expose a smooth, flat stomach, pressing soft, delicate kisses into the flesh around the navel and further downward along the elastic waistband of the matching Calvin Klein boxers.

That did it for Jess. She drew Robin up to her as smoldering deep blue eyes locked firmly onto verdant green, the sensual energy palpable, sucking nearly all of the oxygen out of the room as both women labored to breathe. She kissed the younger woman deeply, while long, slender fingers threaded their way into the soft blonde hair. "Oh, I definitely plan on sticking with the more familiar muffins, Robin." The kisses, now more insistent, were returned in kind, an electric current passing between the entwined bodies. Jess's voice became low and raspy, and her heart seemed to race at least ten times faster as both women ran their hands over every inch of the other's body, unable to get close enough and feeling an all-consuming passion surprising to each in its strength and intensity.

It was both thrilling and scary at the same time, this force seemingly primeval in nature, and Robin, unable to resist its draw, simply let it overtake her. She couldn't help but sense that the connection she and Jess shared was increasing in some extraordinary way, a recognition of a bond far more powerful than either one of them had ever contemplated. She focused steadily on the darkened azure eyes in front of her as a spark of energy ignited a fire beneath her skin like none she'd ever known before. "Good."

It was clear. Something had changed. Something, somehow, had been awakened. And now that a new dimension of awareness and primal sensitivity had been discovered, there was absolutely no going back.

****

Black Point Wildlife Drive. It sounded like an interesting day trip, a drive over to Merritt Island on the Atlantic Coast of Florida, its wetland environment hosting the National Wildlife Refuge situated in the shadow of the Kennedy Space Center and its towering Vehicle Assembly Building. The sun was bright today, hidden periodically by a few puffy clouds drifting lazily eastward, and the air was pleasantly warm with just a slight sea breeze. The true hot weather would come soon enough, though, with its scorching temperatures and sweltering humidity which could prove to be very unpleasant for any period of time longer than ten seconds. But today was delightful, and a good day for an outing, especially after all the horrible stress of the previous several weeks.

The silver Mercedes entered the small town of Titusville less than an hour after departing the Orlando suburbs, the glittering waves of the intercoastal waterway easily visible upon approach. After the lazy Saturday morning the day before, and the extended grocery shopping excursion which subsequently followed, Robin and Jess arose relatively early this Sunday and decided that some outdoor recreation was definitely in order. They packed together a picnic lunch and headed off to enjoy the sunshine and the unspoiled natural habitats that the barrier island had to offer.

The car traveled across the long bridge over the intercoastal waterway, actually a portion of the Indian River Lagoon, toward a small park and picnic area fronting the edge of the wildlife refuge. There were several picnic tables, barbecue grills, covered eating pavilions, ironically complete with electrical outlets, and a couple of boat ramps situated throughout the park area. Many picnickers were already busily cooking their typical barbecue fare, while fishermen of all ages lined up along the small beachfront and boardwalk pier trying their luck at today's catch. Deciding to forego the gathering crowds, Jess and Robin instead headed further on up the road a bit until they came upon an isolated grassy area near what appeared to be a small fishing beach surrounded by low palm trees, a few Flatwood pines, and a hedge of mangroves. It was perfect. Relative privacy and enough shade to keep comfortable.

Jess parked the Mercedes on the well-worn sandy grass path and stepped out of the car, careful to avoid a small rut made by previous vehicles to the site. The brilliant sunlight reflected off of her silver mirrored sunglasses as she adjusted them and made her way back to the trunk of the car to retrieve their picnic supplies. "Go ahead and get the picnic blanket and basket, and I'll carry the cooler." She called as Robin approached. "We have some beach chairs here if you'd rather use them."

"No, the blanket's fine." The smaller woman grabbed her assigned items. "Need any help with the cooler?"

"Nope." Blue eyes twinkled unseen beneath the mirrored sunglasses. "Although you did pack a lot of food."

An slight smirk. "I'm always prepared."

"Prepared for what?" Jess set the cooler down under the shade of a tree in their selected location. "To feed an army?"

Shaking her head, Robin bent down and spread out the blanket, her playful green eyes deliberately peeking above her dark sunglasses. "Someone, who shall remain nameless, insisted that we bring along certain items which I hadn't counted on bringing."

The taller form settled comfortably on the blanket. "Everybody

276

knows, Robin, that you can't have a picnic without the appropriate picnic food."

That drew a light chuckle. "I'd hardly consider fried shrimp sandwiches exactly picnic food, but whatever floats your boat."

"My boat's not only floating, Robin, but it's winning the race."

The blonde woman knelt down on the blanket next to her companion and gave her a quick peck on the cheek. "You're very competitive, you know that?" *And absolutely endearing.*

"That's because I intend to win." *If they don't score, I win.*

"You've already won, and don't you forget it." Another quick peck on the cheek for emphasis, then Robin began unpacking the picnic basket and cooler. "Now, let's see, fried chicken, coleslaw, potato salad for me, fried shrimp sandwiches for you."

"I'll have the fried chicken, please."

Blonde eyebrows lifted. "I thought you wanted the sandwiches."

"You've shown me the error of my ways, Robin. I'll have the chicken."

"But...."

"Didn't you bring enough?" A quick peek inside the cooler. "Seems like there's enough here."

"You really want the chicken?"

"Yes. I love chicken."

Hmmmm. "Fine." Robin removed the chicken from the cooler, then sat back, crossing her legs in front of her. "You know what, Jess?" She placed a piece of fried chicken onto a sturdy paper plate. "I think this whole shrimp fetish thing with you is just a cry for attention."

An incredulous look. That was preposterous. Absolutely ridiculous. "Number one, Robin, just because I have a particular fondness for certain seafood-related items does not mean it's a fetish."

Robin popped the top of a can of soda and took a sip.

"Number two, even if I did have such a supposed fetish, which I don't, I certainly wouldn't need to use it to gain attention."

The blonde head nodded very seriously.

"And number three, I can attract attention, if I want to, completely on my own merits, thank you very much."

"Right." Petite fingers grasped one of the aforementioned sandwiches and placed it on a paper plate. "Here you go, honey."

Damn. She knows me too well. "Thanks."

****

They sat eating their lunch and enjoying easy conversation. It was like that with them, so familiar and comfortable that sometimes, they didn't even have to say a word. Just being together was enough. Robin stared out at the small lagoon near their picnic site watching the tiny waves lap lightly at the edges of the shoreline. A few sea gulls flew by, occasionally dipping down to the water's surface in search of schooling greenback minnows, while a few birdsongs could be heard far off in the distance, carried on the light breeze though the branches of the surrounding tall trees. A young brown pelican stood stationary on a partially submerged piling not too far away, awaiting the receding tide and the arrival of his next meal.

Robin silently reflected on the course of the previous several weeks and the path their lives had taken. It had been on her mind now for a while, this sense of...what? It was a confounding intangible something, hard to explain and even harder to put a name to. She and Jess were definitely growing closer, but that was to be expected the longer they spent together. And yet, there was something else. Something even stronger, something which inspired feelings in her that she'd never felt before, something more...visceral.

Green eyes hidden beneath the dark sunglasses silently observed the taller woman now stretched out on the blanket casually sipping her apricot iced tea, her back resting against the base of a nearby palm tree and her slender legs extending to neatly cross at the ankles. Those same green eyes noted with interest how the shadows of the swaying palm branches danced in random fashion across the statuesque form, the result of a game of hide and seek with the sun's rays which only further served to enhance the captivating presence. *She's beautiful.* One long leg now hitched itself up at the knee, while tendrils of long dark hair blew gently in the breeze, finally settling down to once again frame the chiseled planes of the angular face. It was a compelling scene, striking for its physical appearance, and one of which Robin had more than once taken appreciable notice. Was it that, then? Was it just the considerable physical appeal? Was this the overwhelming feeling she'd been having, one that caused every nerve in her being to become super-sensitized even at the slightest glance? Or was it something else entirely?

The surroundings were pleasantly peaceful and relaxed, nature's ageless treasures laid out before them to admire for their lasting endurance throughout time and progress. Jess, herself, seemed just as lost in thought, perhaps, as Robin now wondered, pondering similar notions. If so, then maybe those concealed azure eyes were privy to an enlightenment which had so far hopelessly escaped the younger woman. The silver mirrored sunglasses kept steadily fixed on a point somewhere amidst the mangrove trees nestled along the opposite shore of the shallow lagoon. *Maybe so.* At last, Robin decided to raise the subject. The problem was, she didn't exactly know just what to say. "You're looking pensive."

The dark head turned slightly. "Just thinking." A silly grin appeared.

That prompted a slight chuckle from Robin. "That's what I said." *Should I bring it up?* Actually, there was no real harm in doing so, was there? "Hey Jess? I was thinking...."

"Pensively?"

A smile. "Yes." Pale eyebrows slowly knit together as words became more elusive. "I was thinking about...well, actually, lately I've felt that...."

Jess sat up a bit straighter, now sensing a more serious discussion. "What is it?" *Did I do something?*

"It's just that I've been feeling that we...you and I..." *What are the words?* This was turning out to be very difficult. "I've always thought that things between us were really great, but lately, I've been feeling...."

What did I do? Jess fought the urge to panic. She removed her sunglasses but was otherwise silent.

"Well, I've sensed that things have... " Robin played with her fingers nervously, then smoothed an imaginary crease in her pale yellow Capri pants. "What I'm trying to say is that I think that lately things seem to have gotten somewhat stronger between us. I mean, sometimes, when I look at you or when we're together, it just seems like it's..." There was simply no accurate word for it. "More."

"More?"

"Yes. More." Robin hadn't yet made eye contact, keeping her dark sunglasses firmly in place. "It's hard to explain, but it just seems that these feelings are...." She again struggled for the right word.

"More." Jess finished.

A relieved smile. "Right." Petite fingers lowered the dark sunglasses and quickly folded them as now unmasked green eyes firmly locked onto crystal blue. "I don't know if you know what I mean, or maybe if you...might feel it, too?"

A large hand reached over and gently enfolded a nearby smaller hand. "Robin, I have thought for a very long time that when I'm with you, things seem to be more intense. Colors and sounds and the smell of everything...it all seems more alive to me." That was certainly the truth. "I've never felt more with anyone else before."

There was a moment's hesitation. "And lately...?" The younger woman was almost afraid to ask, afraid that she'd imagined it all.

Lately? In truth, Jess had avoided thinking about that too hard, although she knew something was subtly different. She took a moment to compose her thoughts, then tried her best to explain. "Well, lately I have sensed something....something I really can't put my finger on. To me, it's almost as though I want...have to be as close to you as I can." *I'm making no sense.* She took a deep breath, searching her mind for a more rational explanation. "Maybe it's just that the longer we know each other, the more in synch we are with each other, and so the feelings we have are just...."

"More." It was Robin's turn to finish.

"Right." An affectionate smile. "More."

"Yeah." The blonde head nodded. "That's what I thought." *At least I'm not crazy.* "I'm glad we got that settled."

Jess gave the hand she held a light squeeze. "You bet." She stood up, feeling the joints in her knees pop slightly before dusting off her faded blue jeans and slipping her sunglasses back into place. "Are you ready to roll?"

"All set. Let's just get this stuff packed up." Robin reached for the picnic basket, casting her older companion a deliberate glance. "You're in charge of the cooler."

"Amazing how light it is now." A nearly inaudible voice playfully quipped.

Petite ears perked. "I heard that."

Chuckling lightly, Robin and Jess gathered together their picnic items and stowed them securely in the car, then headed off down the main road toward the center of the wildlife refuge area. Soon, they came upon a visitor's center and made a brief stop inside to obtain some pamphlets and reading material on the local wildlife habitats and view several of the informational exhibits. Behind the small modern building was a pond with an adjacent nature walk through terrain made up mainly of palm trees, slash pines, scrub oaks, low lying palmettos, and other palm brush set in the middle of a natural wetland. A boardwalk provided a walking trail that led through the wooded area.

Jess stepped outside the back door of the visitor's center, peering down into the shallow pond as three giant goldfish swam by. "You want to take a little walk?"

"I'd love it." Robin surveyed the rustic scenery. "It looks so peaceful here."

"Yeah, this is the original Florida. You can almost picture how the natives lived."

"Native, like you?" A hidden grin.

One slender eyebrow arched conspicuously above silver mirrored sunglasses. "I'm not quite that native, Robin."

They took a few steps inside the entrance to the nature trail and were immediately surrounded by a dense shade with only small hints of sunlight visible through the foliage of the trees. An array of crooked slender oak branches darted haphazardly up above, their bark liberally covered with hanging Spanish moss, some of which had fallen to the ground below in silent camouflage. "This is so cool, Jess." The boardwalk meandered back into the secluded woods. All that could be heard were the calls of various species of birds and the rustle of leaves as small creatures scampered hurriedly beneath the thick underbrush. "There's a red cardinal sitting over there." A petite finger pointed in its direction. "And listen. Do you hear the gray catbirds calling?"

A hushed tone. "Is that what that is?"

"Yeah. They almost sound like cats, don't they?"

"I've never really listened much to bird calls." Jess stood still among the isolated tranquility. It was amazing, all the different sounds echoing throughout the woods, some faint and some close by, things she'd never really heard before. It was...*more.* Yeah, that was definitely the word she'd use to describe her experience with Robin. Everything was more. "Hey, you ready to take that wildlife drive now?"

The smaller woman offered an impish grin as they approached the end of the nature trail. "Lead on, o' native one."

****

The Black Point Wildlife Drive was a seven-mile long journey with several stopping points along the way to view the refuge's wildlife, mostly waterfowl and migratory birds, in preserved habitats of estuaries, salt marshes, sandy mud flats, palm and oak hammocks, and an occasional mangrove-rimmed pond. The refuge itself was supplied with both fresh water from the St. Johns River and salt water from the sea, creating a brackish water environment carefully monitored by refuge personnel for its salinity levels. A five-mile loop foot trail was also accessible, providing a close-up view of the marsh for those inclined to engage in more avid bird-watching activity. For a higher perspective, a raised observation platform enabled panorama viewing of the marshlands and their inhabitants from a distance. It was, of course, a fascinating glimpse of wildlife in its natural environment and offered an appreciation of the joint efforts by NASA and the National

Park Service in protecting the refuge area from the ever-encroaching development along Florida's Space Coast.

The silver Mercedes made its way slowly through the drive route, initially coming across a large marshland filled with a myriad of waterfowl. Stopping by the roadside, Jess and Robin stepped out of their car in order to gain a closer look. Not far away, a large blue heron stood poised in the grassy area near the edge of a pond, as did several snowy egrets further on down the shoreline, their wispy long feathers fluttering delicately in the light breeze. Behind the tall reeds, a lone white ibis, distinctive for its crooked beak, hunted single-mindedly for food in the sand beneath the shallow water. Across the road, mud flats in the distance provided feeding grounds for gathering shorebirds continuously poking their beaks beneath the moist blanket of sand in search of hidden prey, while terns and ring-billed gulls circled overhead ready to swoop down and capture their targets from up above. A large flock of mallard ducks flew in unison overhead, finally settling down gracefully on a distant marsh, their light quacking sounds echoing faintly across the quiet sanctuary.

From this vantage point, varied and diverse habitats could be seen, ranging from the marshlands and sandy mud flats, to the tops of the tall pine trees situated slightly northward, home to ospreys and the American bald eagles. A large bird flew in the direction of the tall pines, and Robin couldn't tell whether it was an osprey or a bald eagle, both similar in appearance from a distance, although Jess was absolutely sure it was indeed an eagle. Both species were said to be protected, with the bald eagle particularly endangered with only ten active bald eagle nests populating the refuge. A type of binocular scope called a Nest Finder assisted wildlife seekers in locating some of the nearby eagles nests.

There were several other wildlife stops along the route, each providing glimpses of the neighboring habitats and some of the species occupying them. Further down the drive trail, remnants of a pine forest ravaged by fire could be seen, the result of a decade-long drought and fire suppression policy that allowed the underbrush to accumulate, causing intense wildfires when struck by lightning. According to one of the brochures, controlled burns were now conducted on a rotating basis in the refuge in order to manage and benefit the wildlife populations. Close by, a yellow-rump warbler's lilting song could be heard seconds before the tiny bird flew from its perch in a mangrove tree on the far side of the road and headed directly for those same charred pine woodlands.

Just as the Mercedes approached the end of the wildlife drive, a slow-moving armadillo crawled its way through the thin grass on one side of the trail, while a barely visible brown cottontail rabbit, ears twitching inquisitively, foraged around in the nearby brush. Alligators had been known to roam the mosquito control ditches on either side of the roadway, selecting suitable locations on the hard mud surface to sun themselves, but none of the crusty reptiles could be seen adorning those side ditches today. The car made its way out of the refuge area and traveled back toward the bridge spanning the Indian River Lagoon just as the sun in was beginning to set for the day.

"Hey, Jess..." Robin took notice of the tops of the tall street light poles as the car passed each one in succession, craning her neck slightly in order to gain a clearer view. "Those look like bird's nests up there."

"Yeah, they do."

Just then, a round head poked itself out from one of the large twig and seaweed nests situated on the platform top of a light pole in front of them. "It's an osprey." Robin was fascinated. "These are osprey nests."

"I never realized they made their nests up there." Jess smiled as a now familiar thought occurred to her. *More.* It was official. Being with Robin was definitely more. "Pretty interesting, huh?"

"Yeah." The blonde head turned toward the car's driver, a contented sigh escaping. "That was a really great day."

"And we even have some food left." Jess quipped.

A purposeful glance. "I'll ignore that comment." The smaller woman surveyed their surroundings more closely. "Hey, isn't this the road that leads to that place where we went fishing that day?"

"Yep"

Hmmmm. "And doesn't it also lead to that particular beach you told me about back there?"

Beach? "Well, there's the Cape Canaveral National Seashore and...." The light suddenly dawned. *Oh.* Jess tried hard to suppress a grin. "You mean the one where clothing is..." There was a ghost of a wink. "Not required?"

A faint blush crept up Robin's face. "Yes." A slight pause. "I was just asking."

A nod. "Right."

The passenger's green eyes focused intently on the road. "Right."

****

It was going to be a relaxing evening, one well anticipated and definitely well earned. Although it was merely the beginning of the week, work had been exceptionally hectic lately, and things were starting to become backlogged. *Of course, that's what happens when you take the entire weekend off.* Robin nestled herself into the far corner of the living room's plush sofa and put her feet up on the coffee table, flexing her toes back and forth to enjoy their freedom from the confining shoes she'd worn that day. *Why can't they make comfortable dress shoes for women?* It didn't seem like a hard question. After all, they could smash atoms into subatomic particles called quarks, manufacture powerful telescopes that could see to the beginning of the universe, and map the entire human DNA sequence, but yet, women's dress shoes remained the most uncomfortable creation known to mankind. *It's a conspiracy.* That conclusion had a lot of merit, she decided, and the business world was the prime conspirator, taking out its revenge against the ranks of professional women attacking its hallowed good ol' boy domain.

It hadn't been a hard day at work, just more running around than usual, trying to file several motions late in the day before the courthouse closed its doors for the night. That, itself, wouldn't have been so bad, but for a few last minute rearrangements of exhibits and the unavailability of any paralegals or runners, which, unfortunately, required that the young associate carry the pleadings to the Federal Building personally, undergoing searches and x-ray screenings before racing into the clerk's office to deposit the documents into the filing bin just as the marshal was locking the doors. *Whew!*

But now, it was good to be at home, the tensions of the day left solidly behind. Dinner had finished a short while ago, with Jess generously offering to wash the dishes and clean up after their quick meal of Chinese take-out. The junior partner had subsequently secluded herself into her home office to prepare a brief which was due the following day, leaving Robin time to relax and unwind. It was working. She was actually starting to catch her second wind as she wiggled her toes and enjoyed the feel of the soft comfortable sofa beneath her. Switching the stereo on to one of her favorite jazz stations, Robin sank further into the sofa and began to idly flip through a magazine she'd found resting on the end table next to her.

It was hard to tell exactly how much time had elapsed before Jess slipped into the living room nearly unnoticed, bearing gifts. "Hi."

Green eyes looked up from the magazine. "Hi."

"I thought you might like these." The older woman stepped over and placed two very fuzzy oversized bunny slippers onto Robin's feet.

"Um....yeah." It was a pleasant surprise. "Thanks."

"You're welcome." Then, just as quickly as she had appeared, Jess vanished down the long hallway, presumably to return to her legal brief.

A few short minutes passed, then quite unexpectedly, the tall form reappeared in the living room bearing another gift. "Hi again."

Blonde eyebrows knit together quizzically. "Hi."

"I thought you might like this." Jess handed Robin a book that the smaller woman had begun reading but hadn't yet finished.

"Um..." A petite hand slowly grasped the book. "Yeah. Great. Thank you."

A quick nod, then just as before, the older woman retreated from the room without another word.

Hmmmm. Wonder what that was all about. Robin returned the magazine to its place on the end table and opened the book, locating the page that she had previously marked. Just as she was settling in to begin her reading, a bit of rattling emanated from the direction of the kitchen, startling her slightly. *What's going on in there?* The younger woman was curious, but not particularly inclined to get up and investigate, so she opted instead to resume her reading.

Exactly one minute later, Jess emerged from the kitchen bearing yet another gift. "Hi."

Cautious green eyes peered over the top of the book, carefully observing the taller woman. "Hi."

"I thought you might like something to drink." Jess set the glass of mango flavored iced tea down on the coffee table in front of Robin, smiled briefly, then turned once again to leave the room.

Okay, that's it! The book closed quickly. "Hold it."

Innocent blue eyes looked at Robin. "What?"

"You know what. What's going on?"

"Going on?" Those same blue eyes blinked several times. "I have absolutely no idea what you're talking about."

She's up to something. "Yes, you do. I'm on to you, Jess."

A shake of the head. "Robin, whatever do you mean?" It was not a very believable protest.

"Don't play innocent with me. First you do the dishes, which was very sweet of you, thank you. Then, you bring me my slippers. Then, you bring me my book. Then, you bring me something to drink, all without me asking. It's not Christmas, and I know it's not my birthday, so what are you doing?"

"Doing?" Jess had to think quickly. "I'm your slave for life, remember? I'm just fulfilling my role."

"Right." Suspicious green eyes narrowed significantly. "Okay, spill it, Jess. I know you want something."

"There's nothing, Robin, I promise."

A frank look. "Just spill it."

"There's nothing...."

Another frank look. "Spill it."

The taller woman slowly approached the sofa, her dark eyebrows now raised almost comically. "Well....now that you mention it..." She knelt down on the floor at the edge of the sofa in front of Robin. "Perhaps, there might be one tiny little thing."

"I knew it!" A satisfied smirk. "Okay, tell me Jess, what is it?"

"I was just wondering...."

"Yes?" Robin was curious.

"Later on, after you've finished reading, if I went into the bedroom and you were to maybe come with me...."

"Yes?"

A long, slender finger made tiny circles on the top of Robin's knee. "And if I were to turn down the lights and maybe put on some soft music...."

"Yes?"

The finger slowly traveled along the length of a petite thigh. "And if I were to maybe lie down on the bed and take my shirt off...."

"Yes?" This was starting to sound interesting.

The finger continued its path upward, drawing idle shapes along the way. "And if you were to perhaps get onto the bed with me, then maybe you could take your hands and...."

"And?"

Twinkling blue eyes glanced up. "Give me a backrub."

Robin tried to stifle a giggle. "A backrub?" She gave Jess an amused look. "You want a backrub."

"Yes." A hopeful expression.

"I see." The blonde head nodded after some considerable thought. "Well, I'm pretty sure something could be arranged."

A pleased grin. "Thanks."

"But tell me one thing, Jess. If you're my slave for life and, of course, you're fulfilling your role, why am I the one giving you the backrub?"

Good question. "Um...I'll get back to you on that."

Robin smiled, then leaned forward and gave the kneeling woman a quick kiss. "How about this? You rub my back, and I'll rub yours."

That was easy. "Deal."

"Perfect." Robin reached for her book and opened it once again to the place where she'd left off. "And then after that you can get started on my neck rub, shoulder rub, and foot rub."

A blank stare. "I can?"

"Yes." A playful pat on the older woman's arm. "I know how desperately you want to fulfill your role."

Um.... Jess contemplated that statement as her eyes traveled from the front cover of the opened book now positioned prominently in her field of vision, down to the fuzzy oversized bunny slippers moving happily from side to side, and then upward to the glass of mango flavored iced tea resting casually in Robin's hand, ice cubes clinking softly in the background. *Damn. She got me.* A tiny smile emerged. *And I used to be so good at bribery, too.*

****

The room had been quiet for quite some time before Robin finally turned over in bed and faced Jess, whispering. "You still awake?"

"Yeah." The moon was bright that night, casting its sharp glow between the small spaces in the Venetian blinds. "You can't get to sleep?"

"I suppose I just have some stuff on my mind." A long pause. "Thanks for the backrub earlier."

"You're welcome. Thanks for my backrub, too. After sitting in that chair all night working on that brief, it sure felt good." Silver-blue eyes focused on nearby gray-green eyes in the dark. "So, tell me, what's on your mind?"

How should I answer that? "I was just thinking about what we discussed the other day....you know, when we were talking about feeling more for each other." The small body snuggled against the older woman. "I don't know what inspires that in me."

A small grin appeared. "I have to say that your grocery shopping lesson the other morning was particularly inspired."

Oh boy. The blonde head burrowed further into Jess's shoulder.

"Hey there." The voice was soft and gentle. "Sweetheart, there's no reason to be embarrassed. It's just me."

"I know." Robin relaxed a little. "Sometimes, I feel a little like I'm almost going to lose control. It's just a bit scary."

Jess sobered. "Come here." Long arms wrapped securely around the smaller body. "Honey, remember what we said? If either of us isn't comfortable with something, we won't do it. I promise you, just holding you is enough for me."

Robin felt safe. "Me too, but I also want more." The contradictory feelings were difficult to explain.

Jess lightly stroked her fingers through the short blonde bangs, trying to soothe away any lingering embarrassment. "Can I tell you a secret?"

The younger woman peered up into silver-blue eyes barely visible in the reflected moonlight. "Okay."

"Sometimes, I almost lose control, too." It was an honest admission.

"Really?"

"Yeah, really. You have that effect on me."

The vibrations of the low voice were comforting. A petite hand reached up to caress the older woman's cheek. "How do you know just the right things to say to me?"

"It's easy when it's all true." Jess brushed her lips across Robin's forehead to reinforce that point more fully.

Contented, Robin nestled the top of her head underneath Jess's chin, then chuckled softly. "We're a pair, aren't we?"

"I wouldn't have it any other way, kiddo."

A slight pause. "Like slippers."

"Slippers?" It seemed a slightly strange analogy. "How so?"

"Well, slippers are warm and soft and cozy and comfortable."

All that was true, but.... An ebony eyebrow slowly edged up. "Are you saying that I somehow resemble your bunny slippers?" There was a definite teasing quality to the question.

"No, what I'm saying is that my Bugs Bunny slippers for me and your Tasmanian Devil slippers for you are cozy and soft and warm and comfortable."

Jess decided to play a little. "And my Tweety Bird slippers aren't?"

"No, Jess, not those big yellow silly looking things." An exaggerated shudder. "They don't fit you."

"But they're the right size for me." The older woman protested.

Robin thought she'd explained all of this before. "That's true, but they don't fit you as a person."

"And the other ones do?"

"Yes." How much clearer could Robin make it? "My Bugs Bunny slippers and your Tasmanian Devil slippers fit us."

"I see." *I'm sure there's a point, here. Somewhere.*

"Right. They fit well."

Jess was trying desperately to follow the logic. "Our slippers are warm and soft and cozy and comfortable, and they fit well."

"Yes. Just like us." Robin smiled. "See, what I'm saying, Jess? We're like a pair of slippers." A petite hand came to rest on the older woman's stomach. "We fit well."

Dark eyelashes fluttered closed at the familiar touch. *Of course.* For some reason, it all made perfect sense. "We fit well."

Exactly. Just like a pair of warm, soft, cozy, comfortable slippers. There was nothing better in the world.

The End.

About the Author

KM lives and works in Orlando, Florida, although she is not originally a native of the Sunshine State. Born in New Jersey, she and her family moved to Florida when she was only six years old. The warm Florida sunshine proved to be a lure her family simply couldn't resist.

A graduate of Florida State University with a Bachelor of Arts degree in Psychology and Criminology, she went on to attend a paralegal school in Atlanta, Georgia before living in Birmingham,

Alabama for several years. Thereafter, she returned to Florida in order to be nearer to her family.

A paralegal by profession, KM always sought more enjoyment from her personal life rather than her working career. She enjoys music and playing the guitar, having been a contract musician for the local navy base before it closed and then volunteering to provide music and voice vocals at local retreats, conferences, and other services. She also enjoys traveling and hopes to explore more of the many fascinating places the world has to offer.

KM is new to writing, having only recently attempted to tap the muse. The mixture and range of emotion she puts into her writing, from sorrow to humor, is often more a reflection of her own personality than of anything else. Her stories are written as a part of herself, and she hopes to continue on with the journey.

Order These Great Books Directly From Limitless, Dare 2 Dream Publishing

Title	Price	Note
The Amazon Queen by L M Townsend	20.00	
Define Destiny by J M Dragon	20.00	The one that started it all…
Desert Hawk, revised by Katherine E. Standelll	18.00	Many new scenes
Golden Gate by Erin Jennifer Mar	18.00	
The Brass Ring By Mavis Applewater	18.00	HOT
Haunting Shadows by J M Dragon	18.00	
Spirit Harvest by Trish Shields	15.00	
PWP: Plot? What Plot? by Mavis Applewater	18.00	HOT
Journeys By Anne Azel	18.00	NEW
Memories Kill By S. B. Zarben	20.00	
Up The River, revised By Sam Ruskin	18.00	Many new scenes
	Total	

South Carolina residents add 5% sales tax.
Domestic shipping is $3.50 per book

Visit our website at: http://limitlessd2d.net

Please mail your orders with credit card info, check or money order to:

**Limitless, Dare 2 Dream Publishing
100 Pin Oak Ct.
Lexington, SC 29073-7911**

Please make checks or money orders payable to: Limitless.

I

Order More Great Books Directly From Limitless, Dare 2 Dream Publishing

Daughters of Artemis by L M Townsend	18.00	
Connecting Hearts By Val Brown and MJ Walker	18.00	
Mysti: Mistress of Dreams By Sam Ruskin	18.00	HOT
Family Connections By Val Brown & MJ Walker	18.00	Sequel to Connecting Hearts
A Thousand Shades of Feeling by Carolyn McBride	18.00	
The Amazon Nation By Carla Osborne	18.00	Great for research
Poetry from the Featherbed By pinfeather	18.00	If you think you hate poetry you haven't read this
None So Blind, 3rd Edition By LJ Maas	16.00	NEW
A Saving Solace By DS Bauden	18.00	NEW
Return of the Warrior By Katherine E. Standell	20.00	Sequel to Desert Hawk
Journey's End By LJ Maas	18.00	NEW
	Total	

South Carolina residents add 5% sales tax.
Domestic shipping is $3.50 per book
Please mail your orders with credit card info, check or money order to:
Limitless, Dare 2 Dream Publishing
100 Pin Oak Ct.
Lexington, SC 29073-7911
Please make checks or money orders payable to: Limitless.

Name:
Address:
Address:
City/State/Zip:
Country:
Phone:
Credit Card Type:
CC Number:
EXP Date:
List Items Ordered and Retail Prices:

List Items Ordered and Retail Prices:

You may also send a money order or check. Please make payments out to: Limitless Corporation.
You may Fax this form to us at: 803-359-2881 or mail it to:
Limitless Corporation
100 Pin Oak Court
Lexington, SC 29073-7911

South Carolina residents add 5% sales tax.
Domestic shipping is $3.50 per book

Visit our website at: http://limitlessd2d.net

Introducing...
Art By Joy

By JoyArgento

Hi, allow me to introduce myself. My name is Joy Argento and I am the artist on all of these pieces. I have been doing artwork since I was a small child. That gives me about 35 years of experience. I majored in art in high school and took a few college art courses. Most of my work is done in either pencil or airbrush mixed with color pencils. I have recently added designing and creating artwork on the computer. Some of the work featured on these pages were created and "painted" on the computer. I am self taught in this as well as in the use of the airbrush.

I have been selling my art for the last 15 years and have had my work featured on trading cards, prints and in magazines. I have sold in galleries and to private collectors from all around the world.

I live in Western New York with my three kids, four cats, one dog and the love of my life. It is definitely a full house. I appreciate you taking the time to check out my artwork. Please feel free to email me with your thoughts or questions. Custom orders are always welcomed too.

Contact me at ArtByJoy@aol.com . I look forward to hearing from you.

Motorcycle Women

Joy Argento

Check out her work at
LimitlessD2D or at her website.
Remember: ArtByJoy@aol.com !

Printed in the United States
46232LVS00006B/85-87